The Philosophy of George Santayana

Dr George Santayana (in 1950)

The Philosophy of George Santayana

Dilip Kumar Roy

With a Foreword by
Pritibhusan Chatterji

Suryodaya Books

Cataloging in Publication Data — DK
[Courtesy: D.K. Agencies (P) Ltd. <docinfo@dkagencies.com>]

Roy, Dilip Kumar (*Reader in philosophy*), 1939- **author.**
The philosophy of George Santayana / Dilip Kumar Roy ; with a foreword by Pritibhusan Chatterji.
– Revised edition.
pages cm
Includes bibliographical references and index.
ISBN 9789392443060

1. Santayana, George, 1863-1952. 2. Metaphysics. 3. Knowledge, Theory of. 4. Aesthetics. 5. Religion and ethics. I. Title.

LCC B945.S24R69 2023 | DDC 191 23

ISBN: 978-93-92443-06-0
First published in 1975 by Progressive Publishers, Calcutta
Second revised edition published in 2023

Printed and published by:
Suryodaya Books
"Suryodaya", D-36A/1, Mohan Garden
Najafgarh Road, New Delhi - 110059
Phone: (011) 25353435
Mob.: 9871394811

Distributed by:
D.K. Printworld (P) Ltd.
Regd. Office: "Vedaśrī", F-395, Sudarshan Park
(Metro Station: ESI Hospital), New Delhi - 110015
Phones: (011) 2545 3975, 2546 6019
e-mail: indology@dkprintworld.com
Website: www.dkprintworld.com

To
my father
from whom
I always humbly sought advice
to be uplifted
morally and spiritually

Foreword

THE present work, as its title indicates, is devoted to the study of the Philosophy of George Santayana, one of the leading thinkers of the modern age. Born in Spain, he came over to the United States at the age of nine. He did his graduate studies in Philosophy at Harvard under the able guidance of two outstanding philosophers of the day, William James and Josiah Royce. Santayana is not only a philosopher, but also a litterateur and he writes in a suave manner. His naturalism may be regarded as one of the most comprehensive philosophies of the present century and he has made significant contributions to the development of contemporary realistic epistemology.

Santayana's philosophical career spread over more than fifty years and it can be broadly divided into two periods. In the first period – during which he published *The Sense of Beauty* (1896) and *The Life of Reason* (5 vols – 1905-06) – he regarded philosophy as a kind of descriptive psychology. He put "mind" in its biological context and drew our attention to its capacity to give an aesthetic and ideal meaning to its surroundings. In the second period which saw the publications of his *Scepticism and Animal Faith* (1923) and *Realms of Being* (4 vols, 1927-40) he switched over to a non-psychological mode of approach and introduced a set of ontological distinctions in the realms of being – Essence, Matter, Truth and Spirit. He sharply distinguished between existence and essence – he characterized the former as temporal and changeable, and the latter as ideal, eternal and permanent. Many commentators feel that Santayana in his formulation of the concept of essence moved away from his early naturalism towards Platonism.

Dr Dilip Kumar Roy, the author of the present treatise, has done an admirable job in presenting the main aspects of Santayana's wide and comprehensive philosophy in a neat and compact fashion. Santayana in his long philosophical discourse dealt with problems relating to Epistemology and Metaphysics, Aesthetics, Ethics and Religion, and Dr Roy has touched on all of them. His work is not only expository and critical, but also comparative. He has instituted suitable comparisons between Santayana and leading thinkers of the West and the East. This critical and comparative approach makes the present work all the more interesting. Dr Roy's method of treatment is thorough and his style is simple and full of force.

Dr Roy started preparing the present work as his doctoral dissertation under my advice a few years ago and I am very glad that he has now decided to publish it. In fact, Santayana does not seem to have received in our country as much attention as he should have and there are not many works on Santayana even in the West. I am sure this treatise will prove to be a valuale contribution in the field of contemporary philosophy and will evoke interest in the study of this great thinker.

21 August 1975

Pritibhusan Chatterji
Department of Philosophy
University of Calcutta
Calcutta

Preface to the Second Edition

IT IS a matter of great satisfaction that this book finds itself in its second edition after a long gap of forty-seven years. In this edition an Appendix on Santayana's Americanism has been included.

Santayana was an American philosopher and one of the leading thinkers of the modern age. He was a proponent of Critical Realism. Critical Realism was a school in the US bourgeois philosophy of the 1920s and 1930s. Among the main advocates of this School we can cite the names of A. Lovejoy, G. Santayana and R. Sellers. Santayana admitted the objective existence of the material world; but what was unique in his statement was that objects would not be cognized directly, but indirectly, through "essences" (that is, through real or possible qualities) as signs of objects. In his understanding of the "essences", Santayana, undoubtedly, was very much close to Plato.

The present work on the *Philosophy of George Santayana* will elicit interest in those who are keen in the study of this great thinker.

I convey my heartfelt thanks to Mr Rajendra Agarwal of Suryodaya Books for kindly accepting the task of re-publishing the book and that with great care and utter responsibility.

D.K. Roy

Salt Lake, Kolkata
24 October 2022

Preface to the First Edition

George Santayana, who combines a versatile intellect with a rare gift of expression, is undoubtedly one of the remarkable talents of the twentieth century. There is hardly a sphere of thought into which he has not probed his mind. All the values of the higher psyche have engaged his attention. He has an elaborate ethical, aesthetic and religious philosophy to his credit. He has tried to scale the dizzy heights of the metaphysics of essence and existence. Epistemological problems also do not escape him. The present work purports to be a systematic study of the aforesaid aspects of Santayana's philosophy.

Santayana's philosophy presents an able statement of systematic dualism. The human mind functions in two ways: it intuits the given (or essence) and believes the non-given (or existence). Here dualism is found between intuition of the given and an animal faith in the non-given. Existence or non-given is approached by belief, and yet it is doubtful to the sceptic. The sceptic would accept nothing but the simple appearance or essence given to intuition. Essence Santayana describes as what is self-identical, devoid of all extrinsic relations, of time, of existence and even of subsistence (since by subsistence he means latent duration). Moreover, each essence, being self-identical, is individual; and again, being denuded of all extrinsic relations, it appears as an ideal term and in that sense, it is universal. Santayana's essentialism does not constitute his whole philosophy; on the other hand, it refers to the transcendental side of his philosophy.

The transcendental side of Santayana's philosophy is a variant of Platonism, no doubt; but it is not absolutely Platonic in spirit. Santayana has carefully distinguished the realm of matter from that of essence. The things which are in the flux of existence can by no means be accounted for by essences which transcend existence. This is a vital point on which Santayana differs from Plato who takes things as appearances of Ideas.

If transcendentalism forms the lofty side of Santayana's philosophy, materialism in his philosophy serves as the presupposition of all natural science and of all deliberate action. Consistency in Santayana's philosophy is marked in two ways: first, naturalism serves as a basis of his idealistic philosophy, and second, essence has a central role to play in his philosophy.

1. In every sphere, in epistemology, in aesthetics, in morality, in religion, naturalism appears as a firm basis. In the case of epistemology, knowledge arises out of the demand of the psyche which is material in nature. The material psyche has a vital demand to act upon the surrounding things. And in its adaptations to the surrounding things it becomes intelligent and creates spirit which, though originating from the material psyche, is not itself material and meets the vital demand of the psyche by selecting essences or "qualities sensed" which serve as descriptive terms of the objects encountered in action. Knowledge finally means description of things.

   Next, for the sense of beauty what are essential as the basic material are vital functions. With a feeling of bodily discomfort we cannot surely have a state of aesthetic sensibility. Art also has a material source; it springs from automatic instinctive action. A useful and automatic instinctive activity becomes art when it is supervened by purpose and conscious expression. What is true in the cases of beauty and art is also true in the case of morality. Santayana understands that the life of impulse is an essential part of human nature. So, instead of extirpating the life of impulse he makes it the basis of true morality. The life of reason by which he means rational morality can be led only when impulses are modified by reflection. The ideal which is to be followed in our rational life is the harmonious adjustment of all impulses and interests of life. Santayana discards the notion of the supreme ideal in the abstract sense and accepts many ideals in the concrete sense. The individual alone is the judge of what shall be his ideal, for he himself feels his own impulses which are to be directed and harmonized in order to give rise to the ideal. Santayana's ethics is naturalistic and individualistic.

Finally, Santayana determines the naturalistic basis of religion. Naturalism, instead of excluding religion, allows for it. Religion is the imaginary extension of the natural. It is the inevitable reaction of the imagination in front of the difficulties of a truculent world. The solution to all the problems of life, since it is furnished by imagination, remains ideal to us, admitting no verification in sense.

2. Essence, which Santayana discovers by the sceptical process, serves as the keynote of his whole philosophy. Its role in epistemology, in ethics and in religion is most important. The role of essence in cognition is to provide the descriptive terms by which we think and speak about the objects. While in epistemology essences are descriptive, in moral experience they are expressive. In epistemology essences are causally connected with the objects external to the psyche, whereas in moral experience, essences bear no such causal connection. Moral essences are selected or preferred as they express vital feeling or the state of the psyche only.

   In religion essence is neither descriptive nor expressive. Here, essences are contemplated ideally; i.e. here, they serve as Ideals. All essences are not ideals at the initial

> stage. An essence becomes interesting to the spirit due to its repeated appearance and as it grows more and more interesting to the spirit, it appears to the latter in a form of beauty; and then it serves as an ideal. Ideal contemplation of essences means spiritual freedom. Spiritual freedom is freedom from oneself, that is, from all allegiance to what is private to each psyche.

This is, in brief, the exposition of Santayana's philosophy. With his philosophic insight has been united the poetic expression of his ideas. His originality as a philosopher lies mainly in his attempt to reconcile the natural with the ideal by making the former the ground of the latter.

Santayana is not easy to understand, for divergent streams of ideas stem from his thought struggling to find expression in his voluminous writings. The present writer does not boast of being an authority on Santayana's philosophy. Indeed, very few writers of the present century can claim to be so. Santayana's comment on Schilpp's edition of his own philosophy makes explicit the truth of what is said here. Santayana says that most of the writings of the said edition are "second-rate for the most part" (Cory 1963: 231-32). Even of the paper of no less a philosopher than Bertrand Russell, included in that edition, Santayana comments, "Bertie's paper is good, but not remarkable except for a few phrase here and there" (ibid.: 234). The philosopher's own comments tend to prove that his philosophy was not properly grasped by a great many amongst its contemporary exponents and critics. Of course, Daniel Cory, who was the personal friend for the last twenty-five years of Santayana's life, can claim the covetable title of being an authority on his philosophy, and this honour was conferred by Santayana himself on Cory. And this was confessed by Santayana in his letter written, in July 1941, to Mr Conant, the then President of Harvard University, Cambridge, Massachusetts. In that letter he writes:

> I will only add that Cory would certainly be the man for the place, if it were thought appropriate that the first incumbent of my Fellowship should be a personal friend of mine and an authority on my philosophy. – Cory 1963: 240

The present writer claims to be an humble student of Santayana's philosophy. He has tried to exercise great care and circumspection in entering into the puzzle box of Santayana's philosophy. So this dissertation is an attempt at disentangling some of the difficulties which easily beset a student of Santayana's philosophy. This work not only expounds Santayana's philosophy critically but judges it also by comparing it with some philosophical doctrines, both Eastern and Western.

The author, in preparing his work, remains indebted to some reviewers and critics of Santayana: P.A. Schilpp, Daniel Cory, Sterling P. Lamprecht, Milton K. Munitz, G.E. Howgate, Irwin Edman; and to many others referred to in the appropriate places. Among those who have given the writer aid and enourgement by words of mouth or through correspondence, he heartily expresses his gratitude to Dr P.B. Chatterjee, Professor and Head of the Department of Philosophy, University of Calcutta. He is especially indebted to Professor P.N. Bhattacharya, Professor and Head of the Department of Philosophy (retired), Presidency College, Calcutta.

In preparing his dissertation the writer faced many difficulties. Sometimes the books needed were not easily available, for Santayana's literature is hardly available in our libraries. Still he is grateful to the authorities of the National Library, the American Library (U.S.I.S.) and the Presidency College Library, Calcutta, for allowing the writer to enjoy their respective facilities.

The writer expresses his gratitude and gives thanks, to Shri Suptokash Basu for the publication of this book.

Calcutta D.K. Roy

Contents

Part One
Metaphysics and Epistemology

1

An Historical Background

I. Introduction

GEORGE Santayana, born in Spain and brought up in America, developed a very uncommon character which exerted a great influence in his system of philosophy. He had a genius which the present century has seldom noticed. A prolific author, he wrote thirty volumes and several essays. His philosophy is the result of his hard and sustained labour for many years. What is noteworthy is that he had been a poet before he became renowned as a philosopher. His mature philosophy takes shape in his *Scepticism and Animal Faith* (1923) and *The Realms of Being* (1942). *The Realms of Being* is a four-volume work. In these volumes, Santayana has carefully distinguished the realms of being which are the realms of essence, matter, spirit and truth.

Santayana disdains metaphysics and proposes to speak of his system not as metaphysical. Now, keeping in mind Bradley's criticism that an opponent of metaphysics must be a brother metaphysician himself with a rival theory of his own (Bradley 1897: 1), it may be asked, in what sense he disdains metaphysics. The further query is whether his philosophy can be called a system as he calls it. Later on, we shall examine whether Santayana admits metaphysics in any sense at all.

Santayana disdains metaphysics in the literal sense of the word; that is, he dislikes that metaphysics which is concerned with immaterial and non-sensuous things. By his *system*, he means natural philosophy which he does not take as metaphysics (Santayana 1923: vii). Natural philosophy arises from speculations about the natural world. In natural philosophy he claims to be the only living materialist (ibid.). His materialism is not metaphysical, though he says that matter is the substance which lies hidden to us. Many may take materialism into the domain of metaphysics on the very simple assumption that matter, its nature being hidden, is unknown and hence suprasensible to us; and we know that metaphysics deals with what are suprasensible and non-sensuous. But Santayana gives a staunch blow with humour to those who think in such a way, by saying:

> If belief in the existence of hidden parts and movements in nature be metaphysics, then the kitchen-maid is a metaphysician whenever she peels a potato. – Ibid.: viii

His materialism is not metaphysical, because it deals with matters of fact which common sense can easily apprehend. Santayana, at several places, insists that he is merely elaborating upon the obvious experience of common sense of all men. He often declares himself to be a scholastic "at heart" and "in principles". He speaks to William James of scholasticism as "common sense carried out consistently" (Schilpp 1940: 499). It may be asked whether Santayana is as good as his word which he utters to James. This is now postponed till we discuss it in the present chapter in Sect. IV entitled "Santayana and Commonsense Philosophy".

Though Santayana disdains metaphysics as a study of immaterial things, he himself cannot help speaking of them. He speaks much of essence, truth and spirit which are immaterial. And, hence, he cannot disclaim being metaphysical. Santayana himself also admits such position of his (1923: vii). Moreover, he poses as if his system is only materilaism. But his materialism is only one wing of his philosophy, the other wing being transcendentalism which ends in essentialism.

There is another point to be noted here. Does Santayana admit metaphysics at all? He dislikes it in the literal and traditional senses of the word, though he likes it in another sense which is proposed by him. Metaphysics should be confined to the realm of matters of fact. In saying so, Santayana seems to side with Hume who takes up an entirely negative attitude towards metaphysics as an alleged science of the suprasensible and with the positivists who regard metaphysical questions about transphenomenal reality as meaningless combinations of words which are incapable of being empirically verified. The positivists come to their conclusion from the general empirical conviction that all knowledge ultimately depends on sense-experience and from the logical analysis of language. If we analyse linguistic statements, we find that compound ones can be ultimately resolved into simple ones conveying some reports of immediate sense-experience. Moritz Schlick, A.J. Ayer and other positivists hold that the structure of all meaningful language represents the structure of the facts of experience.

Bertrand Russell and Immanuel Kant also opine that metaphysics in the traditional sense of a rational system of knowledge relating to non-sensuous realities is impossible. The latter, however, insists that from the standpoint of our moral experience it is necessary that we should believe in suprasensible realities like soul, God and infinity although such belief is not to be regarded as knowledge proper. In fine, he denies knowledge (in respect of transcendent reality) in order to make room for faith. Now, let us see what Russell speaks of metaphysics. Russell contends that sensible facts are the only facts with which philosophy should be concerned. He replaces metaphysics by logic and makes the latter the essence of philosophy. Many philosophical and epistemological problems such as the nature of substance and cause, of relations, universals and the distinction between truth and falsity are really logical problems, i.e. problems of the correct analysis of the forms of logical propositions and their mutual relations.

Santayana, then, fundamentally agrees with the logical positivists and Russell in the fact that there are no transcendental realities. But the contentions of the logical positivists and Russell which Santayana accepts and supports seem not to be correct. Let us, first of all, take the logical positivistic contention that metaphysics is meaningless. This contention is nothing more than a tautology and hence cannot be accepted. If we translate the sentence "metaphysics is meaningless" by substituting for the subject and the predicate the meanings that they themselves give to these words, it is, then, equivalent to: That which deals with the trans-empirical (non-empirical) possesses no reference to the empirical. But such a platitude cannot really stultify metaphysics. Moreover, the fact that metaphysical propositions cannot be verified in terms of sense data does not necessarily imply that they have no meaning. Again, Russell's contention that facts constituted by sensible things and sensible relations are the ultimate facts in the world is merely a dogmatic assumption.

We should not any longer push our criticism against the view that sensible facts are the only acceptable facts. Let us go back to what Santayana understands by metaphysics. It has been already noted that metaphysics, according to him, should deal with matters of fact which can be presented in logical, moral or rhetorical constructions. The dealing with matters of fact in logical, moral or rhetorical constructions Santayana calls "dialectical physics" (1923: vii). Thus, metaphysics is dialectical physics. In such a physics the ideal entities are materialized, harmonies are turned into forces and natural things are dissolved into terms of discourse. What is interesting is that Santayana becomes a metaphysician in a sense in which he discards metaphysics; consequently, he cannot become a metaphysician as he would like to be.

II. Philosophical Traditions of Santayana's Essentialism

Santayana's philosophical view lies mainly in his essentialism which will be elaborately discussed in Chapters 3 and 4. Any philosophical view when it is found in the great stream of the history of philosophy cannot stand apart from all other views which have preceded it. The same is the case with the essentialism of George Santayana which is found to be connected with the traditional idealistic current of thought. His metaphysics cannot be described as radically original. "My system is not mine, nor new", says he at the beginning of his *Scepticism and Animal Faith* (1923: v).

A. PLATONISM OF SANTAYANA, THE POET

The philosophic traditions which have moulded Santayana's thought mainly on its idealistic side are all reflected in his poetry. *Sonnets and Other Verses,* a thin volume written by him, was published in 1894. In 1896 appeared a reprint of *Sonnets and Other Verses,* which includes an additional sequence of thirty love sonnets. This volume is an eloquent expression of Santayana's philosophy in the making. Here are found some fine tributes to naturalism. The love of beauty and of the ideal he speaks of is Platonic, no doubt; but this love is rooted in nature. There is one sonnet which may be said to be a striking tribute to Platonism which looks behind appearance for the deeper and inner significance of the ideal.

Above the battlements of heaven rise
The glittering domes of the gods' golden dwelling,
Whence, like a constellation, passion-quelling,
The truth of all things feeds immortal eyes.
There all forgotten dreams of paradise
From the deep caves of memory upwelling,
All tender joys beyond our dim foretelling
Are ever bright beneath the flooded skies.

There we live o'er, amid angelic powers,
Our lives without remorse, as if not ours,
And others' lives with love, as if our own;
For we behold, from those eternal towers,
The deathless beauty of all winged hours,
And have our being in their truth alone.

What is most revealed in the sequence of his love sonnets can be presented as consisting of three parts, viz.:

1. The earlier experience of the physical passion, but this experience fails to give satisfaction, and
2. hence occur disillusionment and resignation, which
3. ultimately result in an experience more spiritual and what is called more Platonic, with its envisagement of ideal beauty.

The characteristic qualities of Santayana's love sonnets are those of detachment and idealization. And the very same qualities also characterize his later philosophy. The seeds of *The Realm of Essence* (1927) are already sown in the Platonism of Santayana the poet.

Santayana's essentialism, so to speak, is an echo of Platonic Idealism in great many respects. Santayana himself pronounces, "My theory is a variant of Platonism" (1927: 155). By imparting essences a private realm quite distinguished from the realm of existence, by treating them as eternal, universal, immutable and outside space and time, Santayana, no doubt, approaches Plato's Idealism directly. The world of sense is regarded by Plato as a constant flow and in this view of his, he borrows the idea of absolute becoming from Heraclitus. Here also, we find a striking similarity between the ancient Plato and his modern counterpart as partly reflected in Santayana. The latter also quite unhesitatingly asserts that the world of sense which is a world of existence is in perpetual flux. By developing this theory Santayana, like Plato, approaches very near to Heraclitus.

B. ESSENTIALISM AS DISTINGUISHED FROM PLATONIC IDEALISM

It may be said after Santayana that his theory is a variant of Platonism, but not absolutely, since we find some cases in which he departs, rather consciously, from the path of Platonism.

a. Plato in his myths turns the Ideas as supernatural powers. The Ideas have force and can impose their wills as if they were physical agents. But to conceive essence as possessed of a supernatural power and will is, for Santayana, chimerical, for,

   1. first of all, essence or idea which is immutable cannot exercise any power, be it natural or supernatural, like a physical agent, and
   2. second, for Santayana, there cannot be anything like supernatural power.

   According to him, the supernatural is also natural, but here the natural has been extended into the unknown. Thus Santayana, by standing firm against attributing any power or will to essence, opposes Platonism, and refusing himself, rather in a vexing mood, to be a pupil of Plato:

   > I am no pupil of Plato's in all that phase of his thought in which he seems to supply the lack of a cosmology by turning moral and ideal terms into supernatural powers. The supernatural is nothing but an extension of the natural into the unknown. – 1927: 155

b. Santayana stands in sharp opposition to Plato when the latter ascribes subsistence to essences.

   > An insidious remnant of such Platonic mythology adheres to the notion of essences when these are said to subsist.
   > – Runes 1943: 317

By subsistence Santayana means "latent duration" which again means "steady persistence in time". But the essence is beyond time; the eternity intrinsic to it is timeless. Thus to say that essence subsists is a contradiction in terms.

c. The Platonic Ideas bear a threefold significance – ontological, teleological and logical. To judge ontologically, they have real being; they are what they are. The essences of Santayana also have been assigned by him an ontological status. From the logical side the Ideas have three functions: first, to enable us to bring order into the chaos of individual things; second, to recognize the similar and the dissimilar; and lastly, to apprehend the one in many. It has already been said that Santayana cannot tolerate to treat immutable, passive essences as physical agents performing too many functions. The Platonic Ideas have a teleological significance. They are the "primary" patterns of things. All becoming has its end in a being. Each Idea is a perfection of its kind and the ground of the existence of the individual objects coming under it. Thus, perfect whiteness is the ground of the existence of all white objects. The existence of men is explained by the ideal man or the perfect man. Everything is explained by its end. This is a standpoint marked by teleology. And the teleology of Plato finds its culmination in the Idea of Good which stands for the final explanation of all other Ideas and of the entire universe. But in Santayana's philosophy we come to notice that essences cannot have any teleological significance. They, unlike Plato's Ideas, are insubstantial. How, then, can they be the pattern of things which are substantial in character? Moreover, being themselves non-existent, they cannot be the ground of the existence of physical things.

d. Plato, by extending the theory of Ideas to all things, brings the problem of appearance and reality into a new light. The Ideas are the ultimate realities of which things are appearances. But the problem of appearance and reality does not arise in Santayana's Essentialism. The things which are in the flux of existence are by no means accounted by the essences which transcend existence.

The distinction between Santayana's essentialism and Platonic idealism is now manifest, although the latter has influenced Santayana in the formation of his philosophy. Catholicism, medieval scholasticism and the psychology of William James are among other forces which are operative in giving an idealistic pattern to his thought.

C. THE INFLUENCE OF CATHOLICISM UPON SANTAYANA'S ESSENTIALISM

Catholicism as a religious doctrine has its place in Christianity. This doctrine expresses itself not only in Christian symbol and allusion but also in a glowing tribute to faith and in a warm human sympathy. Moreover, there is in the Catholic, whether nominal or devout, a love of finality which makes agnosticism deeply repellent. In his early years Santayana, like his parents, has set himself down officially as a Catholic. From Catholicism he learns "to believe the heart". From Catholicism, again, his heart is led "unto the thinking of the thought divine". In such thought what he finds is arresting and beautiful, but insubstantial. He understands that religion envisions essence. Being aware of its illusory character he yet does not wish to discard it. Like his parents, he regards religion as "a work of human imagination"; but unlike them, he thinks that the works of human imagination are alone good and the whole world is "ashes in the mouth" (Schilpp 1940: 7). This childish conviction which is due to the influence exerted on him by Catholicism becomes soon over (not being, however, totally extinct from his mind) by his attraction towards naturalism.

We find Santayana's deep-seated respect for the claims of naturalism even in the earliest phase of his philosophy. As he states:

> My naturalism or materialism is no academic opinion ... it is an everyday conviction which came to me, as it came to my father, from experience and observation of the world at large, and especially of my own feelings and passions. – Ibid.: 12

His sympathetic attitude and traditional allegiance towards Catholicism on the one hand and his deep-seated respect for naturalism on the other hand create a conflict in his mind in his early years. For him both sides – Catholicism and naturalism – are equally strong and both at once claim to enter into his mind. But these strands of thought, being opposite in their nature, cannot be harmoniously placed into his mind. Santayana's early pessimistic attitude is perhaps due to such conflict.

At last Santayana becomes able to come into a resolve by giving up Catholicism and accepting and advocating naturalism fully. His renunciation of Catholicism in favour of naturalism is perhaps due to his coming in contact with the naturalistic psychology of William James. In his naturalism, James lays stress upon the immediacy of sensation and seeks the springs of consciousness and conduct in physiological processes. Santayana becomes familiarized with the physiological approach to psychology through William James. Being influenced by James, Santayana takes the physical forces as the true matrix, carrying a materialistic interpretation of the universe. Thus, his incipient naturalism, fortified by James' naturalistic psychology, draws his mind heavily to prefer the world of scientific law. He understands that in such preference there is complete disillusion. Let Santayana here speak for himself.

> For my part, I was quite sure that life was not worth living; for if religion was false everything was worthless and almost everything, if religion was true. In this youthful pessimism I

> was hardly more foolish than so many amateur mediaevalists and religious aesthetes of my generation. I saw the same alternative between Catholicism and complete disillusion: but I was never afraid of disillusion, and I have chosen it.
>
> – Schilpp 1940: 7-8

Thus, by choosing disillusion, Santayana tries to put an end to his mental conflict. By abandoning Catholicism he shows that he accepts naturalism. And we hear him speak, "Now in natural philosophy I am a decided materialist – apparently the only one living" (1923: vii). But the question is whether he has been really able to avoid the influence of Catholicism. Is not his essentialism which serves as a keystone of his mature philosophy the outcome of that stage in his early years in which his Catholic mind was charmed by the vision of insubstantial essences? That Santayana has been influenced by Catholicism, at least to some extent, cannot be denied.

D. SANTAYANA'S DEBT TO MEDIEVAL SCHOLASTICISM

Santayana's early acquaintance with medieval scholasticism, it may be presumed, has led him in the direction of essence. The schoolmen took much interest in the discussion about universals or essences. With Saint Thomas Aquinas, scholasticism has reached its most comprehensive and consistent development. He treats God as "the highest intelligible good" to be glimpsed only through the power of intellect in contemplation. This Thomistic conception is prying as if in Santayana's philosophy when the latter speaks of the intuition of essence. It may be said in this connection that the schoolmen often mistook essence for existence, but Santayana has never made such a mistake. Medieval scholasticism owes much to Aristotle. Santayana's devotion to the intensive study of Greek philosophy brings him much closer to a true recognition of essence. Aristotle's conception of "form" on the one hand and Platonic Ideas on the other are no doubt the ingredients which have helped Santayana in the construction of *The Realm of Essence* (1927).

The universality and permanence of essence are ascertained by both Platonism and scholasticism. But that essence can be immediately revealed through sensation has not been marked out by them. In this respect, William James can be treated as a pioneer. Santayana has been very much impressed by James' aptitude for catching and describing essence. To recognize the immediacy of essence as revealed through sensation is to recognize its physical dependence upon existence. Santayana, however, will not admit this, though it is quite definite that he has been influenced by James' sense "for the immediate: for the unadulterated, unexplained, instant fact of experience" (Schilpp 1940: 15).

E. SANTAYANA'S DEBT TO EARLY MODERN PHILOSOPHY

Santayana's sceptical approach to essence has perhaps been made easy by his study of early modern philosophy. The early British and French schools speak of the psychological approach to essence. This is evident when Hume says:

> When I enter most intimately into what I call myself, I always stumble on some particular perception or other, of heat or cold, light or shade, love or hatred, pain or pleasure. I never can catch myself at any time without a perception, and never can observe anything but the perception. – 1739: Bk I, Pt. IV, Sec. 6

This sounds very much like Santayana's intuition of essence. The earliest Germans have discovered the infinity and multiplicity of essence. Spinoza's assertion of the reality as infinite and having the capacity for infinite variations of form and Leibnitz's splitting up reality into the multiplicity of spiritual entities describe essence rather than existence. In the Sect. IIA of Chap. 3, it has been described how Santayana's essentialism differs from, and stands related to, the monadology of Leibnitz. It may be said here that German idealism in treating essence as substance or in speaking of it as if it were purely subjective is not acceptable from Santayana's side, since for him essence is not substance and again it is not subjective or cognate with the mind.

F. SANTAYANA'S DEBT TO B. RUSSELL AND G.E. MOORE

Santayana is indebted in some degree to Bertrand Russell and G.E. Moore, the English realists. Russell and Moore, from the vantage point of mathematics, discern a world of pure, immutable forms which are quite independent of mathematics. The being of these forms, being timeless, is neither mental nor physical. Physical entities have spatial and temporal existence. And similarly, mental entities like thoughts and feelings may be said to exist insofar as they are in time. The pure, immutable forms do not exist, since to exist is to be in time. They merely subsist. But let it be noted here that even the term "subsistence" cannot, according to Santayana, be predicated of essence, for it has reference to time (vide Sect. IIC, Chap. 3). But Russell uses the term to signify the timeless being of pure, immutable form. After his study of Russell, Santayana's frequent and consistent use of essence and existence can be noticed. In "Apologia Pro Mente Sua" Santayana expresses his debt to Russell and Moore by saying:

> When Russell says that, for his part, he still hopes for something better than faith, I wonder if he is not pining for those essences that, as essences, he no longer is sure of. It was he and Moore that helped me, in 1897, to grind fine and filter Platonic Ideas into my realm of essence. – Schilpp 1940: 587

G. SANTAYANA'S ACQUAINTANCE WITH INDIAN PHILOSOPHY

In his early years Santayana was acquainted with Indian philosophy. The Indians hold that all experienced events are illusory appearances. They are given but non-existent. This doctrine of illusion has charmed Santayana most, the Indians' doctrine of transmigration and their mention of some ulterior refuge or substance being superfluous to him: "It is the Indians", says he, "who have insisted most sincerely and intrepidly on the non-existence of everything given" (1923: 51). The Indians' sense for everything given as non-existent is carried out in Santayana's doctrine where we find that the data of intuition are implied in the fact that they are given.

Santayana's statement that the Indians have insisted upon "the non-existence of everything given" is unjustified. It overlooks most of the systems of Indian philosophy which are realistic and treats its idealistic aspects as the whole thereof. Although it is true that the Advaita Vedānta has treated the experienced events as appearances, it is at the same time the undeniable fact that its realism leaves room for empirical reality even of appearances. It has distinguished three grades of experience:

i. certain experiences which an individual gets in illusion, dream, etc. such experiences being private to him;

ii. certain experiences which are common to all individuals under normal conditions; and

iii. pure experience.

The first kind of experience has ephemeral existence (*prātibhāsika sattā*) only.

It is temporal and is contradicted by the second kind of experience which has empirical existence (*vyāvahārika sattā*). This kind of experience has a more stable existence and a greater practical value than the objects which appear momentarily in illusions, dreams and the like. But the world of experienced events is not absolutely real, since it is open to future contradiction. Pure experience or experience as such is present in all particular forms of experience. It is neither contradicted nor contradictable by any experience. It is the absolute experience. The evidence of such an experience can be found in dreamless sleep. It is only realized in a state of deep concentration (*samādhi*) in which all the specific forms of consciousness disappear and what is left is formless consciousness which simply is and, is thus also pure existence.

Thus we get, according to the Indian view, three orders of reality, corresponding to the three grades of experience. In the transcendent order, reality is pure existence–consciousness–bliss which is free from all particularity, duality and finitude. In the empirical order, it is manifested as the particular forms of existence and consciousness. In the apparent order, it takes the form of fragmentary world of subjective appearances. The discussion made hitherto will find Santayana's statement in a slight correct form, viz. it is the Indians who have insisted most sincerely and intrepidly on the "existence" of everything given.

CONCLUSION

The above discussion of the philosophical traditions of Santayana's essentialism enables us to understand the inner implication of his own words, "My system is not mine, nor new". The doctrine of essence of which Santayana speaks is not definitely anything new. This doctrine has been already expounded by Plato and Aristotle and medieval scholasticism. Methinks, there is something novel in Santayana's doctrine of essence. It has been noted how Santayana, being influenced by his predecessors, still differs from them. The points of difference tend to prove that some novelty is attached to his doctrine. There is another sense in which Santayana's doctrine can be regarded as new. The Platonic Ideas, the forms of Aristotle, the universals of schoolmen, being devoid of the character of existence, are said to subsist. But to Santayana, the question is: How do the Ideas or the universals which are held to be immutable possess the character of subsistence, when by subsistence is meant latent duration? Having felt this difficulty, Santayana regards essences devoid not only of existence but also of subsistence. Herein lies the novelty of his doctrine. Santayana's vastness of thought, lucidity of writing, poetic expression and philosophic insight impart to him that originality which is his own. What he says in several places may not be accepted, but still they are his own thoughts viewed from his own standpoints.

III. Santayana's Essentialism and Current Thought

Is Santayana's doctrine of essence a phase of any current movement? Santayana himself answers to this question in the Preface to *Scepticism and Animal Faith:*

> My system, finally, though, of course, formed under the fire of contemporary discussions, is no phase of any current movement. – 1923: viii

It is doubtful or a point of dispute whether Santayana's doctrine has been influenced by any current movement of thought. But that this doctrine bears, a striking similarity with the doctrines of other contemporary philosophers can be easily marked out.

A. SANTAYANA'S ESSENTIALISM AND MODERN PHENOMENOLOGY

Modern phenomenology with which the name of Edmund Husserl is primarily associated can be compared to Santayana's philosophy. Husserl wants to make philosophy radical. Here radicalism is defined as the "absolute freedom from all presuppositions". The radicalism in this sense is also viewed in Santayana's *Scepticism and Animal Faith* which he regards as an introduction to a system of philosophy.

Husserl takes the "phenomenological reduction" as the primary step for the constructive work of philosophy. The phenomenological reduction includes eidetic reduction and transcendental reduction. Eidetic reduction means that essential structures or essences, and not particular facts, are alone of interest. They are non-existent and timeless. They cannot change. They are out of all local relation to the "real world", since they are non-real. They are "immediate data" or "pure phenomena". Thus, Husserl's doctrine of essence comes very close to that of Santayana. Alfred North Whitehead also has come upon essence from the mathematical point of view. He clearly points out to a realm of eternal, individual entities. The eternal entities are sometimes called "sense objects" or sometimes "scientific objects". Therefore, for these entities Whitehead uses the terms which are misleading and adventitious.

The transcendental reduction of which Husserl speaks possesses a technique of "elimination" and "bracketing". Everything contingent can be eliminated or put into a bracket. It may be said here that Husserl adopts the Cartesian method of doubt. And like Descartes, Husserl, by following the method of transcendental reduction, reaches "pure consciousness" of an individual knower. He thinks that philosophy should start from the fact of pure consciousness. Thus, the phenomenological method is subjectivistic. Everything in the world can be doubted, but the experiences referring to the world cannot be doubted without involving contradiction. Here the experiences stand related to the experiencing being. Like Husserl, Santayana also is a transcendentalist. Both of them put the world of contingent things into a bracket.[1] But it should be remembered here that this bracketing for Santayana is not final, since the world he brackets for the purpose of making transcendental flight is accepted from the side of animal faith.

By adopting the same method of transcendentalism, both Husserl and Santayana do not, however, arrive at the same terminus. Transcendental reduction leads Husserl to the "pure consciousness" of an individual knower. But Santayana's transcendentalism leads him to the discovery of essences which are independent of consciousness. The former's standpoint is subjectivistic as against the latter's objectivistic standpoint. One goes back to the Cartesian principle, the other to the pre-Cartesian principle.

Husserl does not give an objective status to the "pure phenomena" or "immediate data". They are all insignificant apart from their relation to the knower. When "being" is spoken of, "known

---

1 Santayana has never used the word "bracketing" which is reserved for Husserl and his followers.

being" is meant. From this, it can be inferred that Husserl's philosophy is under the influence of empirical schools. Like Husserl, Whitehead also invests essence with too tight-fitting a subjectivity. But Santayana, following the path of his Greek predecessors, imparts to the realm of essence an objective status.

We find another point of difference and a very important one, between Santayana's essentialism and Husserl's essentialism. Husserl, by putting essences in relation to the pure consciousness of the knower, cannot advocate the impossibility of knowing them. He says that no one can in truth profess not to know essences. Again, according to him, knowledge of the essences is not representative. They are directly presented to the consciousness of the knower. But Santayana, as against Husserl, says that knowledge of the essences is not possible. Essences can be intuited but not known. Santayana recognizes that essences have a role to play in the field of cognition, but that does not mean that they themselves are cognized. We shall see in Chap. 5 how Santayana establishes his position that essences cannot be known. And it will also be noted there what he means by the intuition of essences.

B. SANTAYANA AND RENÉ GUÉNON

René Guénon, "a pupil of the Oriental School", better describes the realm of essence and in that respect comes very close to Santayana's own findings. Like Santayana, Guénon places the realm of essence above the realm of existence. Again, like the former, the latter holds that a portion of essence can be illustrated in existence; i.e. what is meant here is the realm of truth. The discussion of the realm of truth remains here postponed till we come to Chap. 5.

Santayana's doctrine of essence is, then, formed "under the fire of contemporary discussions". But it can be hardly said that Santayana has been influenced by the contemporary thinkers.

It is not a surprising fact that a philosopher's views can have similarities with the views of other philosophers without being influenced by the latter.

IV. Santayana and Common Sense Philosophy

In our introduction to the present chapter, Santayana's staunch belief in scholasticism has been referred to. By scholasticism he means "common sense carried out consistently". He often declares himself to be a scholastic "at heart" and "in principles". This means that his philosophy is in the main based upon consistently carried out common sense. No doubt, Santayana attaches great importance to common sense philosophy, but still he feels, or rather is conscious of, the dullness and barrenness of this philosophy. To quote him:

> The philosophy of the common man is an old wife that gives him no pleasure, yet he cannot live without her and resents any aspersions that strangers may cast on her character. – 1923: 11

In spite of feeling dullness in common sense philosophy, Santayana does not pause to accept it. He has a great respect for the "orthodoxy which the sentiment and practice of laymen maintain everywhere" (ibid.: v). Even he thinks that common sense is better than the special schools of philosophy, each of which, due to its narrow sightedness, does not explain many facts, although it claims to discover the key to the whole. Common sense beliefs are "ill expressed, but they are well grounded (ibid.). Santayana accepts common sense, not in its crude form, but "in a more accurate and circumspect form (1923: v). He boldly announces, "I stand in philosophy exactly where I stand in daily life; I should not be honest otherwise" (ibid.: vi). A promising announcement, indeed! But has it been possible for him to be sincere to common sense in the long course of his philosophizing? May be, he is a scholastic "at heart" and "in principles", but not in his ways.

Common sense never suspects the existence of the external world. Santayana's view also does not vary from common sense in this respect. In 1904, he wrote to William James:

> The materials which experience is composed of must be credited with an existence which makes them material elements and gives them a mechanical order, since they exist also permanently, potentially and beyond our range.
> – Perry 1935, II: 397

To deny the external world is to reduce it to James's "buzzing, blooming confusion". Common sense belief about the external world is what is called by Santayana "animal faith". Our whole life is based upon our instinctive belief in an independent outer world.

In the introduction to the present chapter, it has been pointed out that Santayana's materialism is not metaphysical if by metaphysics is meant the science of the suprasensible. He claims that his materialism is the product of observation and common sense rather than of any particular philosophic tradition. But his materialism is not the only philosophical presumption. We have pointed out that there is another side of his philosophy, viz. transcendentalism by which he comes to an idealistic conclusion – to the discovery of essence. The *Realm of Essence* is a more original construction than the *Realm of Matter* and is more unfamiliar to the common man. By presuming transcendentalism which leads ultimately to idealism Santayana evidently departs from the path of common sense.

To be absorbed in the intuition of the datum or an essence is not to remain entangled with the busy world to which common sense gives so much importance. Santayana admits:

> This trick of arresting the immediate is in one sense an interruption to life; it is proper only to poets, mystics or Epicureans. – 1927: 156

But is not Santayana himself something of all three? Santayana loves solitude, since it is ideal for the contemplation of essences. He takes solitude as

> the sole path to happiness for the intellectual man, because (he) cannot be satisfied with a good world of perpetual change, defeat and imperfection. – 1922: 120

Santayana, who regards himself as a scholastic "at heart" and "in principles" and who insists that his philosophy is merely the elaboration of common sense experience, should not have spoken like that. But he does so. The changing world does not satisfy him. Only the infinite realm of essence can give that solitude and that confinement which are best suited to his temperament. He is so prone to taking interest in the realm of essence that to him "the rest – the whole real world – is ashes in the mouth" (1940: 7). We find him saying, "I have absolute assurance of nothing save of some given essence" and "the rest is arbitrary belief" (1923: 110). All these utterances sound strange as made by a philosopher who has promised to cast his lot with common sense.

Santayana claims that his materialism is not metaphysical (ibid.: vii). But what is interesting is that a metaphysical element has entered into his materialism. Common sense lays emphasis upon the possibility of knowing matter. Santayana also at first sides with common sense and says, "Nothing can be intrinsically unknowable" (1923a: 8). In Sect. II, Chap. 4, entitled "Is Santayana an Agnostic?" it has been shown why matter, though not unknowable, becomes unknown to us. Matter itself is not unknowable, but to us it remains "dark"; our sense is not so empowered to know it. But matter or substance which Santayana claims not to be unknowable becomes so when he says that existence is "a surd" and "a contradiction". Matter being "a surd" and "a contradiction" ever eludes the grasp of reason or intellect. Thus, it becomes not only unknown but also unknowable. It becomes metaphysical.

Again, Santayana cannot strictly adhere to common sense in respect of knowing objects. According to common sense, objects are directly known. The American neo-realists also maintain this view. Santayana who is a critical realist cannot hold this view of knowledge. His epistemological position as a critical realist is opposite to that of a new realist. The following observations will serve to draw attention to their respective standpoints:

> While the new realist holds that knowing is the givenness of the object, its literal presence to inspection, the critical realist regards knowledge more as an interpreting of a selected and meant object by means of characters discriminated in the field of consciousness. Such knowing is a complicated affair with its meanings and its categories which have gradually been developed in the human mind in its continued response to things.
>
> – Sellars 1929: 288

Critical realism of which Santayana is a distinguished follower makes knowledge respresentative and symbolic. The critical realist's view of knowledge as distinguished from the neo-realist's view of the same would be discussed in Chap. 5, Sect. IB. Here what is to be said is that Santayana's representative theory of knowledge is not the common sense theory of knowledge which is presentative and direct.

Thus, though Santayana promises to make common sense experience of all men the foundation of his philosophy, he fails to keep his promise in the actual course of his philosophizing. He has elaborated his philosophy quite contrary to common sense. He says that essences are known before things, that essence is separated from existence, that spirit comes from matter. Are these the common sense experience of all men, "that shrewd orthodoxy which the sentiment and practice of laymen maintain everywhere"? Santayana himself admits:

> In regard to my intended allegiance to common sense that in several important matters, I have not been able to maintain it.
>
> – 1942: 832

2

Method

Scepticism *and Animal Faith* (1923) and *Realms of Being* (1942) are the two main works which constitute Santayana's mature philosophy. The first phase of his mature philosophy is his philosophic method which is known as the sceptical or doubting method. Now, let us proceed to discuss it.

I. Scepticism

A. SANTAYANA AND DESCARTES

Santayana's motive behind adopting the sceptical method is like that of Descartes. Like Descartes he wants to clear the mind from prejudices and old convictions or beliefs. A true sceptic must clear away all the miasmas of the past and of the present. Santayana's endeavour is

> to think straight in such terms as are offered to me, to clear my mind of cant and free it from the camp of artificial traditions; but I do not ask anyone to think in my terms if he prefers others. – 1923: vi

Descartes's scepticism is forced to halt at the self-certitude of the thinking ego. He is right in affirming the certainty of self-consciousness in some sense or other. Practically all subsequent philosophers have to admit or refute what Descartes had affirmed. Santayana's case also is not an exception. He, in his treatment of what he calls "wayward scepticism" (vide chap. III of *Scepticism and Animal Faith*), has shown how the romantic sceptic feels that when he has doubted everything, his own self or ego remains as the only final certainty. In Santayana's own terms, this point of view, so far from being genuinely sceptical, marks rather an "intensification of affirmation". Nothing could be more wrong-headed than to find ego at the extremes of doubt.

Santayana brings some charges against Descartes:

i. He urges that Descartes sets some accidental limits to his scepticism even about facts, for example, about the fact of his *cogito, ergo sum*. Santayana thinks that as this principle of Descartes has an existential reference, it must, therefore, be a fact, since his view is that every fact must be existent. Descartes takes the fact of *cogito, ergo sum* as self-evident, but Santayana urges that no fact is self-evident (1923: 290).

   Now, it may be said in reply to what Santayana has viewed about Descartes's first principle that he has erred in taking the latter's principle as an "attestation of fact" (ibid.). Though Descartes's *cogito, ergo sum* is the existential judgement, it is the only simple judgement that is self-evident, since it is an intuition. *Cogito, ergo sum* is not derived from any major premise, viz. "whatever thinks exists". On the other hand, this universal proposition has been derived from the particular, "I think, therefore I am". We must first know within ourselves that as thinking beings we exist, before we come to the general proposition, "whatever thinks exists". Thus Descartes's *cogito, ergo sum* is not a syllogism. When it is not a syllogism, it is not a fact also. If it were a fact, it would be derived from another fact: thus it would become a syllogism. But Descartes's *cogito, ergo sum* cannot be called a fact, since it is not derived from anything else. It is purely an intuition.

ii. Santayana declares that Descartes's mind "was not plastic nor mystical enough to be profoundly sceptical" (1923: 289). He thinks that a true sceptic must be a mystic. And Descartes fails to be a genuine sceptic, since he is not mystical-minded.

    That Descartes's mind was not mystical is a hasty, though partly right and partly wrong judgement passed upon him by Santayana. It is hasty, because Santayana does not pause to consider the implications of Descartes's method. Descartes is an intellectualist and a rationalist as well. But intellectualism is broadbased on the self-certifying truth of the self which is not the result of discursive reasoning, for this truth is not rationally but intuitively known. So the roots of rationalism are deeper than those of mysticism. It is, however, debatable whether the intuitionism of Descartes is mystical or intellectual. As a matter of fact, Descartes's intuition is rather the culmination than the negation of reason. Intuition is that non-dubious apprehension of a pure and attentive mind which is born in the sole light of reason ... (1959: 12).

From this point of view, Santayana's charge that Descartes's mind was not mystical is correct. But from another point of view, viz. that reason is something more or even higher than the discursive intellect or that at the stage of intellectual intuition the mind is self-evident or truth is its own witness, Santayana's charge seems open to modification, for in the matter of self-certitude of the thinking ego, mysticism stands on an equal footing with intellectual intuitionism.

B. SANTAYANA'S SCEPTICAL PROCEDURE

Santayana claims to be a sincere sceptic. He pushes his scepticism as far as he logically can, "even at the price of intellectual suicide (1923: 10). But we shall see in Sect. V of this chapter that Santayana does not play fairly as a sceptic. And it is doubtful if he at all has been able to pay "the price of intellectual suicide". Of course, there are some who have praised Santayana's scepticism. For example, Frederick A. Olafson observes:

> Santayana brought to the sceptical task something that is exceedingly rare: a mind genuinely free and detached, and that if scepticism is a viable enterprise at all, he went about it in the right way. – 1954: 44

Let us now see how Santayana follows his sceptical path.

Conventional beliefs are so bred in the bones of man that he cannot easily discard them. Santayana cleverly remarks:

> The philosophy of the common man is an old wife that gives him no pleasure, yet he cannot live without her, and resents any aspersions that strangers may cast on her character. – 1923: 11

But a sincere sceptic must throw off everything which would stand as an obstruction on the way of the clearing of his mind. Religion must, first of all, be doubted, as it is "arbitrary". All the religious beliefs are uncertain and insecure. All established religions must be discredited on account of their variety and absurdity. They are all "fantastic" and "insecure". Santayana says:

> Mere experience and good sense suggest that all positive religions are false, or at least (which is enough for my present purpose) that they are all fantastic and insecure. – Ibid.: 12

After declaring all religions as fantastic and insecure, Santayana proceeds to doubt all histories as "literary fiction". He aslo impugns the belief in physical facts reported by the senses and by natural science. The sceptic can deny all facts and events. Even change can be denied. Actual change, however, may be the object of belief. The more we insist on the idea of change, the more we retreat into the changeless and the immediate, "for evidently the idea of pure change would always be the same, and changeless" (ibid.: 29). Thus, change ends in being self-contradictory.

Thus, all claims to an external world can be discarded. The past is a fiction composed by the imaginative mind in the present moment of reflection. The British and the German solipsists are not consistent to the sceptical mind, as the ideas of which they speak refer to the physical objects of time and space. Thus, solipsism of those idealists is not of the present moment; they posit only remembered experience which can be put to the snare of doubt. What cannot be doubted is solipsism of the present moment. As Santayana observes:

> Any solipsism which is not a solipsism of the present moment is logically contemptible. – Ibid.: 14

The philosophy of the German idealists seems to him a futile, romantic vision. German philosophy, says he, "wore in my eyes a rather questionable shape" (1915: 17).

> Their idealism is a religion of the actual. It rejects nothing in the daily experience of life, and looks to nothing essentially different beyond. It looks only for more of the same thing, believing in perpetual growth, which is an ambiguous notion. – Ibid.: 17

Even the logical principles do not escape from Santayana's ravenous sceptical method. They are arbitrary, according to him. He pushes his sceptical process and says that nothing given exists. What is given is internal or intrinsic to intuition. But existence is not given, as it involves external relations and flux. An existent thing, says Santayana, stands in variable external relations to other existent things and for this very reason to be aware of it involves the awareness of the things to which it is related; but this is impossible, for the relations, if any, of whatever I am aware at any moment must be internal to it. Hence, nothing given exists.

Santayana seeks some authorities to give support to this conclusion of his. He thinks that it is the Indians who have boldly asserted the non-existence of everything given. All the worldly objects are illusory appearances. Thus, the Indians deny change; and in denying change they accordingly deny all existence. They take the principle of existence as an evil principle; passion or sin is the universal source of this illusory existence. If the individual can conquer his passion or sin, that is, if he can be healed morally, he will be liberated from his painful existence. Santayana compares the evil principle of existence to his animal faith. Existence is posited by animal faith.[1] Though it is approached by belief, it is doubtful to the sceptic. Every part of experience is illusion and the animal nature of the individual is the source of this illusion.

The sceptic would accept nothing but the simple appearance or datum given to consciousness. Santayana says:

> The sceptic, then, as a consequence of carrying his scepticism to the greatest lengths, finds himself in the presence of more luminous and less equivocal objects than does the working and believing mind; only these objects are without meaning, they are only what they are obviously, all surface. – 1923: 70

Thus, the logical conclusion of the sceptical process is a kind of timeless intuition of pure essence or quality, absolutely free from references to the external world of physical objects or change. We can doubt or deny that the blue of the sky, the roundness of the sun, the crash of the thunder represent substantial objects, but still we have the blue, the roundness and the crash. Therefore, what is given to consciousness is simple, mute appearance or datum.

---

1 Santayana's meaning of *animal faith* needs to be understood. Animal faith is that tendency to belief which is inherent in the very animal nature of man. We are all instinctively believers. Thus *animal faith* is an instinct.

> It will appear dwelling in its own world, and shining by its own light, however brief may be my glimpse of it: for no date will be written on it, no frame of full or of empty time will shut it in; nothing in it will be addressed to me nor suggestive of any spectator. It will seem an event in no world, an incident in no experience. The quality of it will have ceased to exist: it will be merely the quality which it inherently, logically, and inalienably is. It will be an Essence. – 1923: 73-74

The datum which is ultimately reached by the sceptical process is merely an appearance, not an event. To say that the datum is an event is to see it as existent. And to assert existence of it is to place it in relations which are not internal to it. But any datum may be contemplated to the exclusion of all external relations whatever. Moreover, if the datum be an existent thing, the awareness of it would be an impossibility. And it has already been shown (p. 29) why the awareness of an existent thing is not possible. Hence, it can be concluded that the datum does not exist. A pretty long quotation is requisite here:

> The sceptic turns ... to the immediate, to the datum; and perhaps for a moment he may fancy he has found true existence there; but if he is a good sceptic he will soon be undeceived. Certainly in the immediate he will find freedom from the struggle of assertion and counter-assertion; no report there, no hypothesis, no ghostly reduplication of the obvious, no ghostly imminence of the not-given. (Moreover, all that is obvious and self-evident is that which appears; the fact of the appearance is an after-intuition, another appearance.)
>
> Hence an important conclusion which at first seems paradoxical but which reflection will support; namely, that the notion that the datum exists is unmeaning, and if insisted upon is false. ... That which is certain and given ... is something of which existence cannot be predicated, and which, until it is used as a description of something else, cannot be either false or true. – 1923: 43, 45

Kant was regarded as a sceptic in his day. And his philosophy is called criticism. But Santayana says that Kant's scepticism "was very impure and his criticism, though laborious, was very uncritical" (ibid.: 298). Kant and his followers are not critical as they uncritically assign uniform modes of thought to all men. Kant "posited a transcendental ego, the categories of thought, and a disembodied law of duty" (ibid.: 299). Moreover, "instead of natural substances he posited the unknowable" (ibid.). Santayana says that the true sceptic must throw off all principles of interpretation in his transcendental flight. Kant's scepticism is impure, according to Santayana, in the sense that he posits some principles and categories which should have been put to doubt.

Santayana finds that the sceptic, by his transcendentalism, reaches the peak of ultimate scepticism. This may also be called solipsism of the present moment. Here, he will face nothing but the realm of essence. In such a position, he must be mute, devoid of existence, of life itself. This is the point of intellectual suicide. This condition of the sceptic can be consistently expressed by "silence and death" (ibid.: 168). Santayana says, "scepticism is an exercise, not a life" (ibid.: 69). Indeed, it is an exercise in mental gymnastics. And by such an exercise he denies change, memory and existing facts. If he gazes only at the picture gallery of essences, or, if he reduces himself to the intuition of the obvious, he will thereby renounce all knowledge. But Santayana asserts that the sceptic cannot remain for a long time on the summit of ultimate scepticism where he finds a secure place for himself and remains free from all doubts. He must come down from such a lofty place to the busy world full of events and existing objects.

The simple, mute apprehension of the datum, drained of all external or existential relations, is a blind alley walled up on all sides. How can the sceptic, for whom the continuing apprehension of the essence or essences is impossible, leap over that wall into the existent? By an instinct inherent in him? This instinct instigates him to believe in the existent. This is called animal faith. By animal faith we take for granted the duration and identity of sensations, experience, memory, the self, the external objects and the external world. Scepticism renounces all knowledge, but animal faith establishes it. Santayana develops a theory of knowledge to a fuller extent only on the basis of animal faith. His theory of knowledge will be discussed in Chap. 5.

Thus, in Santayana's *Scepticism and Animal Faith*, we find an absolutely sharp separation of the given and the believed. What is given is intuited. And it has already been noted (p. 29) that nothing given exists. The believed is the not-given. Therefore, in *Scepticism and Animal Faith*, we get the best statement of Santayana's dualistic philosophy.

In retrospect, it may be said that Santayana uses the sceptical method in his philosophical enquiry. And by using this method what he discovers is datum or essence which is inert, mute and drained of all existence. We shall, after a while, see why Santayana chooses the sceptical method for his philosophic speculation. In the meantime, let us take a passing note of the other methods, besides the present one under discussion, referred to by him. These methods also enable us to arrive at what is reached by the sceptical method. That is, these methods also discover ultimately the essence or essences. They, including the sceptical method already discussed, may be called routes which, if followed, lead to the finding of essence or datum. One such route is dialectic.

II. Dialectic

Dialectic means a discourse which involves temporal and progressive existence. The force of the dialectic depends on an instinctive faith in the ability to think and to live rationally. As Santayana observes:

> ... dialectic would lose all its force if I renounced my instinctive faith in my ability to pick up old meanings, to

> think consecutively, to correct myself without changing my subject matter, and in fine to discourse and to live rationally.
>
> –1923: 120-21

Dialectic involves analytical survey of some essence. The essence which is intuited is not simple. It has different parts within it. For example, Euclidean space is a single essence. Yet its character can be analysed in the way that it has three dimensions, is infinite, without scale, etc. Thus, every essence has inward complexity which can be demonstrated by analysis. But analysis is not the whole of dialectic. Dialectic or mental discourse proceeds from analysis to synthesis. The terms in an essence which have been isolated by analysis are synthesized again. For, Santayana observes:

> The force of dialectic … lies in identifying terms in isolation with the same terms in relation; so that even an analytic judgement is synthetic.
>
> – Ibid.: 119

It explores various parts of the realm of essence and "reaches valid insight into their structure" (ibid.: 122).

SANTAYANA AND HEGEL

Here, Santayana's dialectic can be compared to that of Hegel. Both of them advocate dialectic in the positive sense and thus both differ from the Socratic dialectic which is mainly negative. Hegel's dialectic ends in the Logical Idea. Santayana's dialectic also culminates in the apprehension of essence which has the logical or aesthetic being (ibid.: 120). Again, Hegel's dialectic has a progressive movement; and this movement consists of three moments, viz. thesis, antithesis and synthesis. Santayana also calls his dialectic "progressive discourse" (1923: 122), but it consists of only two moments: analysis and synthesis. Unlike Hegel's, it involves analysis only, instead of thesis and antithesis. But the notion of synthesis is involved in the dialectic of both Hegel and Santayana.

III. Aesthetic Experience

Another route by which essence can be directly apprehended is called aesthetic experience. When the sudden impact of beauty attracts our mind, we concentrate upon it to the exclusion of surrounding objects. The charming smile of a child can so fix our mind that for the time being we may forget all ambient circumstances. What is requisite, says Santayana, for looking upon an essence is simple attention or concentration of the mind.

> Awaken attention, intensify it, purify it into white flame and the actual and unsubstantial object of intuition will stand before you in all its living immediacy and innocent nakedness. – 1927: 2

Essence will appear to the attentive mind in its "innocent nakedness", i.e. in a form divested of existential garb.

It is said that aesthetic experience is a method or route by which essence can be discovered or apprehended. But it may be asked, is it a method at all? The answer seems to be in the negative. What is called an experience cannot be called a method. These two are different. Instead of being identical, one leads to the other. That is, we can have an experience of something only when we follow a method. Aesthetic experience is a kind of immediate feeling. It cannot be a method at all. Only it can be said that in such experience is apprehended the aesthetic character of an essence.

IV. Why Does Santayana Choose the Sceptical Method?

So far, we have seen that Santayana puts before us different methods by which we can discover the realm of essence. But he chooses for himself the sceptical method. Now, the query which deserves to be answered is: what is the background to his choice of the sceptical method?

A. PERSONAL BACKGROUND

The root of Santayana's choice of the sceptical method lies in his personal background. He liked solitude from his early years. When he was nine years old, he came with his father from Avila to Boston to be educated there. He faced a new language, new customs and religion which were not at all in harmony with the ways to which he had so long been accustomed. In such a foreign environment, the seeds of solitude developed in him. Naturally, he could not remain encircled within the busy world. He attained gradually an introspective attitude towards life. In solitude he could cultivate his imagination which ended in the discovery of essence, the keystone of his mature philosophy. Santayana says:

> ... they (the works of human imagination) are good, they alone are good; and the rest – the whole real world – is ashes in the mouth. – 1940: 7

From his boyhood, then, Santayana developed the sceptical attitude from his sense of solitude. He says:

> Solitude is the sole path to happiness for the intellectual man, because (he) cannot be satisfied with a good world of perpetual change, defeat and imperfection. – 1922: 120

Intellectual scholars like Spinoza and Kant were enclosed in their own solitary world and their philosophies are the outcome of such a world. The mind of Santayana was drawn towards the heaven of ideas which he called the realm of essences, by renouncing the world of existential objects by his sceptical method. He liked solitude, wanted to retreat into it. And scepticism made a fair job for that retreat.

B. PHILOSOPHICAL BACKGROUND

Santayana's grasp of the sceptical approach to essence was made easy by his study of early modern philosophy, especially the British and French schools.

Descartes and Santayana

All early modern philosophers have adopted the sceptical method. But their scepticism never carries away common sense by violence nor denies the external world. Descartes follows the sceptical procedure. Nevertheless, he proceeds to posit selves, matter and God. And this he does with an 'animal faith' equal to Santayana's. Descartes is not a good sceptic, according to Santayana. The objections raised by Santayana against Descartes' scepticism and the answers to those objections from the present writer's point of view have been already discussed (pp. 26-27). As for scepticism, Santayana carries it further to the solipsism of the living moment. His scepticism is tentative. The same can be said of Descartes also. By using the doubting method Descartes finds out the first indubitable principle, *cogito, ergo sum*. Santayana also by his sceptical method discovers the essences which are all obvious, all surface.

Hume and Santayana

It has been said that Santayana has "Hume in his bones" (1944: 255). To him, Hume is nearer than others. Like the latter he questions beliefs in causality and the self. Santayana's scepticism ends, like Hume's, in the discovery of the ultimate, irreducible sense impression. Hume's arguments against a belief in substance and in the self are in similarity with Santayana's discovery of essence. A thing is nothing more than a collection of qualities. Likewise, the soul is a collection of ideas. We have, says Hume, no idea of substance distinct from that of a collection of particular qualities. To quote him:

> For my part, when I enter most intimately into what I call myself, I always stumble on some particular perception or other, of heat or cold, light or shade, love or hatred, pain or pleasure. I can never catch myself at any time without a perception, and never can observe anything but the perception. –Selby-Bigge 1949: 252

Thus, according to Hume, the passing sensation is the only thing of which we can rest assured. Santayana also says that in the immediate apprehension of the simple datum there can be no illusion.

Between Hume's scepticism and that of Santayana, there is a difference as well. In Santayana's philosophy, both scepticism and animal faith play their respective parts – scepticism in discovering the realm of essence and animal faith in positing the external world. Thus, his attitude towards metaphysics is not destructive. But Hume takes up an entirely negative attitude towards metaphysics. He also says that knowledge of the external world is not at all possible, because such knowledge is not direct or intuitive. Again, when he says that the passing sensation is the only reality, he also fails to recognize the sense impression as the representative character of knowledge. Though he strikes a strong blow against the common sense view that knowledge is indirect, he accepts only the sense impression which is nothing but the representative character of knowledge. Thus, Hume is not consistent, since by his scepticism he drives away common sense which, again, enters his theory in the form of sense impression which he thinks to be the only reality.

Santayana follows the sceptical method of Hume. But he does not distort the vision of common sense, as Hume does. Santayana does not keep animal faith in abeyance in his philosophy. He sets it free from the snare of doubt. Animal faith establishes the existence of the external world, all knowledge, memory, etc. Santayana says in the Preface of his *Scepticism and Animal Faith* that he has a great respect

> for a certain shrewd orthodoxy which the sentiment and practice of laymen maintain everywhere. – 1923: v

We have seen in Sect. IV of Chap. 1 that he fails to maintain his respect for common sense. Finally, it may be said that though with regard to the method Santayana follows Hume, he supports, or rather shows sympathy with, Descartes, Locke and Berkeley who, in their metaphysics, never distort the vision of common sense.

V. Santayana's Method Examined

A. IMPOSSIBILITY OF UNIVERSAL SCEPTICISM

Santayana demands complete scepticism, "even at the price of intellectual suicide". But Bertrand Russell states that complete scepticism is "totally barren and totally useless" (1928: 55). He continues that when a sceptic says that nothing is certain, he must add that some things are much more nearly certain than others. Thus,

> it is much more nearly certain that we are here assembled tonight than it is that this or that political party is in the right. – Ibid.

Russell emphasizes the fact that there are only degrees of probability.

> Therefore, I do not think that we should go in for complete scepticism, but for a doctrine of degrees of probability. – Ibid.

Santayana, however, would say that the doctrine of degrees of probability is a matter of animal faith. Anyway, Santayana promises to carry out universal scepticism, but there are certain aspects at which doubt is forced to halt.

i. Santayana, by his proposed universal scepticism, denies the necessity of the logical principles by saying that they are "arbitrary" and "instinctive"; but these principles are not arbitrary, since all intellectual inquiry whatsoever becomes possible by the application of them. The logical principles are instrumental to the possibility of knowledge. Santayana says that animal faith is an instinct which he does not doubt. Consequently, the logical principles which become amenable to animal faith should not be doubted. They are instinctive in the sense that the mind possesses them by custom or habit from the beginning of one's cognitive life. But by this is not meant that they are innate. Anyway, the necessity of the first principles is unquestionable; they cannot be rejected or denied.

Most of the thinkers give a prior importance to the principle of contradiction. Some, of course, say that the principle of identity is the fundamental law. Santayana by denying the principle of contradiction affirms it. His scepticism cannot be called universal, as it ultimately halts at the discovery of datum or essence. Beyond essence his doubting method cannot proceed. If his scepticism be called universal, then essence should also be doubted; but as this is not the case, so his method, we can safely conclude, is not universal. Thus to practise or propose universal scepticism is an impossible task. And the impossibility of proposing or practising universal scepticism rests upon the infallible truth of the principle of contradiction.

ii. Scepticsm is meaningless if it does not serve a purpose. When Santayana proposes to exercise universal scepticism, it is at least implicitly meant that his scepticism does not care for any purpose. Such a doctrine is absurd and hence untenable. If we posit doubt, no matter if it becomes universal, we also posit indirectly the ability of the mind to know something. Thus, the mental capability to know something which is implied by proposing doubt cannot be doubted further. This is another aspect towards which Santayana's scepticism cannot extend.

iii. Further, Santayana's sceptical method cannot be called universal in the sense that in positing doubt the certitude of self-existence should also be posited. I exercise doubt yet I have no existence of my own – this is contradictory and unintelligible. Self-existence is the firm foothold upon which scepticism depends. It, so to speak, mobilizes scepticism. It may be said in this connection that self-existence is not the first certitude, as Descartes proposes. Awareness of one's own existence is possible through the operations of the intellect which are specified by the objects of its operations. Thus, the intellect becomes aware of itself through the awareness of something other than itself.

B. DOGMATISM IN SANTAYANA'S PHILOSOPHY

From the above we understand that Santayana's scepticism is not more thoroughing than that of Descartes. Though Santayana wants to be a thorough sceptic, dogmatism crawls in his philosophy. Santayana, being himself not conscious of his dogmatic attitude, hints that Descartes's scepticism creates a chance for dogmatism entering into his theory. Descartes is dogmatic in this that he has assumed the principle of sufficient reason. Santayana cannot blame Descartes, because he himself strictly, though unwillingly, adheres to the principle of sufficient reason. There is sufficient reason of Santayana's scepticism for the discovery of essence.

The first principles which are rejected by Santayana are assumed by him. We find him speaking of "self-contradiction". As he says:

> Evidently to deny the truth is to make an assertion, and thereby to allege that there is a truth. Yet a formal refutation of this sort remains rather puerile. It would ignore the depth of irritation and animal courage in that self-contradiction, the scorn of words, the reversion to primitive slumber. – 1938: 122

Santayana in another place writes:

> To deny the being of essence, because it may happen to be unrealized, is self-contradictory; for if it is not realized, it must have a quality, distinguishing it from realized forms. – Ibid.

He, again, applies the law of identity to essences. He says that essences "are what they are" (ibid.: 5). Thus, he assumes the very principles which he rejects.

Santayana, by his transcendental criticism, does not attach existence to essence. The datum or essence is abstracted from existence. Now, such abstraction will be possible if there be any previous knowledge of essence drained of all existence. Thus, here also, dogmatism enters into Santayana's doctrine stealthily. Again, he tells us that the datum or essence is "by definition the whole of what is found" (ibid.: 18) in intuition or "by hypothesis, (it) is the whole of what solicits my attention" (1923: 35). The definition of, and the hypothesis regarding, essence cannot be proffered by a philosopher who proposes universal scepticism. Thus, Santayana's philosophy abounds with dogma or presuppositions. Any doctrine implies dogma insofar as it proclaims positive judgements. Santayana himself recognizes this fact. He says:

> Dogma cannot be abandoned; it can only be revised in view of some more elementary dogma which it has not yet occurred to the sceptic to doubt. – 1938: 8-9

The presuppositions which support Santayana's doctrine can be reduced to two a priori postulates, viz. materialism and transcendentalism. The former explains the source or origin of all things and ends in naturalism. The latter transcends all knowledge of the external world and reaches a realm where there is no existence of anything – it is a realm of essences. Therefore, transcendentalism ends in essentialism. Being encircled by these two presuppositions Santayana moves between them. Let us allow him to speak:

> We must oscillate between a radical transcendentalism, frankly reduced to a solipsism of the living moment and a materialism posited as a presupposition of conventional sanity. – 1940: 17

Both materialism and essentialism will be discussed in Chap. 4.

Thus, the two fundamental doctrines, materialism and transcendentalism, coexist in Santayana's philosophy as postulates. By transcendentalism, Santayana arrives at immaterial essences treating the whole external world as "ashes in the mouth". He says, "I have absolute assurance of nothing save of the character of some given essence" and "the rest is arbitrary belief" (1923: 110). If that be so, he should have strictly adhered to essentialism. But he is not content with living wholly in the realm of essence. He refers to animal faith by which he postulates materialism.

> [The materialism of] Herbert Spencer, I think, taught me nothing. I agreed with his naturalism or materialism, because that is what we start with: the minimum presupposition of perception and action. – 1944: 249

Santayana says that the external world which falls outside the realm of essence is "ashes in the mouth". What are "ashes in the mouth" should be totally rejected or denied. But the external world is not cast away by Santayana. It is accepted by him as "the minimum presupposition of perception and action". The whole thing sounds strange and odd. Yet Santayana speaks like so.

Materialism and transcendentalism[2] are the two doctrines which seem to be irreconcilable opposites. On the basis of traditional philosophy, they suggest two realms different altogether, viz. the realm of matter and the realm of essence. From this point of view, materialism and transcendentalism are the two opposite poles which cannot meet together. Materialism accepts all knowledge, but transcendentalism transcends or denies any knowledge. Santayana places materialism and transcendentalism in his philosophy side by side with total disregard of the commonly recognized contradictions existing

---

[2] By "transcendentalism" is not meant here Kant's usage of the term in the sense of the doctrine of the transcendental presuppositions of knowledge.

between them. So considered, if he is to proceed "logically", he cannot but profess idealism. His scepticism leads to essentialism which is idealism. Transcendentalism in favour of which he stands is the trap of idealism and, once in its claws, there is no escape, even by animal faith.

A reconciliation of materialism and transcendentalism is, however, possible from the naturalistic standpoint of Santayana. As a matter of fact, Santayana does not recognize materialism and transcendentalism as mutually exclusive or contradictroy. Though a materialist, Santayana never says that matter is the only reality. If he said so, the antagonism of matter and essence could arise. What Santayana really insists is that matter does everything, that it is dominant in every existing being, even when that being is spiritual (1930: 100). In this sense of materialism, a reconciliation of it with transcendentalism is possible. The contemplation of essences in a transcendental stage is a function of the spirit and this spirit is material in its origin. The nature of spirit and its relation to matter will be discussed, in Sect. 4 of Chap. 4.

3

Notion of Essence

I. Genesis of the Notion of Essence in Santayana

WE HAVE investigated the first phase of Santayana's metaphysics. His sceptical method, an instrument used to discover essence, which is ultimate and not subject to any further doubt, has been dealt with so far. Let us now approach the second phase of his metaphysics, the notion of essence which stands as the keystone of his philosophy. Essences, says Santayana, have a realm of their own. Metaphysical in its content and meaning, Santayana's doctrine of essence in its origin springs from the psychological demands of his nature. The realm of essence is oft-contemplated by him, as it is best suited to his temperament. It makes him feel solitary and detached from anything existential. The very solitude and detachment which he developed from his boyhood finds its reflection, as it were, in the realm of essence. The realm of essence gave him sincere friendship, solitude and confinement.

II. "Realm" of Essence

Now, the question is: In what sense does Santayana speak of the realm of essence? The term "realm" has spatial and temporal connotations. Does he use the term "realm" in the above sense? Definitely not. As the essences are devoid of all existential reality, the realm, therefore, they constitute is neither material nor temporal, but purely formal. In this realm every essence or datum is merely an appearance devoid of all existence. It is apparent in the sense of being self-evident and luminous; its nature is wholly manifest. Again, it is apparent in the sense of being a specific being which lies simply in its own category. If it is a colour, it remains only as colour. If it is a pain, it is just this pain and not anything else. Each essence is identical with itself. It rejoices in its own quality.

A. SELF-IDENTITY: ESSENCE AND THE MONAD

Thus, the principle of essence is self-identity. Each essence constitutes its own little universe, being devoid of all extrinsic relations to other essences. Each essence is immaterial and inert. It is simply that which it inherently, logically and unchangeably is (Santayana 1923: 39). The self-identity of each essence implies its individuality. One essence is not another essence. The theory reminds us of Leibnitz's "monadology". Leibnitz's "monadology" which splits up reality into a multiplicity of spiritual entities (which are called monads) describes essence rather than existence. Like Santayana, he also says that self-identity is the principle of monad.

But the resemblance that is found between Santayana's essences and Leibnitz's monads is only superficial, their differences being more fundamental. First, each monad is self-identical and yet there is continuity among the different monads in the sense that all represent the same universe in all possible grades of perfection. Santayana, on the other hand, observes that there is no continuity among the different essences. Moreover, all the monads are the same in kind, in that they are spiritual in character. They differ only in their modes of representation of the universe. But essences are different in kind. Each essence has a quality of its own. Further, monads are active in being centres of energy. Otherwise, how can they represent the universe? But essences are inert. Furthermore, monads at least appear to act through space and time which, according to Leibnitz, are due to the confused perception of the monads. But essences are bare of all existential relations. They are spaceless and timeless. But if they are timeless, can it be said that they are eternal? This is a problem to which we shall pass over shortly. Finally, what is important is that all the monads constitute the whole universe. But the realm of essence is not the whole of the universe. Santayana has referred to the other realms of being, the realms of matter, truth and spirit. These realms would be discussed later on, the realms of matter and spirit in the next chapter and the realm of truth in the chapter on epistemology.

B. ETERNITY OF ESSENCE

From the self-identity of an essence, Santayana continues, follows its eternity. When the eternity of an essence is maintained, can it be said to possess an endless duration? Santayana is reluctant to include the idea of duration in that of eternity. "The eternity intrinsic to all essences is timeless" (Runes 1943: 317). That time, according to Santayana, is forever exiled from the domain of eternity is what is also found in one place of his *Scepticism and Animal Faith*. He says:

> Eternity, taken intrinsically, has nothing to do with time, but is a form of being which time cannot usher in nor destroy.
> – 1923: 112

Eternity, being devoid of time, becomes empty; but it does not amount to saying that it is unreal. It is rather real. What is devoid of content remains perfectly silent and eternity, which is also empty and hence internally undisturbed, is "silent". Moreover, eternity which belongs to all essences is "indestructible". If the notion of time be involved in eternity, essences fail to be eternal, for in that case they become moving essences, the notion of which Santayana cannot admit, since to him all essences must be inert. Thus, time, instead of being applied to eternal essences, does apply to the objects of the physical world which are believed to be existent.

This theory of Santayana which relates to the infinity of abstract eternity is what echoes the ancient philosophy of Ideas. Such a philosophy treats Ideas or Forms as eternal in the sense of their being immutable. To say that Ideas are eternal is as good as saying that they are timeless. In the *Timaeus* Plato distinguishes eternity from infinite time. Spinoza also says:

> Eternity cannot be defined in terms of time nor can it have any relation to time. – *Ethics*, V.I, Scholium

But in Henry Bergson, as in modern science, we find that "duration is not a dilution of eternity" (1914: 363). Eternity divested of time, according to this French philosopher, is an eternity of death. Eternity is always living and moving. In it duration is included "as the vibrations are in light" (Bergson 1913: 54). Bergson, then, does not, like the ancients and the modern Santayana, take eternity as immutable and devoid of time, but as absolute duration.

C. ETERNITY AND SUBSISTENCE

The eternity of an essence keeps it aloof from being subsistent. To say that an essence subsists is the same thing as to say that it endures. By subsistence Santayana means "latent duration" (Runes 1943: 317). Hence subsistence is something proper to matter or existence, which is the negation of eternity. Subsistence is not identified with matter, though it applies to it. Subsistence means duration which again means "steady persistence in time". "Existent" is that which comes-to-be, endures and passes away, i.e. in flux. Thus, subsistence forms one of the phases of the existential flux, far from being identified with the flux itself. The notion of existential flux will be carried out more fully in the next chapter, entitled "Essence and Existence".

Russell and Santayana

Russell is of the opinion that subsistence has no spatial reference which existence has. To say that something subsists amounts to saying that it has being. Russell has identified subsistence with being. But Santayana thinks that subsistence belongs to the category of existence, far from being identified with being. It has already been noted that he has not totally separated subsistence from existence, nor has he identified the one with the other. Both Russell and Santayana take existence as the principle of change. But the former does not, while the latter does, take subsistence as duration which implies change.

D. INFINITY OF ESSENCE

If essences, according to Santayana, neither exist nor subsist, to which category do they belong? This is a query to which we shall attend later on, keeping it postponed now. It is here worth mentioning that essences are infinite in the sense that they are non-existent and, therefore, unlimited and undetermined by any extrinsic connotation. That an essence has not appeared to anyone's intuition does not annihilate its being. Whether it appears to anyone's intuition or not, in either case, it maintains its being and in that sense it is infinite. To deny an essence because of not being realized is self-contradictory, for being unrealized "it must have a quality, distinguishing it from realized forms" (1927: 21). Thus, paradoxically, to deny an essence is to admit it.

E. INDIVIDUALITY AND UNIVERSALITY OF ESSENCE

From the self-identity of an essence, as it has been already pointed out, follows its individuality. Each essence is identical with itself. This means that it is self-contained and self-dependent. And it is individuated by its intrinsic character which is self-identity. Each essence is distinct and clear, thus not allowing any shade of vagueness into it. Essences are primary (1927: 138). Santayana contends that the very individuality of each essence renders it a universal as well. It may appear to us that what is individual cannot be universal, since these two terms are contrary. But Santayana affirms that an essence which by its own nature retains its individuality is not (again, according to its nature) loosened from its universality, as he insists that the universal and the individual, instead of being contrary, are identical (ibid.: 19). Each essence is individuated by its intrinsic quality, not by its extrinsic relations. It contains no allusion to spatial and temporal setting. Thus, being divested of all extrinsic relations it appears as an ideal term. In this sense, universality is predicated of essence.

Santayana, Plato and Russell

Santayana's theory of universals keeps its affinity with those of Plato and Bertrand Russell, at the same time not being totally identified with them. Plato's theory of ideas is substantially a theory as to the nature of universals. The "idea" or "form" is eternal, immutable and indestructible. The same adjectives are attributed by Santayana to essence. Plato says that the particulars of sense derive a sort of quasi-reality from the eternal ideas which are universals. Thus, he maintains a causal relation between the universals and particulars. Santayana, however, notes that the universal essences form a realm of their own, much like Whitehead's "realm of eternal objects" (ibid.: 18). Essences which are non-existent cannot be the cause of the particular objects of sense which are believed to exist. Matter, which is the principle of existence, is the matrix of all particular things. This is Santayana's contention which will be referred to in the next chapter.

Russell also holds like Plato that the universals are entities which are eternal and immutable. Santayana also cannot but admit this. He, again, is closely allied to Russell when the latter treats a universal as neither mental nor physical. Mental entities, like thoughts and feelings, and physical objects exist insofar as they are in time. But universals do not exist in space and time. An important point of difference, however, remains between Santayana and Russell. Santayana rejects subsistence with regard to the universals, since it implies duration which cannot be applied to the immutable inert essences. Russell, on the other hand, accepts subsistence with respect to the universals in the sense of their having "being". Santayana also affirms that essences have "being", but not in the sense of being "subsistent". Anyway, he vitally agrees with Russell that universals form a realm of being which is different from the realm of existence, the first being unchangeable and the second fleeting. For Plato, the one is real and the other is semi-real; for Russell, both are real; but for Santayana, the realm of being alone is real, the world of existence being doubtful to him as a sceptic. Let it be noted that the next chapter is devoted to Santayana's discussion about the relation of essence and existence.

F. PURE BEING AND ESSENCE

Santayana considers Pure Being itself as an essence. Again, he takes it as the substratum of all essences. As Santayana says:

> Pure Being supplies, as it were, the logical or aesthetic matter which all essences have in common, and which reduces them to comparable modes on one plane of reality. Pure Being is thus found in all essences as light in all colours or life in all feeling.
> – 1927: 45

Santayana maintains that Pure Being which serves as the universal basis of all essences cannot be existent. It may be said in this connection that the query which we have raised before (p. 49) whether essences which neither exist nor subsist belong to any category seems to have been answered now. Being is a category to which all essences belong. Existence is experienced as a "dull strain". But Pure Being is apprehended through, in the words of Henri Bergson, "intellectual sympathy" which both he and Santayana call intuition. We shall have to rise above the level of sense-experience if we like to apprehend Pure Being. We may now see how Santayana in his theory of Being inclines towards the ancients.

Plato and Santayana

Plato speaks of the Supreme Idea, the idea of Good, as Pure Being which must be perfection itself. Plato never regards Being as a mere abstract concept. It is a concept which comprises and includes all other ideas each of which is also a being or perfection of its kind. Thus, the Supreme Idea, according to Plato, is the ground of all other ideas. But in the Platonic philosophy the theory of ideas has a teleological significance which Santayana vehemently opposes with regard to his own theory. Plato asserts that all becoming, including human conduct, has its end or aim in a being which symbolizes perfection. But according to Santayana, becoming or the realm of existence or matter does in no way aim towards the realm of essence,[1] although the former is continually adopting an essence, but not the same essence always, since it is dynamic or fleeting in nature.

Plotinus and Santayana

Plotinus, as against Plato, urges that Being or God is absolutely one which is beyond all multiplicity. But Plato affirms that the Absolute Being can be no abstract unity, but only a unity in multiplicity. Plotinus cannot follow Plato in this respect. His Being is totally abstract. It is beyond all multiplicity. But still he pronounces multiplicity or the world as somehow coming forth from the one Being. Plotinus is not definitely consistent here, although he, being a mystic, easily evades, the logical absurdities of his theory. Santayana, having placed the realm of essence above the realm of existence which is the realm of multiplicity, leans towards Plotinus. But he disagrees with Plotinus, when the latter holds that the One gives rise to the multiplicity, including matter. Santayana gives a different account of the source of multiplicity. He presumes that the plastic substance or matter explains multiplicity.

---

1 Santayana writes: "No essence ... is the goal of any natural process, much less its motive power." – 1923: 79

Santayana and the Advaita Vedānta in India

In the Advaita Vedānta we get the notion of Pure Being which can be compared to Santayana's concept of essence. The Advaitins demand a supersensible reality, much like Santayana's essence, which, being not within the world of change, is different from the phenomenal, the spatial, the temporal and the sensible. This supersensible reality or Pure Being (*Brahman*) as the Advaitins call it, again like Santayana's essence, is not eternal in the sense of persisting changelessly through time, but in the sense of absolute timelessness and incorruptibility.

But the differences between Santayana's notion of essence and the Advaita view of Pure Being are more fundamental than the similarities existing between them. First, *Brahman* is one while essences are many. Second, *Brahman* is devoid of anything of a like kind or of a different kind and has no internal variety (*sajātīyavijātīyasvagatabhedrahitam*). But Santayana speaks of the differentiation of essence. Each essence being self-contained is distinguished from another essence. Moreover, Santayana refers to the inward complexity of essence, thus admitting its internal differentiation. As he says:

> The datum may seem purely qualitative, like a smell or like absolute Being, and yet some plurality may lurk in its very diffuseness or continuity, giving a foothold for discrimination of different moments or parts within it.
> – 1923: 116

Euclidean space, for example, is a single essence, but its character, being inwardly complex, is subject to analysis, such as it has three dimensions, is without scale, etc. Santayana observes here that each essence may be taken as a unit in spite of its inward complexity.

Santayana speaks of general essence which is shared by all essences in common. This general essence is called Pure Being which keeps much affinity with *Brahman* of the Advaitin.

Each essence has a special quality of its own, but Pure Being of which Santayana speaks has no special form and *Brahman* of the Advaitin also is without any form. Both Pure Being of Santayana and *Brahman* of the Advaitin are absolutely self-identical. There is, of course, a difference between Pure Being of Santayana and *Brahman* of the Advaitin. Santayana lends objectivity to Pure Being, while the Advaitin identifies *Brahman* with *Ātman* (consciousness). To the Advaitin, the purely subjective is the purely objective. But again, we find affinity between the Advaitin and Santayana. The former says that *Brahman* is of the nature of consciousness and yet knows nothing, since empirical cognition is a modification of the internal organ; and like the Advaitin, Santayana also observes that Pure Being or essence knows nothing and empirical knowledge arises out of the demands of the internal psyche (vide Chap. 5, Sect. III C).

G. NON-BEING AND ESSENCE

Each essence, Santayana observes, partakes not only of the nature of being but also of the nature of non-being. To him, it is not a contradiction in terms to state that essence is both being and non-being. Being and non-being are not antagonistic but complementary to each other. Non-being does not mean the absence or negation of being; it is what signifies a privation of essence. An essence partakes of non-being in the sense that it is not being of another sort, i.e. another essence. Thus, non-being is the principle by which one essence is separated from another essence. It imparts individuality to every essence. Non-being, then, belongs to every essence separately, while Pure Being belongs to all essences as an omnipresent basis.

Pure Being also does partake of the nature of non-being. It, being a universal, cannot be particular and is devoid of all specific properties. It is pure self-identity divested of all extrinsic relations. It is perfectly inert and self-contemplated. Both essence and Pure Being partake of non-being, but the latter does so in a high degree. Each essence has a special quality of its own and thus it is distinguishable from any other essence; but Pure Being has no special form, it is purely what it is (Santayana 1927: 57). It may be mentioned as a reminder to the reader that Santayana, albeit he discards the logical principles, has taken the principle of identity as constituting the very nature of essence or Pure Being.

III. What Essences Are Not

Let us now see, after Santayana, what essences are not. We get the following negative results from the fundamental assertion that essences are non-existent.

A. ESSENCES ARE NOT FACTS

Facts mean events in time and space which are found to occur in the existential world. Thus, they are rooted in the external world. But essences, being spaceless and timeless, do not occur in the world of existence. They are all surface forms having no origin or locus in the external world (Santayana 1923: 39). Facts are experienced, but since the appearance of an essence is not an event, its presence is not an experience (ibid.). Again, facts, as they occur in time, are transitory (ibid.: 267), but essences being timeless are eternal. Moreover, facts have the character of contingency, since they are not out of all adventitious relations and every fact that exists in the world might also not exist. But essences being entirely devoid of such relations cannot have "the contingency nor the fortunes proper to an existence" (ibid.: 39). That is to say, essences have a necessity not had by facts. Furthermore, facts have a changing character due to their occurrence in the existential flux; but essence, since it is above all flux, "is simply that which it inherently, logically, and unchangeably is" (ibid.).

B. ESSENCES ARE NOT IMAGES

An image is a representation of percept observed in particular space and time. Thus, though unsubstantial in its appearance, it refers to an existential object; in other words, every image is a replica of a percept. But essences are not images, since they are not representations. Unlike images, essences are original in the sense that they lie simply in their own categories. Again, images as they are bound by space and time are fleeting in nature, but essences are eternal and not determined by space and time.

C. ESSENCES ARE NOT SENSATIONS OR THOUGHTS

Sensations and thoughts belong to the existential order. Sensation means a bare awareness of some object existing in the external world. Thinking is a cognitive process. Both sensation and thought occur as events whenever an object is presented. But essences, as they do not belong to the existential order, are not either sensations or thoughts. And for the same reason they are not events also. In this connection, Santayana's distinction between "eventual" essences and mere essences may be suggested here. Eventual essences are called by him "tropes". Tropes or eventual essences are those which are embodied in matter. Mere essences are those which are given as terms in intuition. Essence, says Santayana:

> never occurs alone, but either as the form of some existing thing or event, or else as a term given in intuition. – 1927: 382

Here, in this saying, he refers to both eventual essences and essences which are not eventual. What is to be specially mentioned is that whether essences are embodied in matter or simply given in intuition, they shine always under the form of eternity.

Santayana writes that an essence may be conceived by sensation or by image or idea, but is not to be confused with them. As an example, he refers to the intuition of essence yellow. If somebody sees a buttercup by opening his eyes, the intuition is called image or idea. If he, again, opens his eyes and sees yellow while there is no buttercup, the intuition is called hallucination. "These various situations," Santayana observes:

> are curious, and worth distinguishing in optics and in medical psychology, but for the sceptical scrutiny of experience they make no difference. – 1923: 91-92

Whatever the process of intuition may be, what appears in all cases is an essence, the essence yellow which cannot be altered.

D. ESSENCES ARE NOT FORMS

Santayana opposes taking essence and form as identical. His distinction between essence and form seems to depend upon his criticism of Platonic Idealism. Plato's Ideas, though placed in an abode separated from the world of things, are regarded as the forms of things. Ideas are the formal causes of things insofar as they constitute the essence of the latter. Thus, they are turned into supernatural powers or "magic powers". On this very point, Santayana disagrees with Plato. Essences which are non-existent cannot be the forms of things which are believed to be existent. Santayana's essences have the texture and ontological status of Platonic Ideas, but the cosmological, metaphysical or moral prerogatives which are attributed to Ideas cannot belong to essences, since essences are "neutral in value".

Santayana, in spite of regarding essences as not forms, often interchanges the words form and essence, so that the distinction between them remains no more sharp and becomes blurred. For example, in one place he says that essences are the "forms of substance" (1930: 219). Again, in another place he observes:

> The flux of nature could not be a flux, nor at all perceptible, unless it was a flux through essences, that is, through forms of being differing from one another. – 1927: 40

It may, however, be said that Santayana's words are contradictory, but his meaning is not. He wants to mean by his theory that essences are not definitely forms. Santayana has not expressed himself as clearly as he should have.

E. ESSENCE IS NOT POSSIBLE BEING

The question of possibility and impossibility cannot arise in the realm of essence, since such a realm is always posited with certainty. It is a realm which is eternal. The notion of possibility or impossibility has applicability only in the field of discourse. In the field of discourse the possible essences are considered to the exclusion of other essences. Thus, here essences are found to contradict themselves. But the realm of essence is such a realm where any one essence does not contradict another, as each is "a little universe, an immaterial absolute theme, rejoicing merely in its own quality" (Santayana 1923: 39).

F. ESSENCES ARE NOT THE CONSTITUENTS OF THINGS

Essences cannot be regarded as the constitutive qualities of things, since each of them is a world apart and shines by its own light. If essences or universals have no existence, how can they constitute the particulars? Santayana gives an example of a man looking at the sky. The blueness and roundness of the sky are not its constituents. They are the qualities which are relative to the observer who happens to observe them. "So when a human eye," says Santayana,

> is turned skyward, the sky truly acquires the quality of looking blue and round: those are its real qualities in relation to such an observer, as certain substances are truly poison for rats.
>
> – 1927: 44

What he means by an essence is the quality sensed. And that belongs no more in some brain cell or nerve tissue than in some sunbeam or thunderbolt outside the body.

According to Santayana, then, essences are the qualities sensed. And they cannot be held to be the constituents of things. Right is he, since any quality cannot be the constituent cause or the substratum in which the effect inheres. The colour of the threads cannot constitute cloth, the threads being its constituent cause. In Indian philosophy, the Nyāya doctrine describes constituent and non-constituent causes as *samavāyī* or *upādāna* and *asamavāyī kāraṇa* respectively. The effect is produced by its material or *upādāna kāraṇa*. The threads are the material cause of the effect, cloth. *Asamavāyi kāraṇa* (non-constituent cause) is the mediate cause of an effect. It determines the character of the effect insofar as it stands as an inherent attribute of the *samavāyī kāraṇa* (constituent cause). The colour of the threads is the mediate cause of the colour of cloth. It has been noted that essence cannot be the constituent cause. Santayana, again, cannot take it as a non-constituent or mediate cause. Since essence is what is independent, it cannot be mediated through, or stand in any intimate relation of anything. Now, if essences or the qualities of the blue and the round be not non-constituent cause of the sky, i.e. if they do not determine the nature of the sky, how, then, is it possible to know and say that the sky is blue and round? Is it possible by animal faith? Santayana would say that any cognitive claim must be an act of faith. And the function of essences in cognitive claims is to provide descriptive terms by which we can think and speak about the objects we encounter. The problem cited here would be discussed in Sect. IIIC, Chap. 5.

G. ESSENCES ARE NOT ABSTRACTIONS

Essences are not abstracted from anything. They are immaterial and as such are not abstractions from matter. What is achieved by the process of abstraction cannot be called universal. But an essence is universal. Each essence is held to be "rejoicing merely in its own quality". This means, it is individual. Individuality indicates independence. An essence, being individual and hence independent, cannot be a product of abstraction. Essences cannot be abstracted from things for the reasons given below:

i. They make experience of things possible. Essences, Santayana observes, "are given before the thing can be clearly perceived, since they are the terms used in perception" (1923: 93-94). This means that they are a priori.

ii. As essences are not parts of things, they cannot be abstracted from the latter. To say that essences are the parts of things is to imply that they are no more independent. Having never been parts of any perceived object, it is impossible that given essences should be abstracted from it.
– Santayana 1923: 94

Thus, each essence, being not abstracted from anything, is "a positive and complete theme" (ibid.) in its appearance. Or, in other words, it is concrete in the sense that it is the exact and total appearance.

Santayana, of course, recognizes that essence can be a product of, and hence an abstraction from, cognitional process in a temporary sense. For example, a man sees an orange which in turn may suggest a sphere. In this instance "roundness" comes as "a late idea", and

> for that person the sphere will be something abstract, not indeed in its essence, but in its mode of reaching manifestation: an act of abstraction happens first to have revealed this essence to this man.
> – 1927: 34

But Santayana never presumes that at first we know objects and then we come to apprehend essences by way of abstraction. It is within our possibility to intuit the essence "roundness" without previously considering a round object (ibid.: 34-35).

It has been already noted (p. 30) that essences appear in intuition. Hence, it is worthwhile to point out the relation between essence and intuition. We find an entire chapter on Essence and Intuition in Santayana's *Scepticism and Animal Faith* (1923).

IV. Essence and Intuition

By intuition, Santayana understands "the light of awareness lending actuality to some essence" (1923: 151). Sometimes he calls it "an act of attention" (1930: 254). However, he means by intuition an immediate awareness. We can have an immediate awareness or intuition of essences. But this intuition is possible through the psyche, since Santayana takes the psyche as "the organ of the intuition" (1923: 151). In *The Realm of Matter* the psyche is defined as a trope of matter, an unconscious movement towards goals and objectives. Let us see after Santayana how intuition arises from the first existence of the animal psyche.

> A psyche, the hereditary organization and movement of life in an animal, must first exist and sustain itself by its "intelligent" adaptations to the ambient world: but these adaptations are not conscious until, by virtue of their existence, intuition arises, and intuition arises when the inner life of the animal, or its contact with external things, is expressed in some actual appearance, in some essence given in feeling or thought.
>
> – 1927: 9

Essences arise in intuition by the special character and movement of both the psyche and the material circumstances. The role played by the psyche here is very important.

Being driven by the psyche intuition is absorbed in its object. In the act of intense contemplation of essence intuition forgets that it springs from the material psyche. Though material in origin, intuition is oblivious of itself and cognizant of immaterial themes. It may be thought that finally essence and intuition of essence become identical. But Santayana does not think so (1923: 128). He says that essences arise in intuition only through the operation of the psyche. If intuition becomes identical with essence, it loses its material source, i.e. becomes disconnected with its organ, viz. the psyche. But being disconnected it completely ceases. And this result leads to a further consequence, that no essences can arise in intuition. Thus, as Santayana shows, to say that intuition is absorbed in the contemplation of essence does not amount to saying that it becomes identical with essence. Essence without arising in intuition is valueless in the sense that it can no more become the object of contemplation, the goal of any effort and the secret ideal of life (ibid.: 128-29).

The distinction between essence and intuition, Santayana says, must be ascertained. There is a profound and certain difference between them. Essence and intuition belong to two different realms of being. The latter belongs to the realm of existence, since it originates from matter. Thus, intuition is existent. That, intuition has an existential character, is also proved by the fact that it has a direction, i.e. it exists for lighting up the essences. Essence is different from intuition in the simple fact that it, being non-existent, does not belong to the realm of existence. Moreover, intuition is an event, as it arises at a point of time; a point of time I should say, since intuition arises "when the inner life of the animal, or its contact with external things, is expressed in some actual appearance" (p. 61). But while intuition is an event, essence is far from being an event, since it is timeless.

V. Summary

Santayana's realm of essence is not existential in character. It is purely formal. Each essence is drained of all existential or external relations. No one essence is externally related to any other essence. Each essence is a world apart. It is individual in the sense of being independent. But its individuality is not at all in contradiction with its being universal. It is its wholeness and rejoices in itself. It is the unity of all multiplicity that is contained in it. It is the pure datum or mute appearance. Again, each essence is inert. Being above the principle of existence which is the principle of change and activity, it remains perfectly inactive, non-existent and unchangeable.

Do essences subsist, when they are not existent? In answer, it is said that subsistence cannot be predicated of them. Subsistence is also an event in time and as such belongs to the realm of matter or existence. Essence, being above time, cannot subsist, since to be subsistent is to be in time.

If essences have neither existence nor subsistence, to which category, then, do they belong? It has been said that essences have "being". But Santayana confuses essence with being. We shall presently refer to it in our criticism of his notion of essence. He speaks of essence as eternal. The eternity of essence does not mean that it has endless duration. The word "eternity", according to Santayana, does not carry the notion of time with it. He refers to some negative aspects of essence which have already been referred to in details (pp. 55-60). He speaks much of essence, both positively and negatively, yet we fail to have an accurate notion of it, since in some respects it appears to us as paradoxical. The paradoxes, some of which shall be referred to in the criticism part of the present chapter, seem to be due to the absence of harmony, which is, of course not for always, between what Santayana intends to mean and his use of language.

VI. Difficulties in Santayana's Notion of Essence

Santayana's notion of essence involves some difficulties which must be examined.

A. SANTAYANA CONFUSES ESSENCE WITH BEING

The metaphysical error lies in his confusion of essence with being. Being is a two-term expression. Being is "what is". In it there are "whatness" and "isness". "Whatness" by which is meant "essence" is only a part of being; it is not the whole of being. Santayana errs when he takes essence as being itself.

Essence cannot be abstracted from being, since the former is the essential part of the latter. It is, however, possible for us to conceive essence apart from being. But to say that essence can be conceived apart from being does by no means amount to saying that the former becomes actually separated from the latter. The candid assertion of Santayana is that essences are not abstractions. Indeed, *essentia* always belongs to an *esse*. The former will be dead if it be divested of the latter. But unfortunately enough, Santayana abstracts essence from being and gives it an independent status. Essence cannot be independent of being. Essence being a part of being cannot be again universal. But it is universal, according to Santayana. At one time he says that essences are not abstractions. At another time he pronounces them as independent and universal; this becomes possible for him to say only by abstracting essence from being. Now, it is up to the reader to decide how far Santayana is consistent here. In this connection we can quote from Etienne Gilson:

> The primary error of the metaphysics of essence is to mistake a part for its whole and to speculate about essences as though they were the whole of both reality and its intelligibility … essentia always belongs to an esse, and even while I conceive it apart, essence never cuts loose from actual being; it is, rather, bound to it by a life-line, and if that line is cut off, essence is dead. No knowledge will ever come out of it. –1952: 202-03

What Gilson says here sums up Santayana's position exactly. Santayana speaks of "inert" essences of which knowledge is not at all possible. Yet, in philosophizing, he treats them as terms used in knowledge.

B. PARADOXES AND CONTRADICTIONS

We cannot have an accurate conception of Santayana's essence, as it sometimes appears to involve paradoxes:

i. In *Scepticism and Animal Faith*, Santayana says that the datum (essence) is an idea (1923: 35). Yet, we find him to utter in *The Realm of Essence* that "it is not an idea" (1927: 41).

ii. In *Scepticism and Animal Faith* we find Santayana saying that we cannot have any knowledge of essences. What is meant by knowledge is "belief in a world of events" (1923: 179). Yet, he admits knowledge of essences when he says, "to know surprise by experience is the only way of knowing its essence" (ibid.: 276).

iii. In *Scepticism and Animal Faith* Santayana pronounces essence or datum as "a pure image" (ibid.: 34). But, in *The Realm of Essence*, he contradicts himself when he says that essence is not "the imaginary" (1927: 29).

iv. Santayana proclaims that essences are "terms of human discourse" (1923: 177). Again, he utters in the same breath that essences are not to be confused with language (1927: 41).

v. In one place, Santayana says that essences are not possible being (1927: 26-27). Yet, in another place, he observes that they are "distinct forms of possible being" (1938: 430). It is not understood how essence which is not a possible being can be a form of the same.

vi. Santayana explicitly urges that essence and intuition belong to two different realms of being, one to the realm of non-existence and the other to the realm of existence. These two realms are opposed, since the one is immaterial and the other material. Yet, Santayana says that essences are given in intuition, and intuition is absorbed in the contemplation of them. That is to say, the immaterial or the non-existent is given in the material or the existent and the material or the existent contemplates the immaterial or the non-existent. It is not clearly understood how this interaction between essence and intuition, the immaterial and the material, the non-existent and the existent, becomes possible.

Again, when it is said that essences appear in intuition, does it mean that they come down to the level of existence from their lofty height of non-existence? If they do, they can no more be called essences, since their immateriality becomes lost. If they do not, they cannot be said to appear in intuition, since due to their immateriality they for ever elude the grasp of the material.

Further, essences are made completely transcendent by being placed beyond space-order and time-order and beyond everything contingent. They are, thus, inert and changeless. Intuition, it has been noted, is an event in time; it is not beyond the principle of change. Now, to say that essences appear in intuition does actually amount to saying that the unchanging essences thrive on change and that the timeless essences roll in time.

Paradoxes and contradictions are so profuse in Santayana's essentialism that we get really confused and perplexed. In such a state of confusion we cannot get the true picture of the nature of Santayana's essence. Anyway, bearing in mind the notion of essence in Santayana's sense, we may proceed to the discussion of the relation of essence and existence which constitutes another important phase of his metaphysics.

4

Essence and Existence

I. Materialism

BEFORE we take up the relation between essence and existence for discussion, it is desirable to explain Santayana's materialism which, as it has been already noted (p. 22), he takes as a presumption. From the earliest phase of his philosophy he cherishes deep-seated respect for the claims of materialism. His conviction is that the materialists are the good observers of the world and of themselves. Materialism is the undercurrent or the main burden of his thought, in spite of its semblance to the contrary.

A. MATERIALISM: NATURALISM

Sometimes Santayana uses "naturalism" instead of "materialism" for the reason that the ambient world produces at any moment effect upon us according to our nature, i.e. according to our sensibility and equipment at that time (1940: 508). But naturalism might include psychologism:

> A theory which fuses the two disparate substances posited by Descartes and maintains that while the inner essence of substance everywhere is to think, or at least to feel, its distribution, movement and aspect, seen from without, are those of matter.
>
> – 1923: 292

Psychologism is well marked in all the Greek naturalists before Democritus. There is, no doubt, that they studied nature attentively, with scientific intent. But they adopted "a false step" of philosophy when

> they mistook both the field of psychology and the field of logic for parts or the whole of the field of matter, or the physical universe. – *The Journal of Philosophy*, January 2, 1964, p. 13

Having sensed that the term "naturalism" might lead to a false step of philosophy, Santayana proclaims that the term "materialism" seems to him "safer" (1940a: 508), since it is unambiguous in its meaning. Matter is that which is the indefinite or undefined. Materialism implies no false realism about itself. Democritus cannot be said to be materialistic, since he creates a false realism about matter when he attributes geometrical forms (which are nothing but essences) to matter absolutely. Matter which is said to be the indefinite cannot be thus qualified. Among the Greek naturalists, Santayana credits Anaximander who, by regarding matter as the indefinite, might seem to have escaped false realism about matter (*The Journal of Philosophy*, January 2, 1964, p. 13).

B. MATERIALISM AS A NECESSARY PRESUPPOSITION

Santayana takes materialism as the presupposition which he cannot live without making. It is "the presupposition not only of all natural science but of all deliberate action" (1940a: 505). Any deliberate action (say, judging, or looking at something) is made possible only on the assumption of a continuous dynamic world external to us. As to the existence of matter Santayana leaves no doubt, since matter is only a name for the principle of existence itself. He warns those who seek to find out the ground of his materialism, since "existence is groundless" (ibid.). To seek the ground of existence would involve us in looking for the ground of that ground and thus we shall be landed in an infinite regress.

C. MATTER AND SUBSTANCE ARE INTERCHANGEABLE

Santayana takes matter and substance as interchangeable terms. "Matter is properly a name for the actual substance of the natural world, whatever that substance may be" (1930: 100). Matter or substance is posited by animal faith. In Santayana's materialism "matter" is specified as that which exists. In *Scepticism and Animal Faith* (1923), *The Realm of Essence* (1927) and *The Realm of Matter* (1930) "existent" has been defined as what comes-to-be, endures and passes away; i.e. "existent" is what is flux. Matter is also defined to mean flux or that which is in flux. Thus, when we say that minds and anything else exist, it means that they are in process and are material. And to deny that they are material is to deny that they exist at all.

D. SANTAYANA'S MATERIALISM IN HIS EARLIER AND LATER WORKS

Santayana's materialism is found in both of his earlier and later works. We find it in *The Life of Reason* (1905) (his earlier work) as "forthright Democritean materialism" which asserts that "existing nature is a system of bodies long antedating sentience" (1905, vol. I: 9) and that in natural philosophy "mechanism is explanation itself" (ibid.: 24). Santayana's earlier Democritean materialism which is mechanistic seems to have changed in *Scepticism and Animal Faith* (1923), *The Realm of Essence* (1927) and *The Realm of Matter* (1930) (his later works) where his materialism treats matter or existence as "flux". But has there been really a shift in Santayana's position from *The Life of Reason* to *Scepticism and Animal Faith*, *The Realm of Essence* and *The Realm of Matter*? Before we come upon this discussion, let us see how his materialism in its earlier and later forms has been dominated and influenced by the theories of his predecessors as well as by modern science.

Santayana and Democritus

Santayana accepts Democritus in this that the inner structure of matter is atomic. But he points out that Democritus has introduced into his physics the radical vice of metaphysics. Democritus holds that the atoms are extended, yet absolutely indivisible. Thus, he has logically denied that his extended atoms are divisible. The cause of such denial lies in his identification of matter, a name for something existent, with Pure Being, a merely logical term. Pure Being is indivisible and matter, being identified with Pure Being, becomes indivisible. Santayana absolves himself from accepting the Democritean thesis (logically inconsistent) that the extended atoms are indivisible. He, however, accepts the atomic theory of Democritus and says that such a theory is alone possible and inherent in physics.

Santayana, Modern Science and Heraclitus

By emphasizing the fact that the extended atoms must be divisible, Santayana comes very close to the modern scientific theory of matter according to which atoms are divisible. The modern scientific theory of matter is called the electronic theory. This theory holds that electron, proton and neutron – in various combinations – make up atoms. Electron is the natural unit of negative electric charge. Every atom contains one or more electrons. Proton is the unit of positive electric charge. The charge on an atomic nucleus comes from the protons in it. And neutron is an uncharged particle. Except for the lightest hydrogen nucleus, every atomic nucleus contains one or more neutrons. Not proceeding further with the electronic theory, we may point out that it asserts atomic matter as active or as always in a process. Santayana also takes the very kernel of the modern scientific theory of matter. To him, as we have seen, matter is flux; it is active.

The very nature of existence, says Santayana, is to be dispersed. Hence, matter is dispersed, but it is also a continuum and is in constant flux. Santayana here is nearer to Heraclitus than to Democritus. In *The Realm of Matter* such a position of his has been exposed in many ways. The insight of Heraclitus is that all things change, existence is a perpetual flux. In this connection we may refer to what Aristotle says. He treats matter not as bodies, but as the surd factor in substances by virtue of which they change and move. Similarly, Santayana's materialism of *Scepticism and Animal Faith* and of *The Realms of Being* (1942), instead of asserting that nature is composed of moving bodies whose actions and reactions exhibit mechanical regularity as that was conceived in classical mechanics, asserts that nature is a process or whatever is going on.

The above discussion facilitates us in conceiving that Santayana's materialism has been moulded by two great systems, its earlier phase by Democritus and its later phase by Heraclitus. Democritus takes existing nature as "a system of bodies", while Heraclitus takes it as a "flux". The one takes nature as a thing, while the other conceives it as a process. Santayana himself observes:

> Two great systems offered, in two legitimate directions, what are doubtless the final and radical accounts of physical being.
> – 1905, I: 23

If either of the two phases of Santayana's materialism is judged separately, contradiction is not found in it. But if his materialism (both of its phases taken together) is viewed as a whole, it seems to involve contradiction. This position of Santayana leads some modern philosophers to think that his materialism has not developed consistently from *The Life of Reason* to *Scepticism and Animal Faith*, *The Realm of Essence* and *The Realm of Matter*.

E. CONSISTENCY BETWEEN EARLIER AND LATER PHASES OF SANTAYANA'S MATERIALISM

The present writer thinks that Santayana's earlier materialism does not differ from his later position concerning it. In *Reason in Common Sense*, volume I of *The Life of Reason*, by matter he understands existence, whatever that existence may be. There he says that material existents are occurent and the state of mind is also said to be occurrent.

> The stuff of external reality, the matter ... is ... continuous with the stuff and matter of our own minds. Their common substance is the immediate flux. – 1905, I: 90

The principle of existence which is implied in *Reason in Common Sense* has been more elaborately and consistently developed in his later works.

Democritean materialism, which forms the earlier position of Santayana, advocates atomic theory according to which force or activity is inherent in atoms. This theory can be distinguished from Plato's theory of force. Plato holds a static conception of matter in contrast with the materialist's dynamic conception of the same. The former attributes the source of all material change to a force coming from without in dead matter, while the latter thinks that motion is native to the material atoms. The Democritean thesis that change is spontaneous to the material existents is carried out consistently by Santayana in his later works in the principle of existence which asserts that existence or matter is flux. Again, Santayana's allegiance to Democritean materialism expresses some negative convictions which are quite in consistency with his later position. Those negative convictions are: that the processes of nature do not require for their occurrence any support or cause beyond them; that the processes of nature require nothing but their own occurrence.

In *Reason in Common Sense* (1905, I: 37) we find Santayana using the phrase "efficacious" order which exists in the world. This usage made by Santayana leads some critics to interpret that beyond the events there are some forces which necessitate order in the world: that is, what they mean is that chaos in the world precedes order established in it by some external agencies.

But Santayana answers, "by chaos we understand a nature" which "must be presumed to have an order" if we give attention to its movement (1905, I: 36). There is in the world change and continuity which are not to be termed as chaos but as order. "Order is accordingly continual" (ibid.). Thus, Santayana's use of the phrase "efficacious" order lies beneath chaos. And we can get down to the bedrock of order and regularity in nature as she is explored further and further.

We see, then, that in *The Life of Reason* Santayana takes the existent nature as rational (in the sense of having order) and as explicable. But in *Scepticism and Animal Faith* (one of his later works) we find Santayana asserting that existence "is necessarily irrational and inexplicable" (1923: 208). The two versions seem to differ. But actually they do not. Existence is called irrational either in the sense that it is not essence of which intuition is possible or in the sense that it defies any control of a priori logic or mathematics. Again, existence is inexplicable either in the sense that beyond existence there are no causes to which we might appeal for its explanation or in the sense that no certain evidence can be given of existence, since existence, on Santayana's definition, is what is believed.

The above observations lead us to conclude that Santayana's materialism maintains a single thread running through from *The Life of Reason* to *Scepticism and Animal Faith*, *The Realm of Essence* and *The Realm of Matter*.

Santayana never claims to be a materialist in the sense that matter is the only reality, since essences and spirit stand in contrast with matter. He is a materialist mainly in that he holds that only matter does anything (1940: 509). He formulates "the great axiom of materialism" as asserting "the dominance of matter in every existing being, even when that being is spiritual" (1930: 100). This great axiom, says Santayana, should be complemental with a truism that matter is no fiction, that it "is no model devised by the human imagination" (ibid.).

II. Is Santayana an Agnostic?

Santayana says that substance, though it is posited by animal faith, cannot be possessed. We feel its pulsations, but we cannot know it. We cannot conceive it, since existence is a flux. Moreover, existence is a surd or irrational, and what is irrational cannot be conceived by reason. As Santayana observes:

> We may enjoy it, we may enact it, but we cannot conceive it; not because our intellect by accident is inadequate, but because existence, which substance makes continuous, is intrinsically a surd, a flux, and a contradiction. – Ibid.: 27

Thus, substance defies our utmost efforts at penetration. In this respect, Santayana tends to stoop towards modern science. Though the modern scientists penetrate into atom and electron, matter itself remains as mysterious as ever. As substance or matter cannot be conceived in its true nature, Santayana, therefore, calls it "dark". But here the term "dark" has a relative significance. Substance seems to be dark, i.e. remains "unknown" to the subject.

Santayana insists that substance is not unknowable, but it is unknown. In this connection, we should be acquainted with the difference in meanings between the terms "unknown" and "unknowable". What is unknown may not be unknowable. What is unknown now can be known afterwards. Therefore, there is a scope for possibility of an unknown object of becoming known. But what is unknowable can never be known. The unknowable remains for ever transcendent to us. Matter is not in itself unknowable. Santayana does not tolerate Herbert Spencer's usage of the term "unknowable". He says, "Nothing can be intrinsically unknowable" (1923a: 8). Though matter or substance is not unknowable, it is, however, unknown and as such "dark" and "alien" to the subject. Santayana treats matter not as unknowable and yet he makes it so when he says that existence is a surd or a contradiction. Being a surd or irrational, it cannot be conceived by reason. Again, being a contradiction, it cannot be brought into harmony with the intellect. Thus, it remains beyond reason for ever, i.e. it remains inscrutable and impenetrable. And what is inscrutable and impenetrable is unknowable also. As a result, though Herbert Spencer's "unknowable" is not welcome to Santayana, he cannot avoid it with regard to matter.

III. Scepticism and Animal Faith

Existence and matter, says Santayana, are what are to be believed. Existent matter is the object of animal faith. Animal faith is only a name for a certain kind of blind impulse. In *Scepticism and Animal Faith* all rational arguments for any kind of belief are discarded. Santayana holds that complete scepticism is not inconsistent with animal faith. By complete scepticism we find out essence or the given which is non-existent; and by animal faith we assert the existence of everything not given. Thus "the admission that nothing given exists is not incompatible with belief in things not given" (1923: 105). Belief in the existence of anything, including myself, is incapable of proof, and this belief rests on some irrational persuasion.

Now, to call an unproved premise "irrational" is hardly warranted. All unproved beliefs are mere expressions of animal faith. But the epistemological problem lies in finding some way of choosing some of these beliefs as more worthy of credence than others. Now, this cannot be done by complete scepticism which denies them all. Nor can it be done by animal faith which accepts them all. If we are going to accept some by rejecting others, then we need some principle intermediate between complete scepticism and animal faith. But Santayana does not provide us with such a principle.

IV. Santayana's Conception of Matter, Psyche and Spirit

A. SUBSTANCE OR MATTER IS PHYSICAL

Substance of which Santayana speaks is not metaphysical, but physical substance (1923: 201). But in his other statements, we find that substance is not conceived as physical. In the notion of substance he includes spiritual entities, intuitions, all remembered experiences and mental discourse (1923: 47). Again, we find, "every event, even if wholly psychological or phenomenal, is a substance" (ibid.: 182). From these varied statements we come to know that substance is not limited to the physical only, though Santayana admits rather emphatically that substance must be physical.

Santayana opines that spirit, being an entelechy, cannot be a substance. It is true that we often confuse spirit with substance. This confusion, however, is due to the incarnation of spirit. Actually, spirit cannot be a substance in the material sense of the term. We find a point of similarity between John Locke and Santayana in their notions of substance. Both of them assert that substance is "what we know not". But while, according to Locke, there may be material and immaterial, incogitative and cogitative substances, according to Santayana, however, all substance must be material or physical, thus banishing spiritual substances altogether from his mind. Hence, Santayana's view becomes just the opposite of the view of Berkeley. According to Berkeley, there is only spiritual substance, the notion of material substance being meaningless to him. Santayana asserts that substance which is not material is only grammatical. Again, he makes fun of Leibnitz and Berkeley as "muscular idealists".

B. DYNAMIC NATURE OF MATTER

It has been hinted at that, according to Santayana, matter is not static or inert. It is dynamic and has least stability. He cannot admit that substance "is". What he accepts is that substance "becomes". The notion of becoming or change is also found in the Kṣaṇikavāda of Buddhism in India, later on in the doctrine of fire of Heraclitus and in modern times in the doctrine of Time of Henri Bergson. William James, whose influence Santayana cannot escape, particularly has a lively sense for the flux of existence. Santayana insists that the flux of matter is not chaotic; it has an order. Its order is maintained by its lateral and forward tensions. Dynamic matter is mechanically guided by forward tensions determined and modified by the force of lateral tensions. Nature is a perfect machine. In the mechanism of nature there is no place for God. Matter moves by itself and in itself; in its movement it is not guided by any supernatural agent or God, Santayana here remains near to the position of the Greek atomist Democritus. Democritus holds that the material atoms are from the beginning in a state of rotary motion. The movement of the atoms is mechanically held. Thus, Democritus also banishes the idea of God in his atomic theory. Santayana is also supported by modern science and the Jainas in India. Both modern science and Jainism hold that the atoms move by themselves and there is no interference of God in the movement of atomic matter.

C. HABITS OF MATTER

Santayana says that matter has habits of its own, i.e. it has some procedures which are habitual in nature. These habitual procedures, which are called "tropes" by Santayana, arise from the dynamic tensions of matter. Tropes are repeated with much regularity. They are mechanical and have spontaneity. In our egotism, we may take them as the laws of nature. But actually they are not so; they are merely the habits of matter. Again, tropes by which are meant repetition and regularity in nature cannot be conceived as manifestations of any fixed law. The concept of a law, says Santayana, is useful as "a measure of events" (1930: 304). By it, events can neither be described nor be produced.

D. REPRODUCTION AND EVOLUTION OF DYNAMIC MATTER

If nature is mechanical, no teleological purpose is served by it. But Santayana admits reproduction and evolution of dynamic matter. Reproduction and evolution are not principles of matter; they are simply its results and these results are due to its movement. As Santayana observes:

> In the first case we speak of reproduction, in the second of evolution; but these words do not stand for different forces or principles but only for different results. In reproduction the flux repeats the same trope, in evolution it changes the trope for one more complex or appropriate, imposed by a new balance of forces. – Ibid.: 325-26

Santayana's theory of the evolution of matter can be compared to the Sāṁkhya theory of evolution which is found in Indian philosophy. The Sāṁkhya theory holds that from dynamic matter the whole evolutionary process takes place. Santayana also maintains the very same view. But the Sāṁkhya system urges that without coming into contact with passive *Puruṣa* (Self) matter or *Prakṛti* cannot evolve. Santayana differs from the Sāṁkhya theory on this point. According to him, matter evolves by itself.

E. PSYCHE AS A TROPE OF MATTER

In Santayana's materialism, the "psyche" has an important place. But what is meant by the psyche? Is it material or not? If it be material, why is it called psychical and not physical? These are the questions which naturally crop up. The psyche, as we know from Santayana, is not different from matter. It is called a habit or trope of matter. The psyche, when it is a habit of matter, is natural. In *The Realm of Matter* Santayana emphasizes that the psyche is a natural phenomenon, a part of matter. The psyche does not admit any mental machinery. On the other hand, it has a physical operation. But what sort of physical operation? The operation of growth, instinct and action. The psyche serves as the biological principle of life in animals. The living organism can defend and express itself due to the presence of the psyche in it. The psyche is integral with life. That is why it is called psychical and not physical. As Santayana says:

> This sort of physical operation is called psychical, because it falls within the trope of a life and belongs to the self-defence and self-expression of a living organism. –1930: 139-40

In *The Realm of Spirit* the psyche is conceived as a hidden power in matter which carries the potentialities of life in its various stages.

F. PSYCHE OR SELF

To Santayana, the psyche and the self are not different. The self is not something immaterial. The self is to be posited, if we want to make our experience possible. We shall discuss, in a separate chapter on Santayana's epistemology, how, according to him, experience becomes possible. Now, the self which is to be posited is the living psyche. Two approaches are distinguished for studying this postulated self or psyche: an external, behaviouristic and an internal, introspective analysis. For his behaviouristic attitude, Santayana is, to some extent, indebted to William James. James' studies in abnormal psychology lead him to a seek the springs of consciousness and conduct in physiological processes. Such a naturalistic psychology serves to fortify Santayana's naturalism. Another approach which may be taken for studying the self is internal. This is the more difficult and dangerous approach. When we try to observe our own selves, we get vague notions about them and never catch hold of them as true selves. The self is what "slumbers and breathes below, a mysterious natural organism" (1923: 149). The same mysterious and hidden nature of the psyche is stressed in *Soliloquies in England and Later Soliloquies* (1922). In *The Realm of Matter*, Santayana indicates that the psyche has a certain amount of pliability; it bends to circumstances in order to sustain itself by its adaptations to the ambient world.

G. PSYCHE AND SPIRIT

From the material psyche originates spirit or mind. According to Santayana, spirit and mind are identical. The psyche itself is unconscious and unintelligent. In its adaptations to alien things it becomes intelligent and creates spirit. As Santayana observes:

> Spirit is bred in the psyche because the psyche, in living, is obliged to adjust herself to alien things: she does so in her own interest; but in taking cognizance of other things, in moulding a part of her dream to follow their alien fortunes, she becomes intelligent, she creates spirit. – 1927a: 66-67

Thus, spirit is an epiphenomenon. In the dependence of spirit upon psyche we have frank materialism. Spirit cannot enjoy free-will; nor can it have mastery over the material body. These two statements are made for the same reason that spirit springs from the material psyche. Spirit being grounded in animal life makes the pragmatic function of physical sensibility possible. But it overleaps this function and becomes associated with the intellectual, moral and aesthetic function. Hence, Santayana encourages pure spirituality in art and life. And with this encouragement exists side by side a pragmatic ethics in Santayana's philosophy. He has referred to fixed aims or ideals of life. These ideals, however, do not lose their charm by the fact that they are grounded in animal life. Herein lies the uniqueness of Santayana's philosophy. His view of morality will be discussed in a separate chapter.

We can here refer to the Indian view of spirit which has, of late, been applauded much by Santayana. The Hindu views that spirit is infinite and is independent of all the accidents of existence have also been approved by him. But the Indians maintain the freedom of spirit at an unnecessary cost of worldly servitude. On the other hand, it has been already noted that on Santayana's view the freedom of spirit cannot be maintained, since spirit takes its origin from the material psyche.

H. SANTAYANA'S CHARGE AGAINST THE INDIANS

Santayana makes a caustic remark about the scientific inferiority of the Indians. He says that they "did not study the movement and mechanism of nature; they had no science" (1922: 210). But this remark is objectionable. Even if by science is meant the study of the movement and mechanism of nature, it may be said that the Indians have to their credit a study of the positive sciences. And this study was no mean achievement considering its antiquity when the much-vaunted scientific progress of Europe was unachieved. In the Nyāya-Vaiśeṣika and Jaina atomism, in the Sāṁkhya theory of evolution, in the Advaita theory of creation, we get enough proof of the scientific pattern of the Indian mind. As Brajendranath Seal says:

> The Hindus no less than the Greeks have shared in the work of constructing scientific concepts and methods in the investigation of physical phenomena, as well as of building up a body of positive knowledge which has been applied to industrial technique; and Hindu scientific ideas and methodology (e.g. the inductive method or methods of algebraic analysis) have influenced the course of natural philosophy in Asia – in the East as well as in the West – in China and Japan, as well as in the Saracen Empire.
>
> – 1915: iii-iv

Thus, the view that Indian philosophy has no science results from ignorance. Perhaps, Santayana's mind was not so prepared to enter into the depths of Indian philosophy.

I. REALM OF SPIRIT

Spirit, according to Santayana, is the highest manifestation of consciousness. It has a reflective capacity and in this it is distinguished from animal or vegetable consciousness. It is intelligence in act. Spirit is not essence, for it is directed at essence. Again, it is not matter, although it may be considered a function of matter. It accordingly forms a new realm of being. Not only spirit is simple awareness or consciousness but also it implies "intent", "belief" and "eagerness". It is a category and by it essences are made appearances and things objects of belief (1923: 274). There are as many forms of spirit as there are essences, each being a distinct "spiritual fact". Spirit cannot be observed as an essence is observed. Nor can it be encountered as a thing is encountered. It "can be discovered only by implication in all discourse" (1923: 275). Discourse is what "is a perusal of essence, or its recurring presence to spirit" (ibid.). The existence of spirit in discourse becomes self-evident.

J. CRITICISM

Matter is the matrix of all life and thought. It is capable of eliciting feeling and thought, since it is the only power or agency in the universe. All things, even those immaterial like spirit, must be reduced to a material plane as "habits" of material substance. Santayana, however, admits that this "may sound dogmatical" (ibid.: 109). He has tried to bridge over the gulf between spirit and matter by the term "psyche". Spirit being rooted in the psyche is related to matter. But the immaterial spirit cannot take its origin from the material psyche. Spirit and matter, as they are antagonistic to each other, cannot be linked by any via media. There is no half-way ground between the realm of spirit and the realm of matter. Santayana says that the "office of matter is precisely to breed mind and to feed it" (1938: 441). This is a contradiction in terms, since it is not at all possible for matter to "breed" that which is not material. Santayana is unable to explain how the psyche comes to generate the spirit. He is content to accept mind and spirit as facts which experience reveals.

V. Santayana and Dialectical Materialism

Santayana's materialism can be understood in relation to dialectical materialism. In materialist dialectic, as in Santayana's materialism, matter is taken as real in its own right, neither deriving its reality from any supernatural source nor dependent for its existence on the human mind. The ancient Heraclitean insight that matter is flux has been shared by both dialectic materialism and Santayana. Motion is an inalienable property of matter. But while dialectical maierialism proposes a dialectical theory of change, Santayana holds a mechanistic theory of change. According to the former, everything, whether it be a physical object or an idea, is in a process of change; it is a unity which turns out, upon analysis, to be made up of oppositely acting elements. This unity or stability, however, is temporary, and what is permanent is change or motion. The law of the unity of opposites as held by dialectical materialism is not found in Santayana's materialism.

Moreover, dialectical materialism suggests that qualities are not something opposed to matter. They form a system of interrelationships in motion. This does not exist as transcendental to the material order, but is the material order. Dialectical materialism also holds that quality is not permanent and unchanging, as metaphysicians think. Santayana, again, differs from such a view of dialectical materialism. He thinks that qualities have a realm of their own. This is called the realm of essence. Essence is the quality sensed. A thing may have characters or qualities. But these characters or qualities do not change with the change of matter; they are essentially unchanging.

Further, the dialectical materialist holds that matter moves, but the universal motion is not aimless, it conforms to patterns expressible as laws. The laws are to be regarded as "a guide to activity and scientific research, not a dogma".[1] Santayana, on the other hand, asserts that the flux of matter does not conform to any law. It functions mechanically but perfectly as an independent power. It may be said in this connection that when we think of the dialectical materialists, Santayana's statement that he is "apparently the only one (materialist) living" (1923: vii) seems to be rather broad. In the criticism of dialectical materialism it may be said that the mechanism of this theory is to some extent of the Hegelian type and hence bears an idealistic

1 *Bolshaya Sovetskaya Entsiklopediya*, 23: 154.

colouring. Santayana's materialism is, however, free from such a defect. He becomes idealistic as regards his theory of essence.

VI. Essence and Existence

We have so far described Santayana's materialism. We have come to know from him that existence is the principle of substance and the object of animal faith. The relation of existence to essence constitutes a main theme in Santayana's metaphysics.

A. DISTINCTION BETWEEN ESSENCE AND EXISTENCE

The distinction between essence and existence was not started fresh by Santayana. It was made by the ancients as well as by the medieval thinkers.

i. *Plato and Aristotle*

Plato teaches that Ideas form a world which exists of itself. They are eternal and unchanging. The earthly sensuous things are merely shadowy images of the bright world of Ideas. The Platonic Ideas are laid up in heaven as patterns to be distantly imitated by the things that exist here below. Aristotle rejects Plato's view that Ideas exist for themselves alone and independent of the particular things. He points out that the essence of a thing is its inner principle which preserves and improves it, explains it and makes it what it is. The essences, according to him, cannot be outside the things of which they are the essences. Both Plato and Aristotle, however, agree that the true essences are relatively few, that they can only be comprehended by reason and that they act on things. Both of them also hold that in contrast with the essences, things are intrinsically deficient and vague. They lay a moral load upon essences by saying that they are good and that they are what things ought to be. The real essence is that whose fulfilment makes the individual truly happy and true happiness is the achievement of the individual's proper good.

ii. *St. Thomas*

Santayana asserts that essences have no "natural being" but only "aesthetic immediacy and logical definition" (1923: 75). Essences are thus the most clearly known and are the true objects of the intellect. Santayana's view is substantiated by the statement of St. Thomas Aquinas that the essence or quiddity of a thing is the proper object of the intellect. Essence, according to Aquinas, is distinct from existence. Such distinction he accepts in the case of created reals. But in the case of God, the above distinction becomes meaningless, since in Him the act of existing is His essence.

For Aquinas essence is distinct from existence and yet it is not antagonistic to the latter. The former is compared to the latter as potentiality to act. The form or quiddity or essence is real but not existent; it is ordered, however, to an existential status. In substances composed of matter and form, three terms must be clearly set apart: form, substance and act of existing. Form is that-by-which-a-thing-is, quo est. Thus, it serves as the principle of existing. Substance is that-which-is, quod est; and by act of existing is meant that-by-which-the-substance-is-denominated-a-being. Form or quiddity is not the act of existing. But it is related to act of existing as "whiteness" is to "the act of being white" or as "light" to "the act of illuminating". Hence, essence though it is not existent is, however, ordered to an existential status. It is to be mentioned in this connection that in intellectual or spiritual substances there remains only form as a subsisting substance; here it is not quo est but quod est. Form is not treated here as a principle of existing or as that-by-which-a-thing-is; it serves as a substance or that-which-is. And in the case of spiritual substances the act of existing is itself the principle of existing (quo est). The act is that-by-which the form is.

For Aquinas, essence is ordered to an existential status, while for Santayana, in contrast, essence stands continually and intelligibly in opposition to the irrational realm of natural entities. In medieval thought, a strong tendency is found to hypostatize essence, not as a substance but as a thought, this tendency being not only present in the realists who identify Platonic ideas with the ideas of God, but also in the nominalists who identify essences with human thoughts of them. Plato also hypostatizes essence as something eternally existent; by such hypostatization he fails to distinguish between essence and existence. Acquinas and later on Spinoza identify the essence of anything with the existence of anything. This is the pantheistic position. This position is, of course, inconsistent with the Christian doctrines of divine transcendence and creation. The medieval distinction between essence and existence is commonly accepted by philosophers today. But does Santayana also make the same distinction? This question can be answered both in the affirmative and in the negative. Let us see how.

iii. *Santayana's Distinction between Essence and Existence*

Santayana makes the logical distinction between essence and existence – the very distinction which is medieval in origin. The distinction he makes between essence and existence is that between what a thing is and that it is, between its character or kind and its occurrence as a case of the kind, between the rosiness of the rose and the fact that it is there. His distinction between essence and existence does not mean the separation between the two. In his "Transcendental Absolutism"[2] he has urged a protest against Royce who says that the gist of Santayana's philosophy is the separation of essence from existence (1940a: 497). Santayana claims his distinction between essence and existence to be logical, not entitative. If this distinction be entitative, it will be as good as separation. But, it will be shortly noticed that Santayana maintains an entitative separation between essence and existence.

---

[2] "If there was insight in Royce's saying that I separated essence from existence, there was not absolute accuracy. I do not separate the two. I merely distinguish them." – Runes 1943: 315

Plato says that to be self-identical is to be eternal. Thus, he confuses logical identity with everlasting existence. This logical flaw is due to his hypostatization of essence as eternally existent. Santayana marks it. But he himself also hypostatizes essence not, however, as existent, but in a realm of its own, the realm of essence. And the logical flaw in Plato's passage from self-identity to eternity is also made by Santayana. The essence of a thing is itself a thing in a realm of its own, different from that of which it is the essence. Therefore, instead of one thing we now have two, the essence (a thing which is self-identical in its own realm) and the thing of which it is the essence. And these two things are not only distinguished but also separated. This is what is called entitative separation. Having thus separated essence from existence, Santayana speaks of the essence as eternal, because it is self-identical. Plato also in an analogous way spoke of a real existent thing as eternal, because it is self-identical. Santayana differs from Plato only in this that the eternal essence is not existent. To be existent is to be in time. To Santayana "eternal existence" is contradictory, since, according to him, "eternity intrinsic to all essences is timeless" (Runes 1943: 317). It may be said in this connection that the entitative separation Santayana makes between essence and existence is not made by the medieval thinkers. Let us see now how Santayana distinguishes between essence and existence.

1. The principle of existence is change, whereas that of essence is self-identity. "Existent" means what comes-to-be, endures and passes away, i.e. in flux. Essence is that which is inert. Santayana regards existence as Heraclitean while essence he treats as Parmenidean, or rather Platonic. For him, as for Plato, the realm of essence is many and infinite; but in the principle of its being it is not different from the one of Parmenides. The cause of this kind of separation is to be found, methinks, in the contradictory demands of Santayana's temperament, at once materialistic and religious, Heraclitean and Platonic.

2. The self-identity of essence implies its eternity, unity and internality of relations. On the other hand, the flux of existence implies disunity, contradiction and externality of relations.

3. Matter which is existent is creative; it is the causative force. But, essence is inert. It cannot produce either itself or anything else. It has no material efficacy.

4. Existence is external to essence. But an essence, says Santayana, can be caught in the flux of existence and incorporated in a substance. In such a state of incarnation the essence acquires a frame of external relations, but it is not identified with the substance which is "more and other than the essence". The embodiment of an essence in substance does not violate the eternal character of that essence. The constant flux of existence enables the essence to elude the grasp of its captor, except to permit momentary external relations. As Santayana holds:

   > It is only by such embodiment in matter that essences can be loosened, as it were, from their essential setting and turned into the characters of facts; or rather – since their essential setting is eternal and holds them even while embodiments of them are passing through existence – it is only by being distributed in the field of action that essences can add for a moment external and variable relations to those which their proper nature involves. –1930:275-76

5. Essences or data of intuition do not exist. What exist are the facts or events believed to occur in nature. These facts or events are intuitions themselves, pains and pleasures, all remembered experiences and physical things and events. Thus, existences, from the epistemological point of view, are facts or events affirmed. It has been said that data of intuition do not exist. Let us suppose that this is not true. Then its opposite, viz. presence to intuition is necessary

for existence, is true. But Santayana affirms that this can be easily disproved by a *reductio ad absurdum*. If it be true that what is present to intuition necessarily exists, intuition itself would not exist. The existence of anything is posited by intuition, but this intuition becomes groundless, if it is posited by any other intuition. Again, if presence to intuition were necessary to existence, then "everything mentionable would exist without question" (1923: 46), and it would be impossible for us to think the non-existent and to deny anything existent since it is present to intuition. What are present to intuition are certain. As a result, there would be no fancy, illusion and hallucination.

6. Santayana says that we believe existence but we intuit essence. Professor Savery makes a remark about Santayana that the latter "believes in eternal essences". Santayana, in his article "Transcendental Absolutism", says that this remark of Professor Savery is objectionable. To believe in anything means to believe that it exists. But eternal essences are such as cannot be said to exist. Existence has no ground in any sense. Existence, says Santayana, is contingent. He differs from the Thomist and the Existentialist on this point. Since there is originally no necessity that you or I exist, there is no necessity that anything exists at all. Thus, the notion that the nature of God is His necessary existence is a chimera. That an essence should entail its existence on the finite plane of objects is finite nonsense. And that it should do so on the infinite divine plane is infinite nonsense.

B. SANTAYANA AND EXISTENTIALISM

Santayana gives primary importance to essence. Existence is secondary, according to him. Existentialism, the latest movement of European thought which has achieved popular success in contemporary France, also distinguishes between essence and existence, but, unlike Santayana, affirms the priority of existence over essence. Martin Heidegger says that existence in its proper form is experienced in the case of self alone. I cannot ask the question, "what I am", without presupposing my own existence. Here existence is primarily given, essence is secondary. Heidegger makes a sharp distinction between essence and existence. When we ask about a thing as to what it is, we are asking about its essence. Having known what it is, we may still ask whether it exists. This shows that essence does not include existence. That essence is not existent is also propounded by Santayana. It is a cardinal doctrine with all existentialists that existence precedes essence and their main concern is with existence. Though Santayana speaks of himself as a materialist, what, according to him, is primary is essence. His main concern is with essence. The notion of essence is the foundation stone of his whole system of philosophy. The primacy of essence in every aspect, epistemological, moral and religious, has been ascertained by him. The role of essence in cognition, the moral function of essence and the religious significance of essence will be subsequently discussed.

As to the notion of existence there is a striking similarity between Santayana and the existentialists. Santayana, as we have already noticed, takes existence as a process or flux. According to existentialism also, "to exist" is not equal to "to be". Existence is an act. True existence implies true becoming and true becoming implies liberty. It implies continuous progress. To most existentialists, existence and being are same in meaning. Santayana, on the other hand, distinguishes between being and existence. He takes being as an essence or as that which is present to all essences. Santayana's concept of being has been already discussed along with the exposition of the notion of essence. The existentialists are mistaken when they regard existence and being as identical. And the same mistake is done by Santayana by making essence identical with being. Being is such as includes both essence and existence. It cannot be identical with either of them. Unfortunately enough, both existentialists and Santayana lack this insight.

Santayana distinguishes essence from existence, but he does not forget to mention their interrelationship. Their interrelationship is as follows:

> The flux flows by flowing through essences; and essences are manifested as the flux of matter or of attention picks them up and drops them. – 1927: 40

Essences render existence intelligible. But there are other essences which are not realized in existence.

The distinction Santayana has made is between the two realms of being – the realm of existence and the realm of essence. Santayana's realm of essence comes as a possibility over against the realm of existence. What are possibles other than existents are essences. That whether the realm of essence can be taken as a possible alternative as against the realm of existence will be discussed shortly in connection with its criticism. Here, we shall refer to the other philosophical views on "possibles" and compare them with Santayana's view of the same.

C. SANTAYANA AND W. NORRIS CLARKE

Both Santayana and Clarke speak of the realms of "existence" and "possible". Again, both argue that possibles are not existents. But Clarke, unlike Santayana, maintains that the existent, the actual, is the only real being; and though not real or actual in themselves, possibles are intelligibly related to the real. The status of the possible is that of esse intentionale. The existence of a thought object or intentional real is not a "to be real", but a "to-be-really thought by a real act of a real mind." Thus, the "reality resides entirely in the real act of the mind thinking, not in the object of this thought (Drennen 1962: 454). Similarly, the possibles, though not real in themselves, are intelligibly ordered to be real.

> Their intelligibility has intentional existence entirely in and through the reality of God, His essence and His act of thought and can only be validly postulated and analysed by us through the mediation of the divine reality, as a necessary consequence of the divine attributes. – Drennen 1962: 456

The possibles, then, on Clarke's view, being not real in themselves, are inseparably linked with existent or real being by a relation of necessary intelligibility –

> a quasi projection of the Supreme Being's own necessary intelligibility as existent, intelligent and all-powerful. – Ibid.

Santayana differs from Clarke mainly in two respects. First, unlike Clarke, Santayana preserves for essences a realm of their own which should be sharply contrasted with the realm of existence. While, according to Clarke, the "really real" is the existent being, according to Santayana, however, the "really real" is essence. Clarke predicates "intentional existence" of possibles. But no kind of existence either intentional or actual has been predicated of essence by Santayana. Second, reality is used by Clarke in the sense of actuality. What is actual is real. In that case the existent being is the only real being. But on Santayana's view, the reality of essence is not an existential reality. Unchangeable and inevitable, its reality is classically real. When an existent changes, essences are not changed, but can be exchanged. At every step, existence casts off one essence and picks up another.

D. SANTAYANA AND HENRI BERGSON

While Clarke inquires into the meaning and status of possibles as possible, Bergson is interested in the "possible" implications of an actual real. The possible is to be judged against the background of reality. According to Bergson,

> reality is global, and undivided growth, progressive invention, duration: it resembles a gradually expanding rubber balloon assuming at each moment unexpected forms. – Ibid.: 460

Reality is in continuous procession and is continually unfolding novelties. Possibles, on Bergson's view, are those which come after this process. They are not simply "there" awaiting actuation; they are not ideally pre-existent. It is actuation which brings forward what has been made possible. Thus, possibility acquires a distinctively "existential" character, being always "after-the-fact". It is "the real which makes itself possible and not the possible which becomes real" (ibid.: 466).

The conception of existence as flux is found in both Santayana and Bergson. Bergson, constant duration being to him the only reality, is perhaps on the right track when he maintains that possibility is not anterior to existence, that possibility, being consequent upon existence, achieves an "existential" character. We find in Bergson's conception of Reality a total system, having no break in it. Santayana does not say that essences or possibles are not anterior to existence; what he says only is that their realm is totally separate from the realm of existence. While according to Santayana essences have no existential character, Bergson's view is that possibles have existential character.

Again, duration or constant change or flux, according to Bergson, is the "really real". Santayana, on the other hand, asserts that the "really real" is essence which is unchangeable. Further, on his view, essences, though not existential, wear an existential garb when they are picked up by existence and are thus realized by us. But, such a view will not get recognition from Bergson who says that the idea

> immanent in most philosophies and natural to the human mind, of possibles which would be realized by an acquisition of existence, is pure illusion. – Ibid.: 464

Finally, while Clarke imparts indirectly "intentional existence" to possibles and Bergson directly communicates existential character to them, Santayana, on the other hand, by separating essences from the irrational realm of natural entities, differs from both Clarke and Bergson.

E. SANTAYANA AND A.N. WHITEHEAD

Whitehead's doctrine of possibility is to be understood against the background of his conceptions of reality and creation. Like Aristotle, Whitehead says that the "fully existent" things are the primary concern of the metaphysical enquiry. He holds:

> The general Aristotelian principle is maintained that apart from things that are actual, there is nothing – nothing either in fact or in efficacy.
>
> – 1929: 54

Thus, what is "really real" according to him is the actual entity or the "fully existent" thing. But, here, Whitehead is to be contrasted with Santayana who holds that the "really real" is essence.

Whitehead conceives "process" as intrinsic to the nature of actual entity. Each actual entity becomes or comes into existence by a process of activity which is not present to this or that actuality[3] only, but is generic to all actualities. Thus each actuality is an individualization of the ultimate generic activity. This ultimate generic activity Whitehead terms "creativity". Creativity is the ultimate source of all creation. But it cannot create something out of nothing. In order to produce an actual entity the whole pre-existing world is to be considered. But this world is composed of other actual entities which again are the previous products of creativity itself. Moreover, in the production of an actual entity, not some, but all actual entities contribute their share of influence, although their effects are not all equally noticed. This explains Whitehead's theory of relativity according to which every event is related to every other event in the world. When we consider the fact that out of an existing world of actual entities creativity has a choice of creating a particular actual entity rather than another, we must recognize a third factor too, viz. alternative possible forms of

---

[3] Whitehead has often used "actuality" as a synonym for "actual entity".

synthesis. These are called "eternal objects". These are called eternal, since becoming, process, and transition are irrelevant to their nature. They are called objects, since they are always "given" for an actuality in becoming.

Eternal objects are the forms of actualities. Actualities become definite by their participation in the eternal objects. Do eternal objects form a realm of their own? As they are "pure potentials" for the determination of actualities, they, therefore, by their nature must have ingression in some actuality or actualities. The eternal forms are "given" as "objects" for present actualities in becoming, only by virtue of their existence in antecedent actualities. Eternal objects are given as possible forms the synthesis of which imparts definiteness to actuality.

The "eternal objects" of Whitehead can be compared to Santayana's essences. One outstanding resemblance between them is that both are recognized as eternal in the sense that they do not undergo any process or transition. Again, Whitehead says that actualities become definite by having ingression into eternal forms. Santayana also with a somewhat similar tone pronounces that an existential event can be described (description implies definiteness of what is described) when it assumes certain essences. In other words, as for Whitehead eternal forms remain as "possible" objects for the determination of actuality, so for Santayana essences appear as "possible" sense-qualities for the description of an object or objects.

Meanwhile, some important points of difference between the two philosophers deserve notice. First, for Whitehead eternal objects remain as ingredients of actualities. But Santayana speaks of a realm of essence sharply distinguished from the realm of existence. Second, there is intrinsic "togetherness" among eternal objects. Whitehead says:

> An eternal object, considered as an abstract entity, cannot be divorced from its reference to other eternal objects, from its reference to actuality generally. – 1926: 198

But Santayana's is the opposite view. He says that each essence is self-identical and independent, and hence forms no intrinsic togetherness with other essences.

F. CRITICISM

1. Santayana's realm of essence comes as a possibility over and above the realm of existence. If there be any duality of existence and something else, it does not strictly mean that that something will be other than existence. Something which is possible other than existence is "possible existence" if there be anything. The duality we get is between existence and possible existence. The "possible" is what belongs to actual nature. An individual can be described not merely in terms of certainties, of what they are and will be, but also in terms of possibilities, of what they may be or do. Santayana, however, maintains that the "possible", instead of belonging to actual nature, belongs to the realm of essence. He says:

   > in the actual universe, its essence being completely determined by the events which compose it, all that is actual is necessary and all else impossible. But this of course does not preclude the possibility of any different world. – 1927: 28

   The possibility of the universe other than the existential universe is here intended to be the realm of essence. Here two criticisms can be made against treating the realm of essence as a possibility other than the realm of existence.

   i. Each essence possesses a nature, incompatible with the word "can". It is said that an essence is what it is, and hence is an actuality; thus, it cannot be said to be a possibility.

   ii. In making a transition from essence to existence we shall see that what becomes metaphysically or ultimately possible is existence, not essence. If the realm of essence is self-complete, the transition from essence to existence is not surely effected by essence itself. The transition is not effected by essence itself for another reason. To make such a transition possible is to attribute activity to essence. But essences are not defined as dynamic. Now, if the transition is not made from the side of essence, it may be effected from the side of existence. And Santayana himself says that existence or matter or spirit "selects" essences. But this selection could not have taken place if the world had not been already existent.

Thus, what is to be metaphysically presupposed is existence. Possibility has a natural basis in the character of what exists. There is no need for a separate realm of essence to house nonactualized possibilities.

2. Essences cannot really exist apart from the act of existence. They are entitative parts of every real being. In real being, essence and existence are not separable since they unite to make "being" be. Essences can, however, be distinguished from existence intellectually. But still an abstracted essence takes on a new (intentional) mode of existence in the intellect. The main upshot is that essence is not separable from existence. Santayana's cardinal error lies in positing essence as the Supreme Reality, since it deprives the mind of the existent reality that is its natural and proper object. The awareness of eixstence is, in the words of E. Gilson, "the beginning of philosophical wisdom". In a technical sense, Santayana never even began to be a philosopher. St. Aquinas is on the right track when he points out that existence precedes essence logically, in that the mind grasps the notion of essence by its apprehension of the essence of some existing thing. The existentialists also deserve much credit, since they become first aware of existence. But they make a common

mistake with Santayana by distinguishing existence from essence. The mind cannot abstract existence from essence, since existence is not a form, but the act of all forms.

3. Existence, says Santayana, is dumb as to its origin or goal. It cannot provide any explanation of itself. It is blind.[4] How does this blind and dumb existence happen to embody selected essences in particular forms and patterns? Incarnation of essences cannot be their own doing, since they are inert. Is this incarnation due to any extrinsic creative power? Santayana does not admit any such power. Then how is this marvellous feat performed? It is by matter itself, the principle of irrational existence. How does matter perform it? Santayana fails to give any definite answer to this question. He says that it just happens. The appearance of essence, its relation to matter and to mind are the puzzles which our philosopher has not tried fully to solve. In fact, Santayana's metaphysics is hardly speculative at all.

4 "Existence ... is necessarily irrational and inexplicable. It cannot, therefore, contain any principle of explanation a priori." – 1923: 208

5

Epistemology

As we have seen, the centre of Santayana's metaphysical problems is, in the main, the notion of essence. This very notion of essence is the key to his theory of knowledge as well. The present chapter undertakes to discuss Santayana's epistemological position in its varied aspects. To understand his epistemological position one must view it in the light of the general development of American realism from 1910 onwards.

I. Development of American Realism

A. NEO-REALISM

In 1910 six American philosophers formed themselves into a group with a view to expounding a new kind of realistic philosophy. The group consisted of Ralph Barton Perry, Edwin Bissell Holt, Walter Taylor Marvin, Edward Gleason Spaulding, Walter Boughton Pitkin and William Pepperell Montague. Their cooperative work is entitled *The New Realism* (1922). They have cast their lot with the common man and maintained that objects are directly known except mainly on the point that while their position is scientific, that of the latter is unscientific. New realism is, broadly speaking, a return to naive or natural realism. The neo-realistic theory of knowledge stands as a criticism of the Lockian theory of knowledge. According to the latter, the external objects are known not directly but indirectly, through the ideas that are in the mind. This psychological argument, however, is not accepted by new realists. Their view is that ideas cannot stand in the way of the knowledge of objects. The subject's having ideas of the object means its having knowledge of it. Ideas do not constitute, according to them, a tertium quid between the percipient mind and the perceived object. Even the dichotomy of the two is called to question and mind sought to be resolved into objects.

The direct theory of knowledge of the new realists is developed into epistemological monism and realism. Holt and some other neo-realists regard knowledge as a response. The subject is what responds and the object is what is responded to. They hold:

> The difference between subject and object of consciousness is not a differencee of quality or substance, but a difference of office or place in configuration. – Perry et al. 1922: 476

With this assertion of the neo-realists, the Cartesian dualism between mind and matter is overcome. Monism in epistemology is finally reached when they relentlessly hold that

> the content of knowledge, that which lies in or before the mind when knowledge takes place, is numerically identical with the thing known. – Ibid.: 34

The object known and the object as it is are one and the same.

The epistemological monism of the neo-realists is supplied by their pan-objectivism. The idealists deny the external world in favour of consciousness, whereas with the new realists the pendulum swings to the other extreme, viz. the denial of consciousness in favour of the external world. They treat "consciousness", "thought", etc. as natural phenomena belonging to the space–time world. Moore's view that "consciousness and its objects are distinct existents" (ibid.: 371) is rejected by Holt. Holt compares consciousness to light. Just as when we suppose that we see light we really see nothing but illuminated things, similarly, when we think of consciousness we really have before us nothing but the objects known.

B. CRITICAL REALISM

American realism does not stop with the neo-realistic theory. It develops further through an important phase, known as critical realism which is substantially different from neo-realism. In 1920, a volume of essays written by seven American philosophers, George Santayana being one of the partners, was published under the title *Essays in Critical Realism* (Drake et al, 1920). This volume is a cooperative study of the problem of knowledge. The names of the other six collaborators are Durant Drake, Arthur O. Lovejoy, James B. Pratt, Arthur K. Rogers, Roy Wood Sellars and C.A. Strong. The epistemological position of Santayana as a critical realist can best be brought out through the contrast of his group with the neo-realists. The contrast is well exhibited in the words of Sellars:

> While the new realist holds that knowing is the givenness of the object, its literal presence to inspection, the critical realist regards knowledge more as interpreting of a selected and meant object by means of characters discriminated in the field of consciousness. – 1929: 288

Critical realism, therefore, makes knowledge representative and symbolic. This is obviously a regression to Locke's representative theory of knowledge with various scientific technicalities brought to bear upon it.

The critical realist does not approve the new realist's epistemological monism and pan-objectivism. The neo-realist's pan-objectivist and a fortiori monistic contention is that everything whatsoever belongs to the objective or physical world. The so-called subjective phenomena, like dream objects and illusory appearances are not due to the subjective stuff of fancy, but belong to the physical world as subsistents, not as existents. This is the view of most of the American neo-realists.

There are some British neo-realists like Alexander who are of opinion that the so-called subjective phenomena belong to the physical world as dislocated parts of the physical objects. The words of Samuel Alexander can be cited here:

> The world of illusion is the same as what we call the real world, but dislocated, its parts taken from their proper places and referred amiss. That dislocation is the mind's own work. Illusion is due to the intrusion of the mind's own idiosyncrasies into the apprehension of reality. – 2016, II: 216-17

Bereft of the subjective world the pan-objective position of the neo-realist boils down to epistemological monism as distinguished from epistemological dualism.

The critical realist cannot accept the neo-realistic position so far as epistemological monism and pan-objectivism are concerned. They argue that the objectivity of physical objects cannot be assigned to the dream objects and illusory appearances, since subjective phenomena are private, instead of being public like ordinary physical objects. Again, the subjective phenomena do not obey the physical laws which are found in the objective world. Further, those who assert that subjective phenomena are the dislocated parts of the physical objects and that dislocation is the mind's own work cannot hold this view when they maintain the identity of the subjective and the objective, the mental and the physical. By emphasizing the fact that dislocation is the mind's own work, they keep the mind in sharp contrast with the external object. Thus, they come, perhaps, unconsciously, to accept dualism which they actually want not to treat with undue favour.

C. BERTRAND RUSSELL AND EPISTEMOLOGICAL MONISM OF NEO-REALISM

Bertrand Russell, the English realist, was once a supporter of epistemological monism. He eliminates ideas as the tertium quid standing between a mind and its objects when he declares that "the faculty of being acquainted with things other than itself is the main characteristic of a mind", and that "acquaintance with objects essentially consists in relation between the mind and something other than the mind; it is this that constitutes the mind's power of knowing things (Russell 1912: 66-67). S. Alexander (1914) also advocates monism in his theory of knowledge when he analyses all knowing into a relation of "togetherness" or "compresence" between a mental act of apprehension and a non-mental thing.

The American realists like Perry (1912: chaps XII-XIII) and Holt (1914: chap. IX) reach the same monistic effect in a different way. According to them, all knowing is a "specific reaction of the central nervous system" and knowledge is the peculiar complex of objects defined by that reaction. What a mind knows depends simply on what the nervous system at a given moment specifically reacts to. Here too there is no room for "ideas".

Russell's monistic position is abandoned in his *An Outline of Philosophy* (1927). In *The Analysis of Mind* (1921) he denies the distinction between sensation and sense-datum. Sensation and sense-data, according to him, are the same neutral entities to particulars which, taken in one context, form the subject matter of psychology, and taken in another context, form the subject matter of physics. In *An Outline of Philosophy* he maintains this standpoint and denies the identity of the percept with the physical object. He says that a man's percepts are private to himself. The perception of an event is "a characterstic reaction which is present when the event occurs and not otherwise" (1927: 223). Russell's view with regard to perception and the physical world is clearly stated in the following lines:

> I take it that, when we have a percept, just what we perceive (if we avoid avoidable sources of error) is an event occupying part of the region which, for physics, is occupied by the brain. In fact, perception gives us the most concrete knowledge we

> possess as to the stuff of our brains, not part of the stuff of tables and chairs, sun, moon and stars. Suppose we are looking at a leaf and we see a green patch. This patch is not out there where the leaf is, but is an event occupying a certain volume in our brains during the time that we see the leaf. Seeing the leaf consists in the existence in the region occupied by our brain, of a green patch causally connected with the leaf, or rather with a series of events emanating from the place in physical space where physics places the leaf. – 1927: 292

The above statement establishes the causal theory of perception. The percept, viz. the green patch of the leaf occupies a certain volume in our brains when the leaf is seen by us. Instead of identifying the percept with the physical object, Russell established a causal connection between the two. This dualistic position with regard to his theory of knowledge is still held in his recent work *My Philosophical Development* (1959: 245f.).

D. RUSSELL AND EPISTEMOLOGICAL DUALISM OF CRITICAL REALISM

The question is: Is, then, Russell an adherent of epistemological dualism which is advocated by the critical realist? Russell's theory is not that of the critical realist and this will be evident from the latter's presentation of theory of knowledge. For the critical realist knowledge is the result of the interrelation of three factors, viz.:

1. a physical object,
2. the subject or the mental state, and
3. a datum or essence.

What we are directly acquainted with is the datum. The datum or the content of the perceiving mind serves as a mediator between the subject and the physical object. The identity between the perceived object (datum) and the physical object is denied by the critical realists, thus giving rise to epistemological dualism.

The epistemological dualism of the critical realists is not the one which is accepted by Russell. For Russsell, as we have seen from his latest philosophical development, knowledge-situation consists of two factors, viz. percept and the physical object. Another point of difference between the critical realist and Russell is that, while the former gives the datum a status independent of both the mental state and the physical object, in the latter's opinion, however, the percept or sensation is identical with sense-datum.

Regarding the nature of the datum with which epistemological enquiry starts, opinions vary among the critical realists themselves. Drake, Strong, Rogers and Santayana maintain that the datum which is given to the knower is not an existent, representing the object. But Sellars, Pratt and Lovejoy opine that

> although what is given is a mere character-complex, it is in reality *in toto* the character of the mental state of the moment, and so is an existent, in spite of the fact that its existence is not given. – Drake et al. 1920: 4

Drake in his essay "The Approach to Critical Realism" shows where lies the reason for the difference of their opinions. Let him be quoted here:

> Our difference of opinion consists in a divergent use of the terms "given ", "datum", etc. Some of us speak of as "given" only those traits that are traits of the mental existent of the moment – traits, that is, that have actual, literal, psychological existence. The rest of us include in the term the traits apprehended as belonging to the object through the attitude, or reaction, of the organism. According to the latter usage – the datum is, qua datum, a mere essence, an imputed but not necessarily actual existent. It may or it may not have existence. It exists just to the extent in which it is, in fact, the nature either of the object known or of the cognitive state (mental existent) of the moment put dash an extent which varies from case to case. Meanwhile, according to the former usage, the datum has *in toto* a psychological existence, and may be spoken of as "mental content". – Drake et al. 1920: 21

II. Santayana's Place in the Critical Realist Movement

Santayana's place in the critical realist movement is an important one. Durant Drake, who wrote the preface of *Essays in Critical Realism*, gives

> especial credit to Professor Strong and Professor Santayana, who, though overseas during this entire period, have kept up a constant correspondence with the rest of us, and thus shared with their cis-Atlantic colleagues the fruits of their many years of consideration of the vexing problem we had chosen attack.
>
> – Ibid.: v

Strong, in turn, acknowledges his indebtedness to Santayana in the following words:

> I had long been convinced that cognition requires three categories for its adequate interpretation; the intermediate one – between subject and object – corresponding to the Kantian "phenomenon" or "appearance" ... but, in my efforts to conceive it clearly, I was continually falling off either into the category of "object" or into that "psychic state". What was my relief when at last I heard Mr. Santayana explain his conception of "essence", and it dawned upon me that here was the absolutely correct description of the looked-for category.
>
> – Ibid.: 224

Santayana's article "Three Proofs of Realism" (1920a) is the clearest presentation of his critical realist point of view. His point of view as a critical realist is shown in his maintaining the transitiveness of knowledge. Knowledge, instead of knowing itself, aims at something beyond itself, the object; i.e. knowledge must be transitive. In his psychological proof of realism, Santayana argues against idealism, which denies the existence of "physical, metaphysical or religious objects", on the simple ground that objects known are not independent of knowledge. Though it denies the claim of knowledge to be transitive with regard to the above-mentioned objects, it asserts the existence of mind and ideas apart from the knowledge of them. Thus, by maintaining the transitiveness of knowledge within the psychological realm, it verges upon the realist point of view.

Belief in time is "the purest and most radical instance of realism (Drake et al. 1920: 176). Transcendentalism of idealism, as it is diametrically opposite to realism, is reluctant to accept anything which is supported from the realistic point of view. Hence, the transcendentalist must deny the reality of time. But Santayana shows that the transcendentalist cannot but accept the reality of time, since his "whole moral inspiration is notoriously bound up with the sense of time, progress and evolution (ibid.). Santayana thinks that we cannot do away with the belief in time which is "the soul of introspective psychology (ibid.: 177). Such a belief is indeed necessary for memory, rational action and hope.

Santayana, thus, through his clever attack upon idealism from different sides, proves and advocates realism. Realism is further proved by him when he adopts the realistic assumption that essences have a status independent of knowledge. They are not independent physically since existence is not attributed to them. Their reality is of a logical or aesthetic character which is immutable, indefeasible and inalienable. This character is, then, "intrinsic, essential, and contingent on nothing else, least of all, of course, on knowledge (Drake et al. 1920: 182). The logical thought of, or pure acquaintance with, essence discovers its reality which is "ontologically far more necessary and fundamental than are physical things or pulses of feeling (ibid.). Ideal contemplation, therefore, is realistic.

III. Santayana's Theory of Knowledge

Santayana's epistemological position now becomes fairly intelligible. By defying idealism as a realist, he advocates dualism which results, again, in a representative and symbolic theory of knowledge. In his *Scepticism and Animal Faith*, where a whole chapter is devoted to epistemological discussion, his mind hovers between two motives, one directed to showing what knowledge is not, and the other to determining what knowledge is. Let us now proceed to discuss this point.

A. INTUITION IS NOT KNOWLEDGE

We have found (p. 30) how the sceptic arrives at the position which is a kind of timeless intuition of pure essence, having no reference to the external world of physical objects or change. The character of the essences does not, however, depend upon their being intuited. Intuition of essences, which is held to be possible, does not mean knowledge of them. The question is: Why is intuition of essence not to be called knowledge? Knowledge means acquaintance with what are existent, i.e. we must know facts. Now, intuition of essences cannot be called knowledge, since essences are not facts and hence are devoid of existence. As Santayana observes:

> So long as a knowledge is demanded that shall be intuition, the issue can only be laughter or despair; for if I attain intuition, I have only a phantom object,[1] and if I spurn that and turn to the facts, I have renounced intuition. – 1923: 170

He shows another reason as to why intuition of essence cannot be called knowledge. Knowledge consists in judgement. What is known is put in the subject–predicate relation. Intuition of essence or datum is not knowledge, since the intuited datum or essence, which stands for nothing else, cannot be expressed in the form of a judgement, although the experience due to intuition of essence becomes contemplative. Santayana points out:

> Judgement is in abeyance; the datum stands for nothing else, and the experience attained is merely esthetic or contemplative. – 1918: 432

---

[1] By "phantom object" Santayana means "essence". As essences are divested of all existence, there can, therefore, be nothing but the fancied vision of them.

It may here be noted that Santayana's use of the phrase "intuition of essence" seems not to be justified on reasonable grounds. That, intuition of essence is not possible, has been elaborately shown in the criticism part (pp. 65-66) of the third chapter of this treatise. Essence and intuition, to take Santayana's own words, contradict themselves by their very nature. Essence is immaterial, while intuition is not so, since its organ lies in the material psyche (1923: 151). Again, intuition which is held to be existent cannot be the principle of beholding essence which is non-existent in character. Intuition and essence – the former belonging to the realm of existence and the latter having the realm of non-existence – cannot be brought under the single phrase "intuition of essence".

If Santayana claims the materiality of intuition, what is, then, possible as a logical conclusion is not intuition of essences, but intuition of things. But to him intuition of things is a "contradiction in terms" (1923: 167). If intuition of things be taken for granted, all possible things, then, should be known immediately and directly. But this is not really the case. Hence, intuition of things remains for ever an impossibility. A query may crop up here. When intuition of things is not possible directly, is it not possible indirectly? That is, can we not know things through their ideas of which we can have intuition or immediate awareness? Santayana answers here also that intuition of an idea is not knowledge, but it is mere contemplation (ibid.: 170-71). In a practical sense, therefore, intuition cannot be knowledge.

B. INTUITION OF ESSENCE AND KNOWLEDGE OF EXISTENCE

Intuition of essence is not knowledge of existence: that is, it is not knowledge in the real or practical sense as has already been pointed out. But Santayana says that intuition of essence can also be called knowledge in a sense other than realistic.

> Literal knowledge is acquaintance with essence, esthetic or logical intuition or construction, the object of which is purely ideal .... – 1918: 436

Intuition of essence is called "sure" knowledge, since in it there is no room for error. Error arises in the case of predication. But essence transcends all predication, being divested of existence.

> Any intuition gives knowledge of acquaintance with an essence, not subject to error, since the intuition chooses its object in the act of determining itself, and asserts no existence of that object. – Ibid.: 432

Intuition of essence or sure knowledge is immediate, since essences are directly apprehended. Again, it is intransitive, since an essence does not stand for anything.

Knowledge of existence is called real knowledge. Unlike sure knowledge, real knowledge is contingent since it is concerned with matters of fact. Again, knowledge of existence is not direct; here things are known through the essences. This point will be discussed shortly. Further, unlike intuition of essence, knowledge of existence is transitive in the sense that it aims at something beyond itself, the self-existing object. The distinction between sure knowledge and real knowledge has been made in the following lines of Santayana:

> We might almost say that sure knowledge being immediate and intransitive, is not real knowledge, while real knowledge, being transitive and adventurous, is never sure. – 1918: 433

Santayana, however, points out that sure knowledge, though it is intransitive, is transitive in the sense that the essences which intuition observes:

> are independent of it, not in existence (for they do not exist) but in character and identity, since whatever is true of any essence is true of it always, whether there be intuition of it or not. – Ibid.

He also says that real knowledge or knowledge of existence, though it is not absolutely "sure" or evident, may contain the highest degree of evidence in the case of the immediate receding past.

C. ORIGIN OF KNOWLEDGE

Henceforward by knowledge we shall mean knowledge of existence only. The question with which we are confronted now is: How do we come to know objects? What is the origin of knowledge? The answer to this question is found in the two volumes of Santayana, first (a) in his *Life of Reason*, vol. 1 *Reason in Common Sense* (1905), vol. 2 *Reason in Society*, vol. 3 *Reason in Religion*, vol. 4 *Reason in Art*, vol. 5 *Reason in Science*, and then (b) in his *Scepticism and Animal Faith* (1923).

a. In *Reason in Common Sense* Santayana shows how we can have an experience of a thing. He points out there that there are two prominent terms in human knowledge: ideas and things. He wants to say that ideas lead to the knowledge of things, concretion in discourse to concretion in existence. Now, what is meant by "ideas"? Santayana seems not to be definite in answering to this. Ideas are sometimes called "ideal terms" (1905, I: 113), sometimes called sensations rendered cognitive (ibid.: 115), and again at the same time called "essences" (ibid.). But in his later works, *Scepticism and Animal Faith* and *The Realm of Essence* (1927), he carefully distinguishes essences from ideas. Anyway, it seems that Santayana in his *Reason in Common Sense* takes ideas for essences. Now, let us come to the actual question: how do we come to know things from ideas or essences? First of all, ideas are to be recognized as separate recurrent sensations. The "togetherness" of those sensations is next noted. Lastly, they are assigned a definite place and object which they may be said to constitute. Thus, in man's discovery of the sun, the ideas of roundness, whiteness and heat were identified first as separate recurrent sensations, second as occurring together, whereupon the sun was marked out as a distinct external object.

b. In *Scepticism and Animal Faith*, Santayana comes into a more elaborate discussion of the problem of knowledge. He says that the psyche is integral with life. Hence, to make life worth living, what is necessary for the psyche is to adjust itself to the surrounding objects. The objects also in turn lay their effects upon the psyche. Knowledge serves as a name for these effects (1923: 164). What Santayana specially points out is that objects are not directly presented to the psyche. Otherwise, the psyche would have possessed direct or intuitive knowledge of them. That, direct or intuitive knowledge of things is not possible, is clearly shown (p. 109). Besides, to Santayana, intuitive knowledge is a contradiction in terms, since intuition and knowledge refer to two different realms, the former to the realm of essence and the latter to the realm of matter. Essences are intuited, but things are known. By discarding the possibility of the intuitive knowledge, Santayana goes against the camps of both empirical and rationalistic philosophers who have accepted intuitive knowledge.

When, according to Santayana, objects are not directly presented to the psyche, the latter in order to adjust itself to them takes a leap – a leap of faith towards them. Thus, in knowledge-situation, the existence of the objects is posited by the faith of the animal psyche. But to posit the existence of the objects does not constitute knowledge of them. Unless the objects are described, knowledge of them cannot arise. Or, more simply, knowledge of things means description about them.

Now, is it possible for the psyche to describe things? The psyche, since it is unintelligent and unconscious as a part of matter (p. 80), cannot do the function of describing which implies the presence of intelligence. Then, other than the psyche, there must be something which can do that epistemological function. The psyche, in its adaptations to the surrounding things, becomes intelligent and creates spirit. Spirit, though originating from the material psyche, is not matter. It is rather a function of matter. It is simple awareness or consciousness. Things are described not by the psyche, but by the conscious spirit.

The question, again, arises: how does spirit describe things? Here on this very point we verge upon essences which have some but important cognitive role to play. The essences appear in intuition by the category of spirit. The psyche produces intent in spirit in its attempt to adjust itself to the alien things, so that the spirit selects those essences by which the things encountered by the psyche can be described (1923: 166). Thus, the spirit makes the pragmatic function of physical sensibility possible. The role of essence in cognition is to provide the descriptive terms by which we think and speak about the objects encountered in action. Let us take an example which is not, of course, cited by Santayana. The existence of an object, say, a table, is posited by the animal psyche. The object which is encountered by the psyche must be described, if we want to have knowledge of it. The spirit performs that fair job by selecting those essences, which are suitable for being descriptive terms of the object. The qualities sensed of the present object or the apposite essences are, say, roundness and hardness. And the object (here the table) is described by saying that it is hard and round. With this description of the table we get knowledge of it.

In any knowledge-situation, then, what play major roles are the psyche, the spirit, intent and essence. These are, so to speak, the conditions of knowledge. The psyche has a vital demand to act upon the surrounding things. The spirit which arises from the psyche fulfils that demand. But how? Through "intent" and the essences. It is "intent" which makes thought cognitive or practical. Intent cannot be finally explained and must be accepted as a mystery. It bridges the chasm between essences and external object, for by virtue of it thought becomes cognitive and practical. Intent is the stick by which the critical realist makes his second leap, the leap of faith. The essences, which are selected by intent, serve as apposite symbols by which the objects encountered by the psyche are described by the spirit.

D. SANTAYANA'S REPRESENTATIVE THEORY OF KNOWLEDGE AS COMPARED WITH THAT OF LOCKE

It is to be kept in mind that Santayana's representative theory of knowledge is not of the Lockian type. Locke holds that the object, itself remaining unknown to us, lays influence upon the knowing mind, giving rise thereby to an idea of itself. The mind knows the object through the idea of that object: that is, the mind, instead of knowing the presentation of the object, knows its representation. To Locke, then, ideas cannot be separated from objects; they are of the objects; their origin lies in the latter. But to Santayana, essences are not, like Locke's ideas, of the objects, but are for the objects. It means that objects are represented through essences which are, however, independent of the former. Thus, when Locke pronounces that ideas are the representations of the objects, Santayana asserts that essences are not the representations of the objects. The former makes ideas dependent upon the objects, while the latter makes objects dependent upon essences, since essences are the only symbols through which objects can be represented.

We must note some points of difference, which are not less important, between Locke's Idea and Santayana's Essence. First, essence which is also called datum or "bare appearance" is not particular, but universal. The datum (suppose, the appearance of a man) is not attached to any space and time, since it may appear in any number of instances without losing its identity. The universality of a datum or an essence is justified in this sense. Locke's Idea, unlike Santayana's Essence, is, on the one hand, particular, since each idea is always of a particular object. Second, an idea belongs to the mind, but an essence, instead of necessarily belonging to the mind, has a realm of its own, which is neither mental nor physical. Thus, an idea is subjective, while an essence is trans-subjective.

E. INDIRECT KNOWLEDGE OF ESSENCE

Santayana, although he denies that intuition of essence can be knowledge, accepts, however, the indirect knowledge of essences. Suppose, I hear now a clap of thunder. Gradually, the physical shock subsides and silence is restored. It is not possible for me now to rehearse the exact pitch and volume of that sound. But when there is a second crash, I may say with assurance whether this crash is longer or louder than the former. Here I know the former crash, which is an essence, not intuitively, but through the memory of it. To quote from Santayana:

> Thus even pure essences can become objects of intent and of tentative knowledge when they are not present in intuition but are approached and posited indirectly, as the essences given on another particular occasion or signified by some particular word. – 1923: 168

Here, the occasion or the word is a natural fact. We know it at first and from the fact we elicit the essence, although this elicitation takes place imaginatively. The occasion or the word is the sign by which the essence or essences are designated. And this designation about them is knowledge.

> Whereas intuition, which reveals an essence directly, is not knowledge, because it has no ulterior object, the designation of some essence by some sign does convey knowledge, to an intelligent pupil, of what that essence was. – Ibid.: 169

F. KNOWLEDGE IS BELIEF

What Santayana finally contends is that "knowledge is true belief" (ibid.: 179). This statement implies two things:

1. First, there must be a belief – a belief in a world of events. The animal psyche cannot but believe in the existence of outer facts. This belief is native to it.
2. Second, belief which is encountered by the psyche about the objects must be true. We have seen (pp. 112-13) that the objects which are believed to exist must be described by the spirit through the essences. When that description becomes appropriate or true, knowledge results.

Thus, true belief by which is meant knowledge means "appropriate description" of things believed to exist outside. It may be asked how description can be made appropriate. We know from Santayana that essences are the symbols or signs in the description of the natural world. Appropriate description depends upon the choosing of the right symbols and to choose the right symbols what is necessary is to give prolonged attention to what actually occurs. Thus any essence is not suitable for describing a fact, although there may be many alternate essences to describe the same. Suppose, the moon that is believed to exist is described by different persons.

> Looking at the moon, one man may call it simply a light in the sky; another, prone to dreaming awake, may call it a virgin Goddess; a more observant person, remembering that this luminary is given to waxing and waning, may call it the crescent; and a fourth, a full-fledged astronomer, may say (taking the aesthetic essence before him merely for a sign) that it is an extinct and opaque spheroidal satellite of the earth, reflecting the light of the sun from a part of its surface.
>
> – 1923: 176-77

Accordingly, we get different descriptions of the moon conveyed by different essences, viz. crescent, Goddess, light or satellite.

All the descriptions are not, of course, appropriate. Here some descriptions contain pictorial elements or infusion of reverie. But the description of the moon given by the astronomer is more appropriate than those given by others, since the

> terms of astronomy ... are the fruit of a better focused, more chastened, and more prolonged attention turned upon what actually occurs; that is, they are kept closer to animal faith. –Ibid.: 177-78

G. LIMIT OF KNOWLEDGE

There is a limit, Santayana opines, to our knowledge of existence. The object cannot be known completely. Complete knowledge of anything means the knowledge of that thing in all its relations, natural and ideal.

> The flower in the crannied wall would not need to reveal God and man to us by any mysterious sympathetic illumination; before we could know all about it we should have had to explore for ourselves the whole universe in which it grows. – 1918: 434-35

But that is not possible, since it is difficult, first of all, to explore all the external relations and affinities which are relevant to the flower, and second, to discern its ideal relations in the realm of essence. Hence, Santayana concludes that it is not possible for us to have a complete knowledge of any object. To have a complete knowlege of any fact, to know a thing in all its relations is to possess the truth of it. The nature of truth and its difference from opinion will be discussed shortly.

The Jainas, who are the Anekāntavādins in Indian philosophy, also advocate, more or less, the same view. They maintain that every object has innumerable characters. It is not possible for imperfect beings like us to know a thing in all its aspects. Each person knows some characters of a thing from his own standpoint. Thus, the knowledge of a thing is relative and not absolute. The Jainas maintain that complete knowledge of a thing may be possessed only by an omniscient person (*kevalī*).

H. WHAT IS TRUTH?

For every fact there is a standard comprehensive description which Santayana calls truth. What does he understand by a standard comprehensive description of any fact? To quote him:

> A comprehensive description (of any fact) includes also all the radiations of that fact – I mean, all that perspective of the world of facts and of the realm of essence which is obtained by taking this fact as a centre and viewing everything else only in relation with it. – 1938: viii

Thus, truth about any fact is infinitely extended and, hence, it is not possible for anyone to repeat it wholly. Although truth radiates from contingent fact and is descriptive of existence, it has no existence of its own.

The implied being of truth is its eternity. Truth is not an existence. It is an essence and eternity belongs to essences only. Though truth is eternal in the sense of being non-existent, it is not timeless, since it is descriptive of existence. It is that segment of the realm of essence which comes to have the special dignity of being actualized in matter (ibid.). And this segment of the realm of essence is called by Santayana the Realm of Truth.

i. Truth and Opinion

Truth which means the comprehensive description of any fact in all its relations cannot be identified with any opinion. An opinion contains a partial description of a fact from a particular perspective. Consequently, it has limitation in scope. Santayana speaks of true and false opinions. Opinions are true when they reiterate the part of the standard comprehensive description of the facts which they envisage. And opinions are false when they contradict the part of the truth about the facts which they consider. True opinions cannot express the truth of any fact in all its relations. What they do is to refer to different aspects of truth. To quote Santayana:

> ... the truth is the field which various true opinions traverse in various directions, and no opinion itself. – 1923: 268

Any true opinion, according to Santayana, is not the absolute truth, since by the latter is meant an all-inclusive and eternal system. If there were no absolute truth, the different views taken by the individuals would themselves be absolute. That various opinions or views are more or less correct and complementary to one another is due to the fact that they all refer to the same standard comprehensive description of the facts which they envisage.

ii. There Are No Necessary Truths

Santayana shows us that there is one absolute truth which gets a partial expression in so many true opinions. True opinions can be called partial truths or simply truths. Santayana's contention is that all truths are contingent since they are descriptive of "contingent" existence (1938: 2). Consequently, there are no necessary truths. We may here briefly note how he establishes this bold contention of his.

1. It is a common conviction that mathematical propositions imply necessary truths. But Santayana asserts that "necessity" and "truth" do attach to mathematical propositions from different quarters. They are necessary, by virtue of the definitions given to their terms. A mathematical equation, say, 2 + 2 = 4, makes explicit certain essential relations between certain terms. Essential relations are all necessary, since they are based on the definitions given to those related terms. Now, this necessity belonging to mathematical science has nothing to do with truth if the terms it connects are not illustrated in existence. Unless mathematics is connected with truth,

it remains a mere play of ideas. When the mathematical propositions become relevant to material facts, it is only in that relevance that they become true, or, in a serious sense, become knowledge. Thus, mathematical truths are not due to the essential relations which exist in certain terms, but rather due to the remarkable and exact relevance of the mathematical terms to material facts. As the truth of mathematics is due to the exemplification of the terms in existence, it is, therefore, contingent.

2. We are confronted with an important proposition that God, or the most real of beings, necessarily exists. On Santayana's view, the existence of God is not a necessary truth. If the proposition that God exists is necessary, its terms can be only essences. In such a case no essence has any power to actualize itself in a fact. On the contrary, if the word "God" be taken as a spiritual moral being exercising an actual power in the spatio-temporal world, His existence can be proved contingently, i.e.

> by the evidence of these natural manifestations, not by dialectical reasoning upon the meanings of terms. – 1938: 10

So, Santayana attempts to establish his view that truth, being a rediation of existence, is contingent.

I. VALIDITY OF KNOWLEDGE

Santayana's discourse on the validity of knowledge deserves notice. In his article "Three Proofs of Realism" (1920a), he refers to some important conditions which, if fulfilled, would make knowledge valid. Those conditions are mainly two: (1) transcendence or transitiveness, and (2) relevance. Knowledge, when it is both transitive and relevant, is valid. Knowledge is transitive in the sense that knowledge does not know itself, but aims at something beyond itself, viz. the self-existing object. The child crying for the moon points at it unmistakably. His bodily attitude, which is "his fixed gaze and outstretched arm", "identifies his object in itself, in its physical and historical setting" (Drake et al. 1920: 170). The object which he identifies is what is also identified by us, since his glances converge with ours. What is true in the case of human beings is applicable in the case of animals as well. Transitiveness is implied in the animal's knowledge of things and this is evident from their "pursuing, touching or recoiling from surrounding things" (ibid.: 172). The "things known exist side by side with the animal they stimulate and prior to the reaction and perception which they occasion (ibid.).

But transitiveness alone is not sufficient to account for the validity of knowledge. It must be supplemented by relevance. Transitiveness and relevance are like the pans of a balance necessary to each other in order to bring forth valid knowledge. That knowledge is relevant means that the essences which are directly present to the mind, resemble, at least in some respects, the object which knowledge aims at.

> Knowledge could not be true knowledge unless, in its deliverance, it specified some of the qualities or relations which really belong to that object. – Drake et al. 1920: 165

Santayana indicates both transcendence and relevance of knowledge by giving an example of a portrait.

> A portrait, to be a portrait, must be distinct from the sitter and must at the same time somehow resemble or be referred to him. – Ibid.

Transcendence implies that knowledge is not indentical in existence with its object (as a portrait is not identical with the sitter). Thus, knowledge becomes something new, "a fresh act". On the other hand, relevance shows that knowledge is identical with its object in essence (as the portrait and the sitter are the same person).

IV. Critical Reflection

In any knowledge-situation, the independent existence of the object should be maintained. Of course, there are some philosophers who are prone to assert the identity of knowledge and its object on the very ground that knowledge and the object are found to have an inseparable relation between them. But this should not be maintained. The fact that knowledge and the object are presented together is not a proof of their identity. Inseparable connection is different from identity. The identity of knowledge and the object snaps the very ground of maintaining the independent existence of the object. In that case cognition is empty of content; the consciousness that there are no external things is empty. If it is said that actually there are no external things and that our consciousness of things as external is illusory, it may be asked, then, if there were nothing external, how can we have an illusion of externality? If there were no such thing as a snake at all, we did not have knowledge of it, we could not imagine it in the rope. Hence, objects exist independent of knowledge. Santayana is right when he maintains that things transcend knowledge and thus have a status of their own.

It appears that Santayana is unerring when he points to relevance as one important condition of valid knowlege. The essence which the mind envisages must be relevant to the essence which actually belongs to the object perceived. Otherwise, knowledge would be invalid. But Santayana's contradictory words with regard to relevance lead us into an obscure position. He asserts that the qualities or relations which the mind attributes to the thing indicated are those of which some at least "really belong to that object" (Drake et al. 1920: 165). But, this assertion of his is not quite compatible with his statement:

> What that object is in its intrinsic and complete constitution will never be known by man. – Ibid.: 172

When the object remains unknown to us so far as its intrinsic nature is concerned, how is it possible to think of the object possessed of some of the qualities which the mind attributes to it? This, really, creates much confusion to anyone who seeks to be acquainted with Santayana's theory of knowledge. But confusion and obscurity seem to be no more when Santayana's words are taken into the meaning more deeply. It is said that the object is intrinsically unknown to us. Naturally, a difficulty may arise for us as regards whether the unknown object possesses any essence or essences and we face another corresponding difficulty regarding relevance between the essences which the mind senses about the object and the ones which are actually possessed by the object. The above difficulties are met along the following lines.

The object may, "in its intrinsic and complete constitution", remain unknown to us; but that it possesses essence or essences is inferred from the fact that it exists. We may, however, be led to doubt, first about its existence and, second, about the embodiment of essence into matter or a thing.

1. Santayana shows clearly that the object exists and the proof for its existence "is given in the fact that we can point to it" (Drake et al. 1920: 172).
2. There cannot be doubt about the embodiment of essence into matter.

The essences which are embodied in matter are called eventual essences to which reference has already been made (pp. 88-89). Now, with the establishment of Santayana's thesis that the object has actually some essences as its forms, the problem of relevance seems to be solved.

V. Further Observations

Before concluding this chapter, some more words are to be said regarding Santayana's theory of knowledge.

1. Santayana, we have seen (pp. 109-10), distinguishes between pure or literal knowledge and discursive knowledge as determined by animal faith. The former kind of knowledge, where discursive thought has been overcome, is the pure immediate knowledge or intuition of the datum or essence denuded of all interpretation by animal faith and of all the particularity which chracterizes its objects. Why does Santayana refer to the pure knowledge or intuition of essence? Probably, being conscious of the dogmatic positions regarding discursive knowledge as determined by animal faith, he seeks for the theoretical knowledge in the intuition of essence. But, there also, Santayana's attitude is rather dogmatic. In pure immediate knowldge, the subject and the object, which are identified, are emptied of all content or concreteness. In such a case it cannot be regarded as knowledge at all. Nor can it be a theory. As Antonio Banfi holds:

   > ... an intuition deprived of all faith, as Santayana says, and deprived of every existential position and activity of the ego – an essence which is neither mere logical form nor mere sensible quality and implies no relation to the world of objects – may be conceivable as position in a dialectic of thought, but cannot be recognized as feature in an experience of knowledge. – Schilpp 1940: 487

   If intuition of essence be not knowledge or a "feature in an experience of knowledge", then it can be regarded as mere aesthetic contemplation and Santayana himself also admits this. But what is most surprising is that intuition of essence cannot be accepted as mere aesthetic experience. Aesthetic experience is compared with empirical experience on the ground that the former is, while the latter is not, free from the objective determinations and connections. But is aesthetic experience truly free from all objective determinations? Does it not conform to a law of constitution? Really it implies a construction according to connections on which depend the universality and individuality peculiarly characteristic of aesthetic image. Thus, aesthetic experience, though not empirical experience, is not totally free from objective determination. Intuition of essence, which is held to be divested of objective determinations and connections, cannot be aesthetic experience. In regarding intuition of essence at one time as pure immediate knowledge and at another time as aesthetic contemplation, though it can be neither as we have just seen, Santayana develops a dogmatic position in his theory of knowledge.

2. In the case of discursive knowledge or knowledge of existence what are essential are the two leaps, viz. the leap of intuition and the leap of faith. The leap of intuition is made "from the state of the living organism to the consciousness of some essence" (Drake et al. 1920: 183). This leap is the primary stage of knowledge. The second stage of knowledge consists in "the leap of faith and of action". It is made "from the symbol actually given in sense or in thought to some ulterior existing object" (ibid.).

   The first leap, which is the leap of intuition, lands us in the realm of the ideal. Essences which are intuited have no existence. Now, the question is: How do we come from the ideal realm to the physical realm? How from the acquaintance of essence do we come to know physical objects? "By the leap of faith", Santayana answers. But this leap, like the leap of intuition, is not ideal; on the other hand, it is realistic. If this leap be realistic, the symbols or essences from which the leap is taken must also be real. Now, if symbols were real, there would be nothing to leap to mechanistically and if symbols are not real, there would be nothing to leap from mechanistically. Since Santayana denies thought a mechanistic character, this leap must be ideal. As a result, the physical object can never be reached. The end of the knowledge-process is, then, the essence which has an ideal existence.

3. Moreover, there seems to be no logical connection between the two leaps. The leap of intuition is made "from the state of the living organism to the consciousness of some essence". In this leap what happens is a change of one state of organism into another. Thus, a continuity is marked here. In such a continuous process the sudden transition from a symbol to an external object appears rather unexpected. In conclusion, let it be observed that Santayana as a critical realist is not "critical" enough in developing his theory of knowledge.

Part Two
Aesthetics

6

The Sense of Beauty

I. Introduction

THE present chapter would concern itself with Santayana's aesthetic theory to which contributions are of acknowledged value. To say that aesthetic theory in America reached maturity with his famous work, *The Sense of Beauty* (1896), is, perhaps, not an exaggeration. This work, a composition of his lectures on aesthetics at Harvard University, exhibits his psychology of taste and proposes to present the nature and elements of our aesthetic judgements. He is eager to construe

> why, when and how beauty appears, what conditions an object must fulfil to be beautiful, what elements of our nature make us sensible of beauty and what the relation is between the constitution of the object and the excitement of susceptibility. – 1896: 19-20

In *The Sense of Beauty*, Santayana has not attempted to give a definition of beauty in the strict sense of the term. He has rather made in it an unfortunate misuse of language which he tries to remove in later works. For example, in *The Sense of Beauty*, beauty is defined, in the first instance, as "objectified pleasure". But in an article published almost thirty years after *The Sense of Beauty*, he writes:

> Nor was the phrase "objectified pleasure" a definition of beauty, a visionary essence utterly indefinable: it was an indication of the conditions and manner in which the momentary apparition of beauty arose and vanished.
> – 1925: 284

The Sense of Beauty, as it is clearly indicated above, investigates the conditions under which beauty is experienced. It is an attempt to describe a kind of human experience, viz. the aesthetic experience. Santayana writes in "Apologia Pro Mente Sua":

> Nor was my book even about the beautiful in its dialectical relations, perhaps to the real or to the good; I wrote about the sense for the beautiful.
> – 1940b: 555

In other words, Santayana's interest here is more psychological than metaphysical. To conclude, in *The Sense of Beauty*, his major work on aesthetics, Santayana does not attempt the definition of beauty itself. What he wishes to define is aesthetic appreciation or the sense of beauty.

Santayana treats beauty as an object of human experience. Hence, his method of studying beauty is neither didactic nor historical, but psychological. His psychological method of construing beauty is referred to when he says:

> We shall ... study human sensibility itself and our actual feelings about beauty.
> – 1896: 11

His psychological approach to beauty has received praise and acceptance from many a writer of today. For instance, C.J. Ducasse of Brown University says:

> My obligations to the writings of Mr. Santayana on aesthetics are overwhelming and gratefully acknowledged. His marvellously acute psychological insight has illuminated for me many an obscure problem.
> – 1929: iv

Santayana describes rather than explaining what is meant by beauty. He treats beauty as a positive fact of experience as a psychologist would do.

Santayana makes a poignant attack against those who cherish "the prejudice against the subjective" (1896: 8). Man generally thinks that what is the outcome of his mind is unreal and insignificant. The ancient philosophers were engaged in speculation on the objective world, without being first aware of their mind, the instrument of all speculation. Modern behaviourism in psychology first deals with the function of perception and the theory of knowledge, and neglects the "human department of imagination and emotion" from which "the great world of perception derives all its value" (ibid.: 7). Santayana who has cast off all prejudice against himself understands that aesthetic judgements, instead of being expressions of objective truth, are the expressions of human nature.

> A judgement is not trivial, however, because it rests on human feelings; on the contrary, triviality consists in abstraction from human interests.
> – Ibid.: 8

A judgement to be significant must have the "function in the ordering and enriching of life" (ibid.).

The value of Santayana's subjective approach in the study of beauty is not to be minimized.

> To feel beauty is a better thing than to understand how we come to feel it.
> – Ibid.: 14

But Santayana is not the first man to treat beauty from the psychological point of view. Kant's approach to beauty also is subjective. That there is many a point of difference between Santayana and Kant as to aesthetical theories will be treated later on. It may be mentioned here that Kant takes a subjective stand on the basis of which he expounds the metaphysics of beauty. This, however, is not accepted by Santayana, since the latter thinks that such a metaphysics is "beyond the reach of verification" (1896: 8). To the poet Rabindranath Tagore, as to

Indian thought in general, beauty is subjective. "In Art, man reveals himself and not his objects."[1]

The subjective approach to beauty made by Indian thought results in aesthetical metaphysics in contrast with metaphysical aesthetics, as posed by the traditional thinkers in the West. We have aesthetical metaphysics when our experience of beauty rules our understanding of reality. Metaphysical aesthetics is that where our idea of reality dictates our understanding of beauty. Santayana's standpoint is neither that of the traditional thinkers in the West nor that of Indian thought. We shall discuss it after we become acquainted with Santayana's theory of beauty.

It may be observed that in his article "What Is Aesthetics? (1904)" Santayana expresses less sympathy with the psychological method than he does in *The Sense of Beauty*. He writes:

> ... mathematics or history or judgements of taste can fall within the psychological field adventitiously and for a third person. An eventual subsumption of the whole universe under psychological categories would still leave every human pursuit standing and every field of experience or faith distinct in its native and persisting hypostasis. ... Aesthetic experience will therefore continue to elude and overflow psychology in a hundred way, although in its own way psychology might eventually survey and represent all aesthetic experience. –1904: 322-23

Thus, psychology may consider aesthetic facts. But, it cannot be said that "because to analyse the sense of beauty is a psychological task, this analysis constitutes a special science (ibid.: 324). Santayana does not treat aesthetics as a separate science.

> A single and complete aesthetic science, natural or ideal, is an idol of the cave and a scholastic chimera. – 1904: 327

1 *Personality*, p. 12.

Any art, abstracted from its practical basis and occasion, and devoid of some intellectual function, is hardly noticed. We cannot hold of the pleasures as beauties,

> if they are attached to nothing substantial and rational, to nothing with a right of citizenship in the natural or in the moral world. – Ibid.: 326

There is another point to be added in our introduction to Santayana's aesthetic theory. His aesthetic theory is not wholly naturalistic. He insists that his analysis will not ignore the insights of the Platonists, but rather explain and justify them. Plato speaks of the eternal ideas in conformity with which all excellence is determined. When we find and declare a thing good or beautiful, we make a categorical judgement that involves a standard or ideal which is "intrinsic and ultimate" for that case: "all ideals are absolute and eternal for the judgement that involves them" (1896: 15). Whenever we make judgements throughout our experience, we always have before us an absolute ideal in conformity with which value is value. But if we attempt to define that ideal,

> we shall hardly be able to say of it anything less noble and more definite than it is the embodiment of an infinite good. For it is that incommunicable and illusive excellence that haunts every beautiful thing. – Ibid.

Thus, Santayana's aesthetic theory is toned with Platonic supernaturalism. But Santayana's naturalistic tone vies equally with the above as it becomes evident from his analysis of the conditions under which the essence of beauty appears.

II. The Sense of Beauty

A. THE THEORY OF BEAUTY: "CRITICISM" AND "AESTHETICS"

The theory of beauty was designated by the writers of the last century as "criticism". The term "criticism" is used in a narrow sense. It implies deliberate judgement and makes comparison with reference to a standard or standards in view. The present-day writers adopt the term "aesthetics"[2] for meaning the "theory of beauty". It means the theory of perception or of susceptibility. In this sense it includes all immediate perceptions, i.e. all pleasures and pains. Thus, the term "aesthetics" is used in a broad sense.

Santayana points out that neither "criticism" nor "aesthetics" does carry a full meaning of the theory of beauty. Each has a partial significance. The two terms taken together impart a full meaning to the theory of beauty. Criticism implies judgement. But sheer intellectual judgement of a thing without having any feeling with respect to that thing is arid and inane. "A sunset is not criticized; it is felt and enjoyed" (1896: 20). So, the scope of criticism is to be broadened to the sphere in which judgements would be concerned with the immediate perceptions or values, i.e with pleasures and pains. On the other hand, "aesthetics" implies perception. But it should include those perceptions which are appreciations; that is, the sphere of aesthetics should be that of "critical or appreciative perception" (ibid.: 21).

B. EMOTIONAL CONSCIOUSNESS IS NECESSARY FOR THE PERCEPTION OF VALUE

After having taken "aesthetics" in the sense of the "perception of value", Santayana proceeds to show the necessary element, the absence of which is followed by the extirpation of all values. For appreciative perception, what is to be first counted is consciousness. But consciousness is a mental state which includes both intellect and emotion. Santayana says that it is not

---

[2] Baumgarten, so far as is known, was the first to use the word "aesthetic" as the name of a special science. It appeared in his doctoral dissertation (1735), "Meditationis Philosophicae de nonnullis ad Poema Pertinentibus" (Philosophical Meditations Concerning Some Things Pertaining to Poetry).

intellectual consciousness, but emotional consciousness that is needed for the perception of value.

Santayana keeps himself close to the facts of feeling in respect of value. When the feeling goes, the value also goes with it. By stressing emotional consciousness for the appreciation of beauty Santayana excludes all intellectual judgements from his definition of beauty:

> A first approach to a definition of beauty has therefore been made by the exclusion of all intellectual judgements, all judgements of matter of fact or of relation. – 1896: 25

Thus, in respect of beauty, he seems to be an anti-intellectualist. What is emotionally approached is immediate and direct. Beauty is immediately perceived.

C. AESTHETIC EXPERIENCE AND AESTHETIC VALUE

"Aesthetic experience" is regarded by Santayana as identical with "intrinsically valuable experience". Then "aesthetic value" and "intrinsic value" are to be considered as identical, though in *The Sense of Beauty* we face some incongruous statements as regards the relation between "intrinsic value" and "aesthetic value". When Santayana first maintains that "all values are in one sense aesthetic", he means that "all values must be ultimately intrinsic" (ibid.: 32). Here he identifies aesthetic value with intrinsic value. But later, he states that all pleasures "are intrinsic and positive values, but all pleasures are not perceptions of beauty" (1896: 39). Here aesthetic value is not made identical with intrinsic value. As a result, we mark an obvious incongruity in Santayana's statements. But that Santayana usually identifies intrinsic value with aesthetic value marks a general position which the present writer will continue to ascribe to him.

Santayana ascertains two main parts in us, one being the rational and the other the irrational. The former is relative, since "mediation, inference and synthesis are the essence of rationality" (ibid.: 24). Reason is a principle by which we can pass from premises to conclusions and synthesize the parts into the wholes. Therefore, the rational part has a relative significance. But the irrational part in us is non-relative or ultimate for reasons to be explained below.

Santayana assigns much importance to the irrational part, since it is the single source from which all values spring. He writes:

> Values spring from the immediate and inexplicable reaction of vital impulse and from the irrational part of our nature.
> – Ibid.: 24

Value accrues to a thing which is appreciated or preferred. "In appreciation, in preference, lies the root and essence of all excellence" (ibid.: 23). Now, what is appreciated or preferred is declared to be ultimate. Aesthetic experience, which is an appreciative perception, is a value which does not follow from the relative (or rational part). All values, including aesthetic values, spring from the natural demand of our life, from the reaction of our vital impulse.

Santayana has distinguished between two kinds of experience, viz. the intrinsically valuable experience and the instrumentally valuable experience. Before we are in a position to understand this distinction we must take note of the function of the spirit as the basis of such understanding. The function of the spirit is twofold: it meets the psyche's need for intelligent action and, again, it subserves the end of its own nature. These two functions imply practical intelligence and contemplation respectively. The psyche, which is substantialized by Santayana, is blind matter which, in living, tries to adjust itself to the alien things. But in order to do so, it creates consciousness or the spirit. Spirit makes the pragmatic function of physical sensibility possible. It comes to make the psyche more resourceful and more intelligent. This it accomplishes by discovering essences. But spirit has another function, viz. that of contemplation. It contemplates essences without any concern for their ulterior use. The pure spiritual function is not always possible for the spirit, since the spirit, having its root in the material psyche, has to come to meet the need of the psyche.

Now, we may try to understand the distinction between intrinsically valuable experience and instrumentally valuable experience. An experience is valuable instrumentally, when the essences discovered by the spirit serve as signs for the description of things – the description or knowledge which the psyche strives for (p. 113). And an experience is intrinsically valuable when the spirit, being oblivious of the psyche's demand, is absorbed in the contemplation of essences. Thus, we may say that all interests, i.e. all the natural demands of life are devoid of intrinsic value. Intrinsic value is limited to a special kind of interest – an interest in a contemplated essence. And this kind of interest is "inwardly integrated" and "harmonious" within itself.

Aesthetic experience is, then, a contemplated state. But Santayana points out that the converse is not true, i.e. all contemplation is not an aesthetic experience. Essences discovered in contemplation are not beautiful unless one takes delight in beholding them. Consequently, aesthetic experience is a species coming under the genus "contemplation".

Irving Singer

Irving Singer has levelled a point of criticism against Santayana's distinction between intrinsically valuable experience and instrumentally valuable experience. An intrinsically valuable experience (or aesthetic experience) is what satisfies, while an instrumentally valuable experience is what leads to further satisfaction. Singer shows that the distinction between these two kinds of experience is undermined, if satisfaction is taken as a criterion of aesthetic experience. It is true that any experience may be both instrumentally and intrinsically valuable, since it may lead to satisfaction and provide satisfaction itself. But what Santayana rejects and Singer accepts is that a practical experience (or instrumentally valuable experience) may be intrinsically valuable. Singer insists that a practical experience is intrinsically valuable "insofar as one appreciates its utility and delights in it as something instrumentally valuable" (1957: 78). Hence, he concludes by saying that Santayana is not justified in maintaining that

> the useful is good because of the excellence of its consequences; but these must somewhere cease to be merely useful in their turn, or only excellent as means; somewhere we must reach the good that is good in itself and for its own sake, else the whole process is futile ... .
>
> – 1896: 32-33

Singer holds that Santayana is mistaken when he maintains that a useful experience is good only because of its consequences and that these consequences are intrinsically valuable only insofar as they are not useful for anything else. An instrumentally valuable experience, says our critic, can be intrinsically valuable as an instrumentality.

Now, one may object to Singer's interpretation of Santayana's view that aesthetic experience should always be "satisfying". An intrinsically valuable experience, by which is meant aesthetic experience, is that in which one gets delight or pleasure in contemplating essences, and this enjoyment occurs independently of all conception of its relations to anything ulterior. Thus, the objector may think that aesthetic experience, which is devoid of all extrinsic relations, is a pure delight which should not be proclaimed as "satisfaction", since satisfaction, being always a relative term, denotes the previous existence of a desire or an interest.

In reply to the above objection, it may be said that Singer's view cannot be set aside, since aesthetic experience can be termed as "satisfaction" for two reasons. First, Santayana speaks of an "aesthetic interest" which satisfies itself in the contemplation of an essence. He himself says:

> The purest asethetic or logical contemplation hardly goes on without a throbbing accompaniment of interest, haste, reversals, and satisfactions. – 1923: 140

Second, the aesthetic interest of which Santayana speaks is not an abstract interest; it is, on the other hand, related to all other non-aesthetic interests of life.

> To attempt … to abstract a so-called aesthetic interest from all other interests, and a so-called work of art from whatever work ministers, in one way or another, to all human good, is to make the aesthetic sphere contemptible. – 1904: 325

Thus, aesthetic experience is a satisfying one, since it, being connected with the non-aesthetic interests, brings about a good to human life.

Aesthetic experience, then, according to Santayana, is, or would be, satisfying. But each satisfying experience should not be called aesthetic. Satisfaction is a necessary condition for the occurrence of aesthetic value. But, it is not a sufficient condition. To say that an experience is satisfying does not thereby imply that it is aesthetic. But, to say that an experience is aesthetic is to imply that it is satisfying. Although aesthetic experience is satisfying, the person undergoing that experience may not definitely be aware of it as a satisfying experience. Santayana affirms:

> The purest aesthetic or logical contemplation hardly goes on without a throbbing accompaniment of interest, haste, reversals and satisfactions; but these dramatic notes are merged in the counterpoint of the themes surveyed, and I think, prove and enjoy without noticing that I do so. – 1923: 140

D. IS AESTHETIC EXPERIENCE TRUE OR FALSE?

The question of truth or falsity cannot arise in the case of aesthetic experience, since the latter is an ultimate emotional experience which is not mediated by any logico-scientific statement. An experience when it refers to something outside which it has to represent or copy can be pronounced to be either true or false.

But an experience, which is ultimate or unique in itself, which has no other "world" for its reference, can be neither true nor false. Yet aesthetic experience is not without significance. But its significance lies wholly within itself, containing to reference to anything outside. Hence, the question of truth cannot arise. Moreover, when Santayana, excludes all intellectual judgements from the definition of beauty, it is clear that we cannot pass any logical judgement upon aesthetic experience.

Keats, Bergson, Rabindranath and Santayana

Thus, aesthetic experience cannot ordinarily be judged to be either true or false. But do we not say after John Keats that beauty is truth? Paradoxical though it may seem, yet it is not so. When Keats speaks of beauty as truth itself, he refers to poetic truth and not to truth as we know it in general. Beauty is, to him, the quality of selfhood which all objects in nature possess. To perceive this selfhood of things is to apprehend their significance, their meaning – is to love them. Beauty is to Keats as perfection is to Spinoza, the essence of Reality; and Reality, in its fullness and completeness – as an object of that love which is the highest form of vision – is beautiful. The supreme vision which encompasses the whole of nature is called by Spinoza *amor dei intellectualis*, and is called by Keats the chief intensity (*Endymion* book I: l. 800). When Keats suggests that truth can be arrived at by vision only, that no logical concepts are involved in it, he is only poetizing.

In this connection, it should be said that the poetic truth which Keats equates with beauty is not a philosophical truth and Keats himself was aware of the distinction between the two kinds of truth. He shows in his poem *Lamia* how all charms fly away "at the mere touch of cold philosophy". Lamia; a serpent, appears to Lycius, a young fellow, in the guise of a fair maiden. Lycius falls in love with the beautiful lady and determines to marry her. In the wedding ceremony the philosopher Apollonius, the teacher of Lycius, presents himself and with his "juggling eyes" looks at Lamia, and she "withers at their potency" remains "no longer fair" and sits there "a deadly white". What this story reveals is that beauty withers at the presence of dry, cold reason; i.e. rational truth is ever antagonistic to beauty.

To Bergson, however, philosophical truth is identical with poetic truth; for him philosophy should base itself on intuition; reality is to be intuited as it escapes intellect. But Keat's view is different from that of Bergson. To Keats, poetic truth which is imaginative apprehension of reality is like beauty and ceases to be intellectual. He says:

> Imagination may be compared to Adam's dream – he awoke and found it truth . ... Adam's dream will do here.[3]

Truth of imagination is beauty and has a kind of reality which satisfies the mind. Keats recognizes this and hence gives a high status to poetry. But poetic truth or truth of imagination is not philosophical truth which is arrived at through reasoning or conceptual thinking.

Thus, we see that Keats has never turned philosophy into poetry, rational truth into beauty. To him, philosophy may be poetical or poetry philosophical, but without losing their essential identities. Keats is well aware that poetry or beauty is always a vision, truth (rational) or philosophy is always a thought. He never confuses between the two values.

To Rabindranath, rational truth is not truth proper, it is what he calls "fact". Truth proper can be achieved through intuition or vision and not through reason. Beauty Rabindranath equates with this truth proper and this he does since in these values he finds a common character of harmony which reveals itself in truth as consistency and synthesis, and in beauty as unity and proportion. Intelligence provides us with fact or a combination of facts. But the truth lying hidden in the facts is revealed to us

---

3 Letter no. 29: To Baily, 22 November 1817.

through intuition. The distinction between fact and truth can be illustrated by taking an example. Inquiring of a gardener what flower it is we see yonder, he answers, "a lily". This is a mere fact, a bare information. But when this is described in a poem as the "lady" of the garden, this very fact comes to us as a beauty, as a truth tuned with our own heart.

The truth revealed through intuition, says Rabindranath, reveals also our self. It is the harmony between the object and our consciousness. "Aesthetic delight", the poet observes:

> is such a sense of harmony beyond the object that it does not delay in merging with our consciousness. In this case the revelation of the truth of the object is the same as the revelation of my consciousness.[4]

When Keats equates truth with beauty, he means by truth poetic truth and not intellectual truth. Rabindranath also keeps the beautiful away from the intellectually true or what he calls "fact". We have also come to know what Rabindranath understands by truth proper and how he makes it identical with beauty. Like both Keats and Rabindranath, Santayana also holds that truth (intellectual) is not at all the same as beauty (1938: 115). He says that beauty is a good, the possession of which is a free intuition, whereas the possession of truth is knowledge which satisfies the intellect and which is necessary to a man's moral integrity. Thus, Santayana separates the realm of truth from that of beauty.

Santayana, however, opines that the true is akin to, but not identical with, the beautiful in some respects. He says that when an idealistic meaning is rendered to truth, i.e. when by truth is meant the inner potentiality or perfection of all things, we indeed divine the principle of beauty also.

A further affinity between truth and beauty, Santayana contends, consists in their freeing the spirit from private entanglements. Of course, truth and beauty perform this

---

[4] *Sahityer Pathe* (1343 BS), 45.

function of liberating the spirit in their different ways. In the case of beauty the deliverance from the travail of existence is spontaneous. "But the deliverance that comes through the truth comes through sorrow: it is redemption by the cross" (ibid.: 117). The more we recognize (however painful it may be for us to bear) our illusory existence, our insignificance, the more we approach to the realm of truth. Pure insight into truth means total deliverance from finitude and ignorance. But Santayana says that for us it is only possible to be acquainted with a part of truth. But that part of truth, seen under the form of eternity, does not remain external to us; it becomes united with the rhythm of our life and thus turns into clear joy for us.

E. MORAL, AESTHETIC AND INTELLECTUAL JUDGEMENTS

Both moral and aesthetic judgements, Santayana holds, are judgements of value as contrasted with judgements of fact. Value-judgements are based upon some felt appreciation.

> ... unless there is in us some trace of passionate reprobation or of sensible delight, there is no moral or aesthetic judgement. – 1896: 24

Intellectual judgements in contrast with value-judgements are concerned about matters of fact or relation. In such judgements we do not appeal to actual feeling.

> If we approach a work of art or nature scientifically, for the sake of its historical connections or proper classification,we do not approach it aesthetically. – Ibid.: 25

Of the value-judgements, Santayana mainly deals with the moral and aesthetic ones. He distinguishes between them as follows: First, the value with which aesthetic judgement is mainly concerned is the positive value of enjoyment. Morality, on the other hand, is mainly concerned with the avoidance of evil and prevention of suffering.

In the second place, aesthetic judgements are "necessarily intrinsic and based on the character of the immediate experience" (ibid.: 28), while moral judgements merely perdict that something is instrumental to a desired experience. Aesthetic pleasure does not consist in the consequence of the utility of the object. It lies in the immediate perception of the object. Thus, aesthetic pleasure is ultimate in its value. But moral worth is not ultimate. Since moral judgement has to do with the avoidance of evil, its value comes as a consequence of the benefit that is achieved by such act of avoidance. This point of distinction between aesthetics and morality makes one thing explicit, viz. that while aesthetic value has immediacy, moral value has not.

A legitimate question emerges: Is the ugly an aesthetic value or a moral one? Or, is the value of the ugly positive or negative? Santayana answers that the ugly in itself is a source of amusement (ibid.: 29). As such, it is a positive value and comes under the sphere of aesthetics. But if the sight of the ugly is appalling and causes pain, its value is no longer aesthetic; we, then, take a practical and moral attitude towards it.

Moral principles are instrumental to further values. The goals towards which moral principles lead are intrinsically valuable and exist for their own sake. Santayana adds here that our attitude to moral principles, such as honour, truthfulness and cleanliness, is aesthetic, since it is based on "constitutional sensitiveness" (1896: 35), rather than reflection or benevolence. It may be said against Santayana that a reaction based on reflection is no less aesthetic for having a cognitive effect. Now, we may ask: What is "constitutional sensitiveness"? Constitutional sensitiveness is a feeling. The man who has constitutional sensitiveness feels emotions of sympathy and affection in the presence of moral virtues mentioned by Santayana. Having refused to limit aesthetic experience to mere contemplation, we may now consider these feelings as possibly aesthetic, just like everything else which satisfies.

Though Santayana distinguishes between moral and aesthetic values, the distinction made is not vital or real. He confesses:

> I can draw no distinction – save for academic programmes – between moral and aesthetic values. – Schilpp 1940: 20

According to him, aesthetic value and moral value are really the same. Let Santayana speak for himself,

> ... beauty, being a good, is a moral good; and the practice and enjoyment of art, like all practice and all enjoyment, fall within the sphere of morals – at least if by morals we understand moral economy and not moral superstition. On the other hand, the good, when actually realized and not merely pursued from afar, is a joy in the immediate; it is possessed with wonder and is in that sense aesthetic. – Ibid.

F. AESTHETIC PLEASURE IS NOT PHYSICAL PLEASURE

Santayana states that all pleasures are intrinsic and positive values, but they are not all related to the sense of beauty. Aesthetic pleasure and physical pleasure are not to be identified on the ground of semblance between them. Both kinds of pleasure are immediate and positive. Again, both have physical conditions. Like bodily pleasures, aesthetic pleasures also have a bodily seat. They "depend on the activity of the eye and the ear, of the memory and the other ideational functions of the brain" (1896: 39).

But aesthetic pleasure, in spite of having semblance to physical pleasure, is to be clearly distinguished from the latter. Physical pleasures are those which call our attention solely to some part of our own body. But the range of aesthetic pleasure is not limited to its bodily seat. In such pleasure the soul forgets its connection with the body; it enjoys the illusion of disembodiment and is carried to some external object. While bodily pleasure is centripetal, aesthetic pleasure, on the other hand, centrifugal.

G. IS DISINTERESTEDNESS THE DIFFERENTIA OF AESTHETIC PLEASURE?

In the contemplation of the essence of beauty there is an impersonality of the enjoyment. The painter does not look at a beautiful woman with the eyes of a satyr. In aesthetic contemplation, says Santayana, there is disinterestedness in the sense that the soul forgets its bodily connection, that pleasure "is not sought with ulterior motives, and what fills the mind is no calculation, but the image of an object or event, suffused with emotion" (ibid.: 42). But he says that this disinterestedness is not the differentia of aesthetic pleasure. The sense of beauty, is not totally bereft of any interest of desire. He says:

> Appreciation of a picture is not identical with the desire to buy it, but it is, or ought to be, closely related and preliminary to that desire.
>
> – 1896: 41

The absence of our interest in beauty means the absence of our aesthetic faculty.

> If we were not interested in beauty, if it were of no concern to our happiness whether things were beautiful or ugly, we should manifest the maximum, but the total absence of aesthetic faculty.
>
> – Ibid.: 42

Santayana, Kant and Schopenhauer

In the Kantian doctrine of aesthetic contemplation disinterestedness makes its debut. Aesthetic pleasure, according to Kant, is a pleasure which is wholly emancipated from all interest and desire. To Kant and other philosophers also, disinterestedness is the fundamental differentia of aesthetic enjoyment. Disinterested pleasure felt in aesthetic experience is what Schopenhauer describes as "pure, will-less, painless, timeless" (1818: 231). Again, disinterested pleasure is represented by Lipps as aesthetic empathy. He distinguishes between empathy and aesthetic empathy. Empathy is, while aesthetic empathy is not, characterized by interest. Lipps says:

> Empathy is practical when it is concerned with the reality of what is felt; aesthetic empathy, on the contrary, is not so concerned. ... Aesthetic empathy is empathy under the condition of pure aesthetic contemplation. – 1903, II: 35

The notion of disinterestedness is fundamental both in Kant's and Schopenhauer's aesthetics. They, however, differ in the fact that, while Kant's approach to the problem of disinterestedness in aesthetic contemplation is logical, the doctrine of disinterestedness being the precondition for the universality of the judgement of taste, Schopenhauer's approach to it, on the other hand, is psychological, for it is concerned with the state of consciousness during aesthetic contemplation. Santayana differs from both Kant and Schopenhauer in this that he does not take disinterestedness as the differentia of aesthetic pleasure.

Even Santayana's reading of Schopenhauer makes us conversant with the fact that some sort of interest gleams through the latter's theory of beauty. We can quote Santayana here:

> The desire of individual objects, indeed, is absent in the perception of beauty, but there is still present that initial love of the general type and principles of things which is the first illusion of the absolute and drives it on to the fatal experiment of creation. So that, apart from Schopenhauer's mythology, we have in him the recognition that beauty gives satisfaction to some dim and underlying demand of our nature, just as particular objects give more special and momentary pleasures to our individualized wills. – 1896: 41

We can support Santayana by saying that aesthetic experience or imaginative experience is the intensification of life. It is the gratification of a need, the response to an interest in the fullest sense. Like Santayana, Kant speaks of the subjectivity of aesthetic experience, but the latter does, while the former does not, divorce sensation from aesthetic experience. As a result, Kant's aesthetics becomes abstract, while Santayana's is not. Kant fails to realize that aesthetic experience is not any isolation but

> the integration of impulse, emotion, sensation, thought, volition flowing from, and leading to, an unimpeachable comprehension of reality. – Knox 1958: 26

Santayana truly understands that aesthetic experience is born of an intense sensitivity for life and beauty.

H. IS UNIVERSALITY THE DIFFERENTIA OF AESTHETIC PLEASURE?

Santayana, Kant and Lotze

Kant, the greatest name in aesthetics, contends that aesthetic experience is attested by a universal satisfaction and such satisfaction is not due to any interest or inclination of the subject. It is disinterested and is not based on such variable factors like interest or desire, but grounded on what is universal, or what may be presupposed in all men. Thus, Kant speaks of the universality of aesthetic judgement which is based on the universality of the subjective conditions for judging of objects.

That all mankind possesses a capacity for the appreciation of the beautiful has been rightly affirmed by Kant. But this human capacity has been explained by him in terms of his own metaphysics. So, Kant ignores the wealth of emotional contents with which aesthetic experience is replete. By ignoring or transcending the feeling aspect of aesthetic experience, he postulates certain a priori categories by reference to which the judgement of taste is rendered universal.

Santayana says that the doctrine which takes universality as the essence of aesthetic pleasure cannot be supported, since on this view the perception of beauty becomes a judgement rather than a sensation. Beauty is sensed differently by different persons, since "no two men have exactly the same faculties ..." (1896: 44-45). While Kant speaks of the general appreciation of the beautiful, Santayana, on the other hand, tells us that

> if our appreciation were less general, it might be more real and if we trained our imagination into exclusiveness, it might attain to character. – Ibid.: 47

Kant's assertion of the universality of aesthetic judgement has not been accepted by Hermann Lotze. Beauty, according to the latter, attains value only when living spirit feels it. Like Lotze, Santayana speaks of the sensuous appreciation of beauty. What is beautiful to one man cannot be beautiful to another, since their senses and their associations and dispositions are not similar. By discarding universality as the differentia of aesthetic experience, Santayana proceeds to show that the differentia of aesthetic pleasure lies in its objectification.

It may be mentioned in this connection that in *The Sense of Beauty* Santayana says that the ground of the beautiful lies wholly in the subjective condition, while Lotze maintains that the ground of the beautiful lies neither wholly in the subject nor in the object: it consists in the agreement between the subject and the object. Lotze says that beauty consists in the spiritual feeling of enjoyment and the external order of things stimulates the spirit to experience this feeling. Thus the ground of the beautiful, according to him, is subjective–objective, while it, according to Kant and Santayana, is merely subjective. While Kant's aesthetics, being subjective, is devoid of all sensation and emotion and is thus formal, Santayana's aesthetics, in spite of being subjective, includes sensation and emotion, and is thus concrete. While Kant's formal aesthetics tends to be universal within the subjective sphere, Santayana's concrete aesthetics, within the same sphere, tends to be exclusive and individualistic.

I. AESTHETIC EXPERIENCE AS OBJECTIFICATION OF PLEASURE

According to Santayana, then, the beautiful is a kind of pleasure; but it is neither physical, nor disinterested, nor universal. The differentia of aesthetic pleasure lies in its objectification: it is "the transformation of an element of sensation into the quality of a thing" (1896: 47). Santayana does not accept the views of those according to whom beauty has an independent existence which we perceive when our senses come into contact with it.

He, on the other hand, says that beauty "exists in perception and cannot exist otherwise" (ibid.). If it does not exist in perception, it will be a pleasure not felt; and it is a contradiction.

Thus, Santayana holds that the ground of the beautiful is the subjective sphere. Beauty is an emotional element, a subjective pleasure, and yet it is perceived as a quality of a thing. This illusion is inherent in all beauty. We get an idea of a thing by the process of abstraction from the mass of perceptions and reactions which that thing effects. But such abstraction cannot take place in the case of aesthetic idea:

> The aesthetic idea is less abstract, since it retains the emotional reaction, the pleasure of the conceived thing. – Ibid.: 50

Santayana argues that aesthetic pleasure is not a kind of ordinary pleasure. Most of the pleasures caused by an object can be distinguished from the perception of that object. Sweet, when applied to a particular organ, like the palate, produces a pleasure which is taken as an effect and not as a quality of the object. But aesthetic pleasure is of a different sort. When the process of perception is itself pleasant, we have a pleasure which is intimately bound up with the thing and is taken as its quality which is given the name of beauty. So, beauty, on Santayana's view, is a pleasure objectified.

Beauty taken as objectified pleasure is not, however, Santayana's final contention. In his article "The Mutability of Aesthetic Categories" (1925a) he takes beauty as a "vital harmony" or pleasure which is viewed as an essence under the form of eternity. Then it need not to be objectified as an image felt to be beautiful, since it, as an essence, is already an object of intuition.

III. Criticism

We have, on the whole, tried to present Santayana's theory of beauty by comparing it specially with that of Kant. We have not yet discussed Santayana's dealing with aesthetic elements which form a vital part of his aesthetics. Leaving room for discussion of the aesthetic elements in a separate chapter next to the present one, we are now prepared for the criticism of what has been discussed hitherto.

a. i. In *The Sense of Beauty* (1896), Santayana has formulated beauty as "pleasure objectified". The aesthetic experience as depicted by him is a completely absorbed pleasant experience, a total experience that makes no reference beyond itself, just as it makes no distinction between subject and object within it. The efforts of a person undergoing aesthetic experience "are concentrated on not asserting and not implying anything but simply noticing what he finds" (1923: 16). Pepper (1945: 42) gives a like interpretation of Santayana's doctrine of objectification as follows:

> When, however, a situation is such that pleasures are objectified and appear to be incorporated in an external object along with the colours and textures of the object, then this object is aesthetically perceived. What this limitation means in practice is that the spectator is so absorbed in the object that he forgets himself or loses himself in it, and all of his experience is merged into one pleasant or even ecstatic whole. There is no split then in his perception setting this much of it on one side as due to him and that much of it as due to the object. Santayana thus virtually describes the aesthetic field as that of completely absorbed pleasant experiences.

Pepper's account of Santayana's aesthetic experience represents it as mystical, since it speaks of an absorption into the eternal essence – an extinguishing of all particularity and the gaining of a complete calm through the cessation of all the wear and tear of life. But Santayana's view of aesthetic experience as one of completely absorbed experience cannot be acknowledged, since a "split" comes to happen in aesthetic perception. Our pleasure cannot be said to be objectified unless we are cognizant of an object and also aware of its hedonic effect upon us. If the observer's experience "is merged into one pleasant or even ecstatic whole" and if he, in such ecstatic state, forgets himself, how can the pleasure be said to be "objectified" rather than subjectified?

ii. In his article "The Mutability of Aesthetic Categories" (1925a) Santayana writes:

> Pleasure ... does not need to be objectified in order to be fused into an image felt to be beautiful; if felt at all, pleasure is already an object of intuition. – 1923a: 17

Against such formulation of his aesthetics, a point or two can be pressed. In his *Scepticism and Animal Faith*, Santayana says that a solipsist enjoying a momentary scene before him never conceives himself as a separate body, nor "his enjoyment as anything but its beauty" (Ibid.). A solipsist who is unable to distinguish himself from the object of intuition will not be able to ascribe his enjoyment either to himself or to his object. Further, Santayana says that beauty is a pleasure or "vital harmony felt and fused into an image under the form of eternity" (1925a: 284). Here enjoyment is merged into the essence contemplated. If that be so, how can it be said that the enjoyment itself is an object of intuition?

Thus, we see that both the earlier and later formulations of beauty given by Santayana are unreasonable. He is not clear in some other respects as well. As G.W. Howgate shows, Santayana has not specially referred to the point of distinction between beauty and other objectified pleasures such as humour (1938: 94).

b. Santayana says that in aesthetic experience, beauty is perceived as a definite or determinate quality. He also says that beauty or value is an indefinable quality that simply is what it is. Our contention is that when beauty is taken as a determinate quality, it must be definable. To take a word as determinate is to bring it under interpretation and classification. But Santayana seems to hold that in aesthetic experience, which is a kind of immediate experience, we have the intuition of the quality of beauty which is determinate, but bereft of all interpretation and signification. According to him, all interpretation, classification and signification apply to mediate experience only.

A datum, say, whiteness, cannot be held to be determinate unless it is distinguished from a sound or a tactual impression or a kinaesthetic feeling. If it were not associated with other colour data, it could not be seen as a definite whiteness. Similarly, we cannot hold beauty as a definite and determinate quality unless it contains analysis and interpretation. When we take something as beautiful, we mean that it has a tendency to participate in an aesthetic experience. It is the unique complex of class and sign-relations, together with the fact that the organism is firmly accepting instead of doubting what is revealed to it, that makes the quality of beauty determinate in its own way.

G.E. Moore says:

> The most important sense of "definition" is that in which a definition states what are the parts which invariably compose a certain whole. – 1922: 92

In his article "Hypostatic Ethics" (1911), Santayana inclines toward Moorism when he says that a word is indefinable unless one can specify the constituents of what it denotes.

Beauty like "good" is simple and has no parts; hence it is indefinable. But a definition of a word may not always be given in the sense prescribed by Moore. As John Wisdom in his *Interpretation and Analysis in Relation to Bentham's Theory of Definition* (1931) holds, a word can be defined by giving an analysis of what we mean by it. He also says that for defining a wood it is not necessary to give a statement about the constituent parts of the object denoted. We define "brother" by showing how our meaning for it is composed; "brother" means "male sibling". In a similar way, we can define the predicate "beautiful". When we say that something is beautiful, we mean that it has the capacity to participate in aesthetic experience.

c. Santayana contends that aesthetic experience should always be immediate. This contention of his cannot be admitted on the following ground. An experience to be aesthetic must satisfy. This satisfaction we may have not only from immediate experience but also from mediate experience. In mediate experience we are concerned with the procedure of inquiry, the process of doubting what is given, etc. So long as these satisfy, mediate experience can be called aesthetic.

d. When Santayana in his theory of beauty proposes to combine "criticism" with "aesthetics", he says that his concern in the field of aesthetics would be with "instinctive and immediate" judgements which are also appreciations and enjoyments. Here, Santayana makes a confusion which creates a serious defect in his theory of beauty. A judgement about the beauty of anything need not be enjoyable. Conversely, an enjoyment or appreciation can be aesthetic without accompanying a judgement about the beauty of the given object. Our philosopher simply makes a confusion between aesthetic experience and the experience of taking something as beautiful. It is true that confusion naturally occurs since these two experiences often coexist.

e. In one place, Santayana says:

> If we approach a work of art or nature scientifically, for the sake of its historical connections or proper classification, we do not approach it aesthetically. – 1896: 25

And then in another place, he insists:

> If the direct effect were absent, and the object in itself uninteresting, the circumstances would be immaterial. – Ibid.

From these two observations we come to understand that Santayana quite legitimately makes a distinction between our direct experience of the object and our knowledge about that object. But his insistence that the "direct effect" of the object upon somebody, and not his knowledge of its historical relations, makes the object aesthetic cannot be acknowledged. Our theory demands that both the experience of an object and the knowledge about that object have the possibility of being aesthetic. When we look at a painting, the colour seen creates a direct effect upon us. And we may get an aesthetic delight from such a direct effect. It is likely that we may be bored by looking at the painting, but we may enjoy it when we know the different conditions or historical connections under which such a work of art has been made. Here, the direct effect is not aesthetic; on the other hand, the experience of gathering facts about the natural product becomes the aesthetic effect.

7

Aesthetic Elements

I. Introduction

IT HAS been hinted at in the beginning of the preceding chapter that Santayana has not attempted to give a definition of beauty in *The Sense of Beauty* (1896). He has stated there only how we come to have the sense of beauty or the aesthetic feeling. Beauty, as it is felt, is indescribable. It is difficult to say what beauty is. Now, the aesthetic feeling, as it is by nature subjective, leaves no room for being described by itself, since it "has no parts" (1896: 261). Hence, for the description of the aesthetic feeling Santayana adopts what is called the psychological method. Mind, being a "fluid" of thoughts and ideas, feelings and emotions, admits of no easy description. But still psychologists attempt to give a description of mind by describing a physical counterpart of it. To quote Santayana:

> Our whole classification of mental facts is borrowed from the physical conditions or expressions of them. The very senses are distinguished because of the readiness with which we can isolate their outer organs. Ideas can be identified only by identifying their objects. Feelings are recognized by their outer expression and when we try to recall an emotion, we must do so by recalling the circumstances in which it occurred.
>
> – Ibid.: 260

The method, which is followed by the psychologists in order to describe mental facts, is applied by Santayana to describe the aesthetic feeling. He distinguishes the elements of the object and treats the aesthetic feeling as if it were composed of corresponding parts. The description of such feeling consists in the contributions of these elements. But the feeling itself is not aware of contributions.

> It is an affection of the soul, a consciousness of joy and security, a pang, a dream, a pure pleasure. It suffuses an object without telling way; nor has it any need to ask the questions. – 1896: 261

Let us now see how Santayana proceeds to consider the different elements which contribute, separately or in close union, in producing the aesthetic effect.

II. Sensuous Element

A. THE BASIC MATERIAL FOR THE SENSE OF BEAUTY

The basic material for the sense of beauty, according to Santayana, is constituted by the vital functions. The human body depends upon certain vital functions, on the cessation of which it is dissolved. We are not normally conscious of the vital functions, like blood circulation, digestion, assimilation of food and glandular secretions. A slight disorder in these processes at once produces painful changes in consciousness. Really, it cannot be denied that

> the whole temper and tone of our mind, the strength of our passions, the grip and concatenation of our habits, our power of attention and the liveliness of our fancy and affections are due to the influence of the vital forces. – Ibid.: 58

Santayana now points out that our aesthetic sphere, which is subjective or mental, depends, for its existence, upon the efficiency and perfection of our vital processes. That we are attracted towards play or art or speculation is due to the surplus energy furnished by the vital functions. Aesthetic sensibility or insensibility depends on what G.F. Stout calls "the common sensibility" or the "coenaesthesis" which is again due to the vital processes in our body. When we are overfed, a feeling of bodily discomfort arises and with it we have a state of aesthetic insensibility, since due to such feeling of discomfort our imagination is kept back, although the senses remain aware. On the other hand, we have a state of aesthetic sensibility, when we feel a bodily pleasure or comfort which comes with pure and refreshing air.

B. BEAUTY RESTS ON DEFINITE IMAGINATION AND PLEASANT EXPERIENCE

Santayana says that what can be definitely imagined and enjoyably experienced are to be propounded as aesthetic. Since in most cases social objects are not definitely imaginable, they are not aesthetic. They are abstract and verbal rather than sensuous in their materials. If we "pursue happiness conceived merely in the abstract and conventional terms, as money, success, or respectability", we shall "miss that real and fundamental part of happiness which flows from the senses and imagination" (1896: 68). Of course, in some cases social objects can be definitely imaginable, and in that respect they acquire a great aesthetic value. "Home", for example, is a concept of happiness in its social sense; but when it is materialized into the image of cottage and garden, it becomes an aesthetic concept.

The senses of touch, taste and smell have been called by Santayana the "lower" or "anaesthetic" senses. But he says that when they are blended with imagination, they acquire an associational importance for arts such as sensuous poetry. What he denies is that gustatory, olfactory and tactile sensations can themselves be made into works of art. Smell and taste, for instance, are not suitable for the representation of nature, because they are not intrinsically spatial, and nature "allows herself to be accurately conceived only in spatial terms" (1896: 69).

The disadvantage, which the "lower" senses have, applies also to the sense of hearing; that is, hearing also has no intrinsic spatial character according to the consensus of psychological opinion except that of a few like William James and Henry J. Watt. But sounds have comparable pitches and durations. Hence, they can be organized, classified and distinguished from one another. Santayana says how auditory qualities, such as intensity, pitch or timbre, contribute to the sense of beauty. All auditory sensations are pleasant only between certain limits of intensity. A sound will be a note, if the waves of air strike upon the tympanic membrane at regular intervals. The pitch of tones is determined by the rapidity of such regular beats. And the timbre or the quality, by which we can distinguish one sound from another sound, is due to the different complications in the air. We find music in the vibrating air as we have the capacity to discriminate the various waves in it.

C. CONFLICT OF AESTHETIC PRINCIPLES

In this connection, Santayana describes an important conflict of aesthetic principles. They are the principles of purity and interest. We perceive a note, when we cannot discriminate a set of regular vibrations in the chaos of sound. Thus, the perception of this artistic element is due to the purging from the field of attention of all elements which do not occur at regular intervals. This is called the principle of purity. This principle accounts for the enjoyment that we get when we hear an elemental sound or the tone of a tuning fork. The principle of interest which demands variety and expression is the principle of interpretation and discursive comprehension. These two principles, then, are not coordinates. The principle of purity accounts for sensuous charm, while the principle of interest demands something more than mere sensory excitement. The conflict of the above principles is expressed by Santayana in the following way:

> The child who enjoys his rattle or his trumpet has aesthetic enjoyment, of however rude a kind; but the master of technique who should give a performance wholly without sensuous charm would be a gymnast and not a musician, and the author whose novels and poems should be merely expressive, and interesting only by their meaning and moral, would be a writer of history or philosophy, but not an artist.
> – 1896: 74

Thus, in distinguishing between purity and interest, Santayana insists that the former is essential to aesthetic effect. Purity, being unaccompanied by interest, would result in a "tedious" beauty, but beauty nevertheless. Interest without purity would fail to produce beauty, since it would lack the sensuous appeal, the basic material of beauty. Santayana insists upon the necessity of satisfying both the principles. Yet if he inclines to one side more than to the other, it is to the side of purity.

D. THE AESTHETIC EFFECT OF COLOUR

As hearing is raised to a level of aesthetic importance above that of the lower senses, sight is elevated above hearing. Beauty is "derived mainly from the pleasures of sight" (ibid.: 76). The visible is spatial and easy to organize and classify. Form, the second element of beauty, "is for us usually something visible – it is a synthesis of the seen" (ibid.). Prior to the effect of form comes the effect of colour which is "purely sensuous" and a readier element of beauty than other qualities.

Form and meaning can be presented only in something sensible. We enjoy form when we discriminate and recognize its variations. This form becomes meaningful when the emotional value, which it gives rise to, allies the presented object with other experiences, which involve similar emotions. The form of sunset, for example, becomes enjoyable, when its different colours, the brilliance and softness of which charm the eye, are discriminated and recognized. And the emotion that is gathered from such experience, being associated with similar emotions involved in the experiences of heaven and the evening, helps the object (the form of sunset) to acquire a meaning which intensifies the charm.

E. IMPORTANCE OF SENSUOUS BEAUTY

Sensuous beauty is not the most important element of aesthetic effect; but it is the element which is "the most primitive" and "the most universal" (1896: 80). The effect of material underlies that of form: the latter is only enhanced by the former. The beauty of the object attains "a certain poignancy, thoroughness and infinity" (ibid.) only through the artful use of materials. That is why, the Parthenon is made of marble, the king's crown of gold and the stars of fire. Santayana says that insensibility to the primitive and fundamental effect of beauty proves a natural lack of aesthetic sense.

> If a man demands light, sound and splendour, he proves that he has the aesthetic equilibrium. – Ibid.: 82

Santayana concludes:

> The beauty of material is thus the groundwork of all higher beauty, both in the object whose form and meaning have to be lodged in something sensible and in the mind, where sensuous ideas, being the first to emerge, are the first that can arouse delight. – Ibid.

III. Formal Element

A. FORM AS "THE UNITY OF A MANIFOLD"

Santayana takes the beauty of form to be the most important aesthetic element. Form is defined as "the unity of a manifold" (1896: 98). But this unity is not absolute, since it has material constituents which are distinct, though coordinate parts; otherwise, there would not be a perception of form. Form does not appeal to the inattentive. Since the inattentive do not survey the parts and appreciate their relation, what they get from objects is only a vague sensation and thus what they find in objects is only the value of the material, not that of form. Santayana takes the beauty of form as higher in the hierarchy of values than any other kind of beauty. Those who are endowed with aesthetic nature can have sense of beauty of form. Thus, we find Santayana saying:

> Beauty of form … is what specifically appeals to an aesthetic nature; it is equally removed from the crudity of formless stimulation and from the emotional looseness of reverie and discursive thought. The indulgence in sentiment and suggestion, of which our time is fond, to the sacrifice of formal beauty, marks an absence of cultivation as real, if not as confessed, as that of the barbarian who revels in gorgeous confusion. – Ibid.: 99

B. SYMMETRY AND MULTIPLICITY IN UNIFORMITY

Santayana has made a learned discussion of symmetry and multiplicity in uniformity. The value of symmetry lies, in some cases, in the comfort and economy that come from muscular balance in the eye. In some other cases, "symmetry appeals to us through the charm of recognition and rhythm" (ibid.: 94). Symmetry always avoids ugliness and imperfection. We experience symmetrical beauty when "the very process of perception is made delightful by the object's fitness to be perceived" (1896: 95).

Symmetry is held to be the principle of individuation. The different parts of a thing so coalesce that they form a single object, the unity and multiplicity of which are based upon the rhythm and correspondence of its elements. Symmetry has no value in those objects that are too small for composition. Again, symmetry loses its value in the very extensive objects, for example, a large park, since such objects, due to their large size, cannot contribute to the unity of perception. Greek temples which are not very large are symmetrical on their façades.

The perception of space is taken by Santayana as a perception of form. Such perception illustrates multiplicity in uniformity or unity in variety. The sense of extension, which is a feeling of relation, is the realization of different directions. Here the relation of point to point is vaguely but inevitably given. The effect of extension, being different from that of material, is still found in conjunction with the latter. The form of absolute uniformity in extension is mostly allied to the material. By the former the latter is made real and perceptible. The effect of extension, in order to be long satisfactory, is to be superinduced upon some material beauty;

> the dignity of great hangings would suffer if they were not of damask, but of cotton and the vast smoothness of the sky would grow oppressive if it were not of so tender a blue.
> – Ibid.: 102

The form of multiplicity in uniformity is best illustrated in the case of the starry heavens. First, the continuum of space is broken into numerous points and thus we get the idea of multiplicity. We are aware of their individuality since they are distinct and vivid. Second, we sense the dark background with the throbbing fire of the stars. This material beauty goes along with the sublimity of the effect of the starry heavens. Santayana does not forget to assert that the form of multiplicity in uniformity has the disadvantage of creating monotony. This monotony becomes painful when the repeated impressions are acute and when they make a constant appeal to the same sense.

C. INDETERMINATE, DISCURSIVE AND DETERMINATE ORGANIZATION

The most interesting portion of the chapter on form is his treatment of what he calls "indeterminate organization". Indeterminate objects are those that are not determinately organized. They are vague, incoherent and variously interpretable (1896: 131). They are obscure and uncertain in their effects. The artist who has no mastery over a theme employs an indeterminate form to express it. Such an artist "sketches and never paints; he hints and never expresses; he stimulates and never informs" (ibid.). As an indeterminate object Santayana takes the example of a landscape. A natural landscape contains so many diverse perspectives as to allow the eye to move indiscriminately. It suggests "an infinity of different scraps and glimpses given in succession" (ibid.: 134), and hence its different elements are not integrated aesthetically.

An indeterminate work of art has two drawbacks:

a. The emotion which such a work of art stirs is hardly pleasant; "it brings a desire rather than a satisfaction" (ibid.: 148).

b. The emotion, being not embodied, is not aesthetically relevant.

Santayana speaks of a kind of determinate organization which is too discursive. We can take here the example of discursive landscape painting. It represents the sum of our positive observations of a particular scene so fully that its work is sure to be perfectly intelligible. But it makes each scene unnecessarily determinate and it is sure to be dull, since it has no sensuous appeal.

To sum up the result, Santayana finds no beauty of form either in indeterminate or in discursive organization. He finds beauty of form only in a harmonious unification of diverse components. The observer need not further interpret an object which is presented to him in a definite and determinate form. As a determinate organization, Santayana takes the example of the cloud which may be seen as a camel or a whale. If the cloud appears like a whale, without giving any reference to the associations of the idea of the whale with those of the sea or fishermen's yarns, we intuit a determinate form.

> We speak simply, of the intrinsic value of the form of the whale, of its lines, its movement, its proportion. This is a more

or less individual set of images which are revived in the act of recognition; this revival constitutes the recognition and the beauty of form is the pleasure of that revival. – 1896: 115

IV. The Element of Expression

In the final section of *The Sense of Beauty* the aesthetic component called "expression" is discussed. The material and formal aspects of the aesthetic object have already been explained. There is present, with the immediate perception of the object, a certain tendency and quality, not original to it, an emotional overtone, which colours the sensation and our memory of it. This aura, "acquired by objects through association is what we call their expression" (ibid.: 192). Santayana distinguishes the element of expression from those of materials and form.

i. In form or material there is one object with its emotional effect. In expression, on the other hand, there are two objects, the first being the word, image or physical object which is actually presented and the second being "the object suggested, the further thought, emotion, or image evoked" (1896: 194). The first object is called "the expressive thing" and the second object is termed as "the thing expressed". In the case of expression "the emotional effect belongs to the character of the second or suggested one" (ibid.: 192). By passing to the suggested object, our pleasure will be embodied in the memory of that object, while the suggestive thing will be overlooked. An object acquires the value of expression when the images of memory evoked by association with it gild it. Thus, a word is often beautiful only by virtue of its meaning and associations.

ii. The value of expression is as inherent in the object as that of material or form. But while the value of expression accrues to the object from the "association" with it of further processes, the value of material or form accrues to the object from the bare act of perception.

The beauty of material and form can remain separated from the beauty of expression. As for example, we may be charmed by the colour, the line and the shape of a painting, although we may remain ignorant of what this painting expresses. The beauty of expression, on the other hand, cannot be possible without being subordinated to that of material or form. Expression occurs only when the two terms, "the expressive thing" and "the thing expressed", "lie together in the mind" (ibid.: 194).

Matter and form, then, constitute aesthetic value in the first term, whereas, expression is value in the second term. The latter value is found in the associations, the moral values, history, etc. – all of which may go with the presentation of a work of art. Those associations, accompanying the work itself, are raised to the level of beauty, when in themselves they present a joy and sweetness which transcend the utilitarian character that they ordinarily have.

Croce and Santayana

As an eminent advocate of the Expressionist Theory of Art, Benedetto Croce can appropriately be compared with Santayana. Croce and Santayana are contemporaries. A comparison of their views on beauty may bring Santayana's concept to bold relief. Their contrast is determined by their fundamentally different philosophical positions. For example, Santayana is a realist, while Croce is an idealist. Let us, however, concentrate on their respective approaches to the meaning and content of beauty.

Croce upholds the expressionist theory of beauty. For him, art or beauty is intuition and intuition is expression. He holds that art is the expression of emotions and expression is the objectification of feelings by way of representative images. It is impossible to separate the image from its physical embodiment. "L'intuizione pura" and "la pura expressione" are for ever one. Pure intuition is essentially lyricism, "liricita", which signifies the representation of states of mind, passion, feeling and personality (Croce 1949: 22-23).

For Croce, then, art cannot be separated from expression. His expressionist theory of beauty is, in other words, known as the linguistic theory of the same. He identifies aesthetics with language. Language is essentially expression and expression is the fundamental aesthetic fact. Let us compare the Crocean position with that of Santayana, so far as it bears on art as expression.

a. While Croce identifies art with expression, Santayana does not do so. The latter, on the other hand, takes expression as one of the elements of the aesthetic effect.

b. From the standpoint of Santayana, Croce's identification of art with expression seems to be wide of the mark, for the term "expression" is far too comprehensive for the narrow limits of aesthetic experience. The spontaneous and involuntary expression of fear or anger, of grief or delight, or of any other violent emotion, is surely in itself neither beautiful nor expressive. On the whole, his use of the term "expression" is too broad to be taken as identical with aesthetic experience. Santayana, on the other hand, uses the term "expression" in a more specific sense. Expressiveness is a property of being meaningful. It may belong to any object without being an aesthetic value, until it is subordinated to the intuition of the material and formal characteristics of the object. When expressiveness takes on aesthetic value, it becomes expression which constitutes an important element of aesthetic experience.

c. For Croce, as we know, art or beauty cannot be separated from expression. But, for Santayana, though expression is one of the elements of beauty, it is possible to have aesthetic experience where the element of expression is not incorporated. Santayana cites an example:

> The decorative inscriptions in Saracenic monuments can have no beauty of expression for one who does not read Arabic; their charm is wholly one of material and form. – 1896: 194

Here the expressive thing, the decorative inscriptions in Saracenic monuments, does not suggest to one by association any further thought or image since he is ignorant of Arabic, i.e. he has no study of the object. Hence, "the expressive thing", without being assisted by "the thing expressed", fails "to arouse a pleasure which would be incorporated in the present image" (ibid.). Yet he derives pleasure from the material and formal characteristics of the expressive thing.

Santayana and Collingwood

Santayana's conception of art differs from R.G. Collingwood's conception of the same. The latter's theory reflects the worldwide influence of Croce, the great protagonist of Expressionism. Both Santayana and Collingwood, of course, suggest that art must be expressive. But while, according to Santayana, art is always an expression of mind in matter, Collingwood, on the other hand, conceives art to be a merely imaginative expression of emotion. The latter says:

> A work of art in the proper sense of that phrase is not an artefact, not a bodily or perceptible thing fabricated by the artist, but something existing solely in the artist's head, a creature of his imagination. – 1938: 305

But this view of Collingwood comes in conflict with that of Santayana. Santayana maintains:

> Until art arises, all achievement is internal to the brain, dies with the individual and even in him spends itself without recovery, like music heard in a dream. – 1905, IV: 15

Santayana and B. Bosanquet

Bernard Bosanquet is another contemporary of Santayana. *Three Lectures on Aesthetic,* which was delivered at University College, London, 1914 and which was first published in 1915, is Bosanquet's best work on aesthetics. The famous work *The Sense of Beauty* was written by Santayana when he was quite young.

But Bosanquet's *Three Lectures on Aesthetic* was written in the latest years of his life. So far as the two philosophers' views on the subject of beauty are concerned, their difference is again determined by the fact that Bosanquet is a Neo-Hegelian while Santayana is a critical realist. Let us see how Bosanquet's views in aesthetics stand in relation to those of Santayana.

a. Both Santayana and Bosanquet make a psychological analysis of the attitude of aesthetic contemplation. Both hold that aesthetic experience is a feeling of pleasure. Bosanquet distinguishes this feeling from other pleasant feelings. The aesthetic feeling of pleasure is a stable feeling, for it endures more continuously than the pleasures of the lower senses. Again, this feeling is a "relevant" feeling, since it is attributed to a specific external object.

   Santayana also, though not in the manner of Bosanquet, distinguishes the aesthetic pleasure from other pleasures. Other pleasures are easily distinguished from the perception of the object. For example, an edible object, being placed upon the palate, may cause pleasure. Here, the pleasure which is localized in an organ is recognized as an effect and not as a quality of the object:

   > But when the process of perception itself is pleasant … when the intellectual operation, by which the elements of sense are associated and projected, and the concept of the form and substance of the thing produced, is naturally delightful, then we have a pleasure intimately bound up in the thing … . – Santayana 1896: 50-51

In other words, the distinctiveness of aesthetic pleasure lies in its "objectification". Here, the feeling of pleasure is subjective and yet it seems to be a quality of the object.

b. For Santayana, as for Bosanquet, contemplativeness is a characteristic of the aesthetic attitude. The latter holds that, in contemplating the object, the object is not altered for the attainment of some useful purpose. Santayana also tells us, in a similar tone, of the aesthetic pleasure which

> is not sought with ulterior motives, and what fills the mind is no calculation, but the image of an object or event, suffused with emotion. – Ibid.: 42

That is to say, detachment is the soul of the aesthetic attitude.

c. Both Santayana and Bosanquet lay emphasis upon the formal aspect of beauty. Bosanquet says that aesthetic experience is a response to the inner organization of the object, i.e. a response to form. But form abstracted from matter has no appeal to one having an aesthetic attitude. For Santayana also, form which is "a synonym of beauty" is a synthesis of what are seen; that is, he also recognizes that form is always accompanied with matter, that the effect of material underlies that of form.

d. Again, Bosanquet holds that many objects are capable of being analysed into component parts. A painting may be seen as a juxtaposition of shapes, as a relation of colours and so on. Full appreciation depends on the ability of the observer to see these elements as related in a harmony. Only the attentive can experience the inner organization or form of the object. Does Santayana not also hold the same view? A form, he says, must have elements. And the manner in which the elements are combined constitutes the character of the form. A man who is not conscious of the distinction and relation of parts cannot have a perception of form. Beauty of form appeals to an aesthetic nature.

Although there is much parity between the views of Bosanquet and Santayana, we cannot fail to notice how one differs from the other.

i. Bosanquet urges that the aesthetic feeling is common because it can be shared and is increased by sharing. By upholding this view, Bosanquet comes very near to Leo Tolstoy whose famous work on aesthetics, *What Is Art?*, was published in 1896, in which year Santayana's *The Sense of Beauty* was also brought out. Art, according to Tolstoy, is the intentional communication of feelings. In a work of art, the artist creates something which he feels and his feeling is capable of being shared by others. Thus, art must originate with the feeling of the artist. And genuine art, which needs no critics, has a universal appeal.

Santayana differs both from Bosanquet and Tolstoy when he says explicitly that the differentia of aesthetic pleasure is not its universality.

> It is unmeaning to say what is beautiful to one man ought to be beautiful to another. – 1896: 44

Two persons can have the same aesthetic feeling if

> their senses are the same, their associations and dispositions similar ... . – Ibid.

But since no two men have exactly the same faculties, they cannot have a common aesthetic feeling.

ii. Bosanquet gives prime importance to the factual content, the expressive thing and not upon what is expressed or, in his words, represented. Green trees remind us of summer and bare trees of winter; smiles denote happiness and tears sorrow. Here, the factual contents are green trees, bare trees, smiles and tears. The represented symbols or things are summer, winter, happiness and sorrow. Bosanquet tells us that we cannot and should not ignore factual content. As a medium of expression, it has aesthetic value.

Santayana, like Bosanquet, acknowledges the beauty of the expressive thing. When the expressive thing does not contribute to expression, its intrinsic value (the beauty of material and form) may be neglected, but by this is not meant that its intrinsic value is lost, since the expressive thing shines by its own charm. But unlike Bosanquet, Santayana says that very often the expressive thing

> is the source of stimulation and the acuteness and pleasantness of this determine to a great extent the character and sweep of the associations that will be aroused. – Ibid.: 203

And we cannot neglect the beauty of expression which accrues to the present object from its associations.

V. Criticism

Santayana's exposition of aesthetic elements rebounds to his credit in many respects. His unique presentation of the theme in the graceful style, which he always tries to maintain in all of his writings, captures notice easily. The first element, the beauty of material, is neglected by many writers in aesthetics. Santayana's admiration of pure sensuous beauty is as ingenuous as it is profound. His discussion of form, specially of symmetry and multiplicity in uniformity, is in his best veins. It is difficult for a critic to give an accurate estimate of Santayana's position, since the critic's judgement is moulded by his romantic affinities. Still what seem to be relevant criticisms can be presented thus.

a. When Santayana says that values spring "from the irrational part of our nature" (1896: 24), he expresses his naturalistic outlook on value. But he comes close to a variety of Kantian idealism in his consideration of the imaginative and synthesizing character of mind by which the world of objects and the beauty therein is constructed. George Boas also points out Santayana's adherence to this idealistic tradition which makes one feel that the "mind" is more intrinsically worth than the body (Schilpp 1940: 253).

b. Santayana's contention that form is composed of the materials cannot be held true, though it can be recognized that form organizes the materials. The sonata form is not composed of sounds, but rather of the three movements, themselves composed of smaller formal units. The artistic form, instead of being an "aggregation" (1896: 98) of the elements, is a perceptual unity of something seen, heard or imagined, i.e. the configuration, or Gestalt, of an experience. Artistic form is "organic" which cannot be expressed by the term "aggregation".

c. Santayana gives paramount importance to the formal element of beauty. At times he takes form as "a synonym of beauty" (1896: 76). Not only Santayana, but many modern art critics also have dealt with formalism in aesthetics. E. Souriau, a French philosopher, is a champion of formalism. He says that aesthetics is the science of forms, "la science des formes" (1929: 180-81, 388). A strong formalist tendency is to be found among many other critics. Clive Bell has urged that the value of the work of art lies, not in its emotional or intellectual content, but in those relations of line, colour or volume which constitute what he calls "significant form". Roger Fry, an eminent critic, also takes form to be the most essential feature in art. Sir Herbert Read, a recent exponent of art criticism, defines beauty as "a unity of formal relations among our sense perceptions" (1951: 2). And art he finds as "an attempt to create pleasing forms" (ibid.).

The positive value of the attitude of Santayana and other art critics to aesthetics resides in the stress it lays upon form as an essential ingredient of beauty. But what can be said against them is that aesthetics cannot be reduced to a science of forms or it cannot be made synonymous with form, because aesthetic experience is deeper and wider than the mere enjoyment of symmetry, balance and proportion.

d. Santayana's assertion that matter, form and expression are the elements of beauty hardly seems to be true. What is to be said is rather that they are the elements residing in a physical object, e.g. a painting has some colours and lines which are again organized and their organization expresses something of which it is the painting. To take another example, a statue may be made of marble, cut to form a particular shape which expresses or represents a certain person. Thus, we see that matter, form and expression are the elements of a physical object.

Although matter, form and expression are not the elements of beauty, they have the capacity to participate in aesthetic experience, that is, each of them can give rise to some aesthetic effects when it is experienced and interpreted in some ways. The colour which constitutes a material of a painting may excite in us feelings of awe, surprise, etc. and to that extent it gives rise to emotional aesthetic effects. Again, it provides sensible aesthetic effects when it is experienced as something in particular, similar to some colours and distinct from others. Further, it becomes a cognitive aesthetic effect when it is seen as determinate and meaningful and in a variety of relations. These three aesthetic effects also participate in our experience of "form" and "expression".

e. By aesthetic elements we mean three aesthetic effects mentioned above. A work of art can be said to be beautiful when it has the capacity to provide a complex of aesthetic effects that are enjoyable as a whole. If that be so, then Santayana's statement that an object may be a work of art if it has only beauty of material or form seems to be unjustifiable. The sound of a tuning fork may not be "interesting", but since it has beautiful materials, it is taken by him as a work of art. But this is unreasonable, since it provides nothing but only sensible aesthetic effects. For anything to be a work of art, all the three kinds of aesthetic effects must participate in it.

Now, we can conceive aesthetic unity as a harmonious coordination of the three kinds of aesthetic effects. Our conception of aesthetic unity obviously differs from Santayana's conception of the same. According to him, aesthetic unity occurs when the element of expression is subordinated to the elements of matter and form. But the case of subordination does not arise in our conception of aesthetic unity. The aesthetic unity of which we speak demands the harmonious participation of the different aesthetic effects.

8

The Theory of Art

I. Introduction

Two foregoing chapters engaged our attention to Santayana's aesthetics. His theory of art has not been expounded so far, but the discussion of his aesthetics will remain incomplete if his theory of art be not explained. Santayana assigns to art a very high place in *The Life of Reason* (1905). In *Reason in Art*, the volume four of *The Life of Reason*, he supplies us with much data of art. The reader of the volume referred to discover in his treatment a concreteness of details frequently missed in the other volumes. Here, Santayana shows how art, founded on automatic self-expression, develops into what is called fine art. Of the fine arts, music and poetry deserve special mention. But he does not confine art to the sphere of fine art only. Art is widened to include most of man's creative effort and thus it cannot be independent of the moral values which govern life and promote happiness. We are accustomed to think that art is for art's sake. But Santayana thinks that art is for life's sake. He insists upon the intimacy between art and life.

II. The Nature of Art

A. ART IS PURPOSIVE

Instinctive adaptation and spontaneous action, Santayana considers the material source and condition for the existence of art. He thinks that art springs from instinct and yet it is not a return to instinct. It is a function which is purposive as well as rational. He says:

> If the birds in building nests felt the utility of what they do, they would be practising an art; and for the instinct to be called rational it would even suffice that their traditional purpose and method should become conscious occasionally.
>
> – 1905, IV: 9-10

A useful and automatic instinctive activity becomes art when it is supervened by purpose and conscious expression.

B. ART IS PRACTICAL

According to Santayana, art by which is meant a creative process is practical and useful. It is the most complete embodiment of reason and the expression of mind in matter. By such expression the outer world is remodelled and moulded "into sympathy with inner values" (ibid.: 15). Art cannot lie hidden in the mind. It is always a rational expression, a progress "bettering the conditions of existence" (ibid.). The aesthetic value which is possessed by some works of art is one of the satisfactions which art offers to human nature as a whole.

III. Types of Artistic Process: Fine Art and Servile Art

Santayana has mentioned two types of the artistic process, viz. (a) the aesthetic process of art, and (b) the non-aesthetic process of art. The first is called fine or liberal art and the second servile art. Fine art is an operation which one undertakes for its own sake. Such art has an intrinsic or aesthetic value. Servile art is an operation which is not its own end, that is, which is not performed for its own sake and which is undertaken as an instrumentality for some ulterior purpose. To put it simply, servile art has an instrumental or extrinsic value which is non-aesthetic in character.

THE DISADVANTAGE OF SERVILE ART

Santayana has shown that the cultivation of servile art suffers from a disadvantage. Industrial or mechanical art illustrates what is called servile art. Industrial art and its products are to be estimated by the ultimate interests they subserve. A man who practises industrial or mechanical art only indulges himself into a mere physical drifting. His occupation becomes sordid, instrumental and justified only externally. Industrial arts are indispensable no doubt, since they support a person's practical life, but if they occupy human attention *in toto*, they are definitely "pure burdens" (1905, IV: 23) for those who, as rational creatures, should vindicate their prerogative to spiritual freedom.

HARMONY BETWEEN SERVILE AND FINE ARTS

What Santayana wishes to do is to bring harmony between fine art and servile art. Servile art makes the ground easy for the cultivation of fine art. An advantage which accrues to servile art lies in the diminution of toil, for such diminution of toil in the mechanical field serves as an opportunity for employing energies in other fields, so that the total accomplishment may be greater. Servile operation, since it is a non-aesthetic process, is menial, but if it be accompanied by the ideal representation of ends pursued, it becomes an anagram of spiritual freedom. Fine art, for its existence, needs the material conditions provided by the servile process of art. To separate the aesthetic element from the non-aesthetic ones in a fine art is not practically possible. "The rose's grace", says Santayana,

> could more easily be plucked from its petals than the beauty of art from its subject, occasion and use. – Ibid.: 17

Thus, according to Santayana, servile art and fine art do not subtend to each other. They are rather two stages of art, one being subservient to the other. Let Santayana speak here:

> Art has accordingly two stages; one mechanical or industrial, in which untoward matter is better prepared, or impeding

> media are overcome; the other liberal, in which perfectly fit matter is appropriated to ideal uses and endowed with a direct spiritual function. – 1905, IV: 27

Servile art prepares matter and makes it useful. And matter thus prepared is used by fine art to serve some ideal function.

IV. Fine Art

Santayana maintains that initially action remains always spontaneous and automatic. It is also, in its initial phase, tentative. By experiment, certain tendencies are fortified and others are cancelled. As a result, habit and wisdom are formed. Then action remains no longer spontaneous. It is accompanied and guided by foresight. It becomes purposive and is expressed consciously. In other words, it becomes a rational function and that is art.

Fine art lies midway between two extremes. At one extreme lies spontaneous action and at the other extreme pure utility. Spontaneous action leads to art when it is performed rationally. An art, like dance, originates when automatic self-expression gives way to conscious and rationally disciplined actions. Again, any utilitarian activity is not art, but "utility leads to art when its vehicle acquires intrinsic value and becomes expressive (ibid.: 30). A servile art, like war, is utilitarian, since it is externally justified. But

> out of the pomp and circumstance of war fine arts may arise – music, armoury, heraldry and eloquence. – Ibid.

A. MUSIC

Santayana pays great tribute to pure music as a fine art. "Pure music is pure art" (1905, IV: 42). It is an ideal world of forms and more vital in their emotional content. The rhythm of music gives it a superior emotional power.

Barbaric and Modern Music

Santayana sees no difference between barbaric musicians and modern musicians. Barbaric music is nothing but loud and unceasing cry. Barbaric musicians are too much carried away by their performance,

> all are performers and the crowd is only a stimulus that keeps everyone dancing and howling in emulation. – Ibid.: 39

What is suggested by the primitive art of music is only "performance". That music has an inherent value is not recognized by barbaric practice. Modern art of music, Santayana maintains, does not improve much in comparison to barbaric art of music. Only "instead of vague custom we have schools and instead of swaying multitudes academic example" (ibid.). A modern musician indulges himself in so many suggestions and in the tumult of production. But Santayana thinks that this is sheer wastefulness. The practice of music lies in an ideal function which it subserves and not in any external suggestion.

The Transcendental Aspect of Music

Music, abstracting itself extremely from material trammels, creates a new realm of form by its entire spontaneity. When we are carried in such a realm, we are simply impassioned by its musical form. Music, since it is an ethereal art, is not confined to mortal obligations. In it, there are "no imperious needs calling us back to reality" (ibid.: 44).

Its Affinity to Life

Santayana says that "expression is never art while it remains expressive to no purpose" (1905, IV: 30). Music, since it is an art, is expressive of a purpose. It "interests humanity most when it is wedded to human events" (ibid.: 42-43). The alliance between human life and music becomes possible only through the emotions aroused by both. The absence of music is followed by the absence of emotion. If music breaks in upon us when we remain busy in other activities, we may remain inattentive to it or we may be swayed into the realm of sound and enjoy the ideal musical form. Music helps to arouse from our animal heart many a suppressed feeling and by such arousal we are led into an ideal world of forms from which we do not, for the nonce, feel any imperious urge to come back to reality. Thus, music as an art elevates our experience and makes life better.

B. POETRY

Three Requirements of Great Poetry

Santayana's dealings with poetry as a fine art proves his deep understanding of this art. Great poetry, according to him, must have three requirements. First, it should have a perfectly determinate form. The images invoked must form a picture. The recognition of sounds should be according to definite rhythmic schemes. Second, with the formal beauty of great poetry is to be added its material beauty. Its material elements are sounds, words and images. In any great poetry sounds are melodious and musical, words are rich and suggestive, and images are graphic and stimulating. Each of these three material elements should be presented in a determinate form. Third, a significant world outlook should be expressed by great poetry. Great poetry is always rational. Reason is universal in its outlook. Rational or philosophical poetry "would present in graphic images the total efficacy of real things" (1905, IV: 80). Such a poetry is deeply rooted in human experience. It presents a meaningful interpretation of both the human condition and the cosmic scene.

Is Rational Poetry a Fine Art?

The last requirement of great poetry, then, consists in the formulation of a metaphysics that will account for experience itself. Now, to formulate such a metaphysics it has to undergo a kind of laborious and discursive thinking which is reserved for intellect rather than for imagination. Should we, then, call such poetry a work of fine art when we know that fine art must take an imaginative flight?

We can seek the answer to this question from some portions of Santayana's *Three Philosophical Poets* (1910). He maintains that

> if we think of philosophy as an investigation into truth, or as reasoning upon truths, there is nothing in philosophy akin to poetry.
> – 1910: 8

But he insists that philosophical or rational poetry is possible, since the vision of philosophy may be poetic and imaginative. Discursive reasoning and investigation which we find in philosophy are "only preparatory and servile parts, means to an end" (ibid.: 10-11), but ultimately they may be led into intuition which is "a steady contemplation of all things in their order and worth" (ibid.: 11). And he says:

> Such contemplation is imaginative. ... A philosopher who attains it is, for the moment, a poet; and a poet who turns his practised and passionate imagination on the order of all things, or on anything in the light of the whole, is for that moment a philosopher.
> – Ibid.

Great Poetry vs Greatest Poetry

The above three requirements suffice to define great poetry, but not greatest poetry. Santayana says that Goethe, Lucretius and Dante are great poets, but they are not greatest ones. They are great poets, since each of them expresses, in beautiful and determinate form, a large and penetrating vision. But each is limited in his outlook. One's intuition is to be supplemented by the intuitions of the other two if greatest poetry is to be brought into existence.

Santayana holds,

> Goethe is the poet of life; Lucretius the poet of nature; Dante the poet of salvation.
> – 1910: 204

Goethe portrays a world that is constituted by human feelings and ideas. But his vision should be combined with that of Lucretius who has an insight into the substance of things. But neither Goethe nor Lucretius possesses that insight which is supplied by Dante. Dante understands the life of contemplation and spiritual harmony. The harmony of these three intuitions can give rise to the greatest poetry. The greatest poet, according to Santayana, is he who understands the inner substance of things, appreciates the textural wealth of experience and possesses the vision of the good and the contemplation of perfection.

Santayana's Final Statement of Poetry

We should not take the above view of Santayana as his final statement of poetry. An article of Santayana "On My Friendly Critics" (1921) was published in the *Journal of Philosophy* seven years after *Three Philosophical Poets* appeared. In that article he recants his view that "the noblest poetry also must express the moral burden of life and must be rich in wisdom". He now finds:

> quite sufficient perfection in poetry, like that of the Chinese and Arabians, without much philosophic scope, in mere grace and feeling and music and cloud-castles and frolic. – Ibid.

Answer to Santayana's Statement

But Santayana is mistaken when he maintains in the abovesaid article that philosophic scope is unnecessary for the noblest poetry. To say that a work of art contains philosophic scope does not amount to saying that it has a literal truth value. "Lying is a privilege of poets", says Santayana (1905, IV: 73). A poet indulges in a fanciful fiction. But that fiction should be taken as a device for communicating to us an imaginative interpretation of the everyday world. The poet's interpretation of life may be erroneous from the scientific or metaphysical standpoint. But still a philosophic scope remains for a poet to render an imaginative interpretation of life. It should be remembered in this connection that poetry, in order to be a fine art, should contain philosophic scope and with it the emotional appeal and sensuous attraction.

V. Plastic Art

Plastic arts grow from man's plastic impulses which are spontaneous and expressive. A man, who depends on things for his experience, changes these by his automatic impulse so that there is every possibility that his welfare should be promoted by his action. Now, the change brought in the things by the impulse fortifies that impulse and as a result a reactive habit is formed, and that act is done with foreknowledge of its benefits. Thus, the plastic impulse becomes art. Plastic art, says Santayana, may be constructive or representative.

A. CONSTRUCTIVE ART

Constructive art is illustrated in decoration. If a man happens, by the movement of his hand, to turn a flowering branch into a garland and if the new form given to the object interests him, then he will have discovered a decorative art. His plastic impulse, which brings a change in the environment in this way, being fortified by the new discovery, tends to repeat that action. If the same plastic impulse remains operative, it will be attended with knowledge and criticism of its happy results. Santayana says:

> Self-criticism, being a second incipient artistic impulse ... may to some extent modify the next performance. – 1905, IV: 85

Decoration is an independent art. It is to be practised for its own sake, "in obedience to elementary plastic instincts" (ibid.: 94). Again, it is fundamental in design, since it lends sensuous impression by its unique structural effect.

Cases Where Plastic Construction Faces Obstruction

Plastic art develops if the plastic impulse admits anything new. There are specific cases where art cannot make progress. One such case is conservatism. Primitive art is conservative. The idol of the primitive artist "must be the self-same hereditary stock, or at least it must have the old sanctified rigidity and stare" (ibid.: 85). Art cannot also make its progress in society which contains an inert custom. In a Christian society, Christian architecture is determined by an inert custom, i.e. a fancy of building churches in the shape of a cross. Builders here cannot conceive any alternative to that convention. Customs prevailing in society are the "debris of old perceptions which choke all fresh perception in the soul" (ibid.: 88). In such a situation, plastic construction becomes impossible.

B. REPRESENTATIVE ART

This type of art emerges, when the plastic impulse does not construct anything new, but reproduces or imitates a form which is decorative in itself. What is to be noted is that representation or imitation does not mean a literal repetition of the object. In an imitative art, the copy is not primary. Here what is fundamental is the reproduction of a form in a new medium, giving it a different function. Santayana maintains:

> Imitation is far more than similarity. ... It has a representative and intellectual value because in reproducing the forms of things it reproduces them in a fresh substance to a new purpose.
> – 1905, IV: 103

Thus, imitative art has its progress, since reproduction of a form of thing is made for a new purpose.

As an example of representative art, Santayana refers to sculpture. This type of plastic art not only reproduces the material form which is interesting but also renders it an ideal expression. The sculptor has a task to harmonize the attitudes momentarily achieved or vaguely imagined. Again, sculpture is to depend on its model. The model must be refined, if

> the statue is to be ideal, i.e. if it is to express the possible motions and vital character of its subject.
> – Ibid.: 107

VI. Critical Review

Santayana is right in defining art as a rational function. Art is not sheer self-expression. It is a conscious activity which offers satisfaction to human nature as a whole. The definition of art as rational includes within it the notion of "artistic criticism". Artistic criticism means the varied interpretation by the artist of what he has done. He goes through the process of artistic criticism when he interprets whether the work of art carries significance, maintains its relation with other effects, draws praise from the audience. On the basis of such interpretation, the artist will be satisfied or dissatisfied with his product. Artistic criticism the artist cannot ignore, since it enables him to undergo a more perfect performance. As Santayana says:

> Self-criticism ... may to some extent modify the next performance. – 1905, IV: 85

According to Santayana, art is for the sake of life. By cherishing such a view he goes against those who advocate art for art's sake. Indeed, he keeps his view as a challenge to the view held by the rival party. Santayana asserts that art is not a separable sphere of human activity, it does not escape life and does not create realms of beauty fancy-free. It is his credit that he makes art an organic part of the sum total of life.

Santayana maintains that though artistic activity; which consists in imposing an ideal form upon matter, is preoccupied with imagination, its concern is wholesome, since it fashions facts according to ideal preferences; it

> alters the material conditions of sentience so that sentience becomes at once more delightful and more significant. – Ibid.: 155

Thus, art is an achievement, a step forward towards the goal of rational living. "What nature does with existence, art does with appearance" (ibid.: 119). In our concrete experience we meet life with misery and unhappiness, with rivalry and vanity. But art fancies a world in which we find a picture of rational living and where life instead of being mixed with unhappiness and rivalry is united with peace and equanimity. As Santayana says:

> Art supplies constantly to contemplation what nature seldom affords in concrete experience – the union of life and peace. – Ibid.

Santayana's theory of art has some disadvantages which are so grave that it loses its glory to a great extent. They are stated below:

a. The distinction Santayana draws between servile art and fine art cannot be maintained. He says that fine art is, while servile art is not, intrinsically valuable. And what is intrinsically valuable is not instrumental to any other thing. Our contention against Santayana is that servile art, like fine art, may be intrinsically valuable and fine art, like servile art may be instrumental.

   We have already noted (p. 138) that any satisfying experience may be intrinsically valuable. Fine art, being clean a most complete embodiment of reason, gives satisfaction to human nature as a whole and hence contains an intrinsic value. Servile art, Santayana says, is instrumental and justified only externally. It prepares matter and makes it fit so that the fine artist can use it for some ideal function. When Santayana says that servile art prepares matter, he by no means precludes the possibility of its being enjoyable. Since the servile process of art satisfies by virtue of its function as an instrument, it has intrinsic value.

   Again, fine art, like servile art, is instrumental. Santayana says clearly that art is "the best instrument of happiness" (1905, IV: 155). As instrumental, the process of fine art, like that of servile art, may be intrinsically valuable at least to the extent that it satisfies by virtue of its utility. Thus, we see that both fine and servile arts are instrumental.

And since both satisfy by virtue of their function as instruments, they may be intrinsically valuable. So, the Santayanian distinction between fine and servile arts stands meaningless. The distinction, however, becomes meaningful if the two are made to differ in the degree of instrumentality. Fine art is less instrumental than servile art.

b. Santayana observes that art consists in imposing an ideal form upon matter. We find him saying:

> Art needs to find a material relatively formless which its business is to shape; and this initial formlessness in matter is essential to art's existence. – 1905, IV: 26

Art, then, according to him, gives a propitious form to matter. Suppose, the sculptor faces an unhewn block of marble and his rational function as an artist will be to bestow a propitious form to that marble. The ideal which he will impose upon the formless matter is a character or quality which he has previously experienced or which he has imagined. Thus, here the ideal serves as a conscious and determinate end according to which the sculptor will proceed to chisel the marble. And then we can expect an exact resemblance between the final product and the ideal according to which it is produced.

But the conclusion that is reached can be hardly maintained. In both representational and non-representational art, the exact similarity between the production and the ideal according to which it is produced is rarely attained. The artist may be inspired by what he has seen or imagined. But that seen or imagined thing can rarely serve as a conscious and definite end which is to be modified or reproduced. Sometimes the artist's work can hardly resemble what he has already experienced. This is possible since the artist works with an attitude which is called "artistic criticism". His production is not the embodiment of any prior ideal.

It is rather the culmination of an experimental process in which judgement and satisfaction or dissatisfaction lead to further experimentation, which is judged and modified and then again judged and modified and so on until the artist stops working and finds himself most satisfied.

c. We can once again quote from *Reason in Art* the portion where Santayana refers to the two stages of art. He says:

> Art has accordingly two stages: one mechanical or industrial, in which untoward matter is better prepared, or impeding media are overcome; the other liberal, in which perfectly fit matter is appropriated to ideal uses endowed with a direct spiritual function. – 1905, IV: 27

Thus, a distinction has been made between the phase in which the artist prepares matter and the one in which he uses it for an ideal function.

But such a distinction is not tenable. Let us consider the function of the sculptor facing an unhewn block of marble. The sculptor as a fine artist has an ideal function, viz. to chisel the facial features in the marble. The preliminary function, viz. to render the marble an attractive texture by cutting it down to a manageable size and by polishing or cleaning it, is performed by the servile or industrial art. Santayana will say that this servile operation is instrumental to the above-mentioned ideal function. But this contention of Santayana cannot be maintained. What is the true function of the artist? Definitely to produce an object that will satisfy in every respect. If the production of the sculptor is to be most satisfying, what he should do is to give not only a certain outline but also an attractive texture to the marble. If he only chisels the facial features upon a marble having an ugly texture, surely this ideal function will not give a total satisfaction. Marble with a certain texture is not instrumental to marble with a certain outline. On the other hand, both are instrumental to a total effect that the artist wants to attain.

9

Santayana and the Indian View of Beauty and Art

I. Introduction

THE preceding three chapters have carefully considered Santayana's theory of beauty and art. In the present chapter a comparative study has been made between his aesthetics and Indian aesthetics. Such discussion, very brief as it is, seems not to be meaningless, since we can have a better understanding of a theory in the light of comparison.

It may be mentioned here that there is a notable point of difference between Western aesthetics and Indian aesthetics. In the West we meet so many rival theories of aesthetics and miss a connecting thread underlying those theories. Indian aesthetics also bristles with many theories. It has been enriched by Bharata, Ānandavardhana, Abhinavagupta in the past and by Rabindranath, Abanindranath and Nandalal among others in the last century. But modern Indian aesthetics bears a close relation to the traditional aesthetics of India. This is, perhaps, due to the peculiar philosophic outlook cherished by the Indians, both in the past and in the present. Spiritualism, which forms their philosophic outlook, remains at the basis of their aesthetic attitude also. Aesthetic delight, to the Indians in general, is a spiritual awakening and a joy divine. Thus, we can bring about a single character of Indian aesthetics, whereas we fail to do so in the case of Western aesthetics. Anyway, let us see how Santayana's aesthetics differs from the traditional theory of Indian aestheticians of the past.

II. Santayana's Aesthetics and Indian Aesthetics of the Past

To Santayana, as to Indian thought in general, beauty is subjective. But the aesthetic experience of which Santayana speaks is mainly sensuous experience. Beauty, according to him, is a positive value, a pleasure experienced immediately by our emotional consciousness. The Indian aestheticians of the past, unlike Santayana, maintain that aesthetic experience is *rasāsvādana* which is spiritual and a joy divine. *Rasa* is the keyterm in Indian aesthetics. Hence, the theory of *rasa* needs to be explained.

THE THEORY OF RASA

The literal meaning of *rasa* is taste. The doctrine that *rasa* is the essence of poetry started from Bharata (first century CE) and advocated by Abhinavagupta (tenth century CE) and Viśvanātha (fourth century CE). The theory of *rasa* arises from the theory of suggestion or Dhvanivāda. The essence of poetry, Indian aestheticians hold, lies in *dhvani* (suggestion). Now, what is the meaning they attach to *dhvani*? As the gracefulness of a lady is something over and above the structure of the different limbs of her body, so the poetry of the great poets expresses something more than words, meaning and style embodied in it.[1] This

---

[1] *pratīynmānaṁ punaranyadeva vastvasti vāṇīṣu mahākavīnām* ।
yattathprasidhvavayavātriktaṁ vibhāti lāvaṇyanivāṅganāsu ॥
– *Dhvanyāloka* 1.4

[But the implied aspect (of meaning) is quite different (from the expressed aspect of meaning). In the words of great poets, it shines out supreme and towers above the beauty of the outer parts even as charm does in ladies.]

extra something is called suggestion (*dhvani*) which implies a different world transcendental to the literal meaning of poetry. An example can be cited. Kālidāsa, a great Indian poet, speaks of Pārvatī in his *Kumārasambhava*:

> *evaṁ vādini devarṣau pārśve pituradhomukhi* ।
> *līlākamalapātrāṇi gaṇayāmāsa pārvatī* ॥

> When the great sage was thus speaking, Pārvatī sitting beside her father counted the petals of the toy lotus with her face lowered in blush.

Here the excellence of poetry lies in a rich suggestion that transcends the literal meaning expressed by it. The phrase "the counting of the petals of toy lotus" suggests something transcendent, viz. modesty of courtship.

The theory of suggestion proves that Indian aestheticians do not, while Santayana does, fail to understand that aesthetic experience is deeper and wider than the mere enjoyment of symmetry, balance and proportion. Now, suggestion which constitutes the essence of poetry is always of some or other *rasa*. We realize *rasa* when we feel the aesthetic sentiment or emotion, devoid of all of its usual conative tendencies. This emotion is suggested by the representations in art of those objects that excite it in nature, such as characters, their actions and their physical expressions of emotions in the case of drama and words, figures of speech, rhythm, etc. in the case of poetry. Now, the emotion, which, being thus variously suggested, is awakened in the mind of audience, has a different quality from that aroused in real life. It is at once dislodged from the specific object (by which it is aroused in life) and from the particular subject who enjoys it. It is apprehended in the aesthetic attitude in an impersonal manner. It is no longer felt as a personal psychical affection, but as an impersonal ideal object of contemplation.

The theory of *rasa* also suggests that in aesthetic experience the self is placed above narrow egoism and assumes an impersonal contemplative attitude. And the contemplative self, being free from all craving and external necessity, is blissful. Thus *rasāsvādana* is a kind of relish of one's own blissful consciousness.

According to the Indian theory of *rasa*, aesthetic experience is spiritual, through which knowledge of the self in its contemplative aspect becomes possible. The desire to know the true nature of the self lies at the root of the philosophical speculation of the Indians. Aesthetic experience also, according to them, gives us a glimpse of the nature of the self in its true aspect.

But Santayana, like Indian aestheticians, does not take aesthetic experience as the realization of the impersonal contemplative aspect of the self. He regards beauty as a naturalistic fact. The aesthetic pleasure of which he speaks is a simple psychological experience. Santayana, like Indian aestheticians, refers to the contemplative state of aesthetic experience. But while, to Indian aestheticians, contemplative state is an active state of enjoyment, to Santayana, on the other hand, contemplation is a passive state of enjoyment.

Santayana says that in all "expression" two terms can be distinguished:

> The first is the object actually presented, the word, the image, the expressive thing; the second is the object suggested, the further thought, emotion, or image evoked, the thing expressed.
>
> – 1896: 194

Santayana attaches paramount importance to the first term, viz. "the object actually presented", while the advocates of the theory of *rasa* attach importance to the second term, viz. "the object suggested, the further thought, emotion, or image evoked, the thing expressed". That to Santayana the first term is of primary importance can be proved from his saying:

> Beauty in the first term – beauty of sound, rhythm, and image – will make any thought whatever poetic, while no

> thought whatever can be so without that immediate beauty of presentation. – Ibid.: 203

But Indian aestheticians hold the quite opposite view. They say that poetry, as a species of art, can be excellent when a central emotion is suggested and evoked by the word, meaning, style and rhythm embodied in it. In this connection we can suggest one point of the *rasa* theory of poetry. Emotions which are aroused in poetry are of two classes, viz. (1) permanent or dominant emotions, and (2) transient emotions. The latter are subservient to the former. In a poem, transient emotions appear and disappear, but a certain dominant emotion, suggested by them, remains always steady. The aesthetic delight or *rasa* is derived from the contemplation of this central dominant emotion. The essence of poetry, Santayana would say, lies in the meaning of words, in harmony, rhythm, that are expressed in it. As he says:

> ... poetic language is language at its best. Its essential success consists in fusing ideas in charming sound or in metaphors that shine by their own brilliance. – 1905, IV: 76

But the Indian aestheticians hold that the essence of poetry lies, not in the rhythm, but in the aesthetic delight had from the contemplation of a dominant emotion expressed in it. They, of course, say that rhythm, figure of speech, meaning of words have their utility in helping to arouse the aesthetic delight. The poet Rabindranath Tagore also says:

> Rhythm is not the essential element in a poem. Its essence lies in the aesthetic delight; rhythm only reveals this delight and is an accompaniment. – *Sahityer Swamp* 35

III. The Aesthetical Theory of Rabindranath Tagore

We have briefly compared Santayana's aesthetical theory with that of Indian aestheticians of the past. Rabindranath Tagore can be viewed as an important figure in modern Indian aesthetics. Let us compare his aesthetical theory with that of Santayana.

Rabindranath has been inspired by traditional Indian aesthetics. But his extraordinary genius, instead of remaining confined to the traditional Indian thought, absorbs all that is essential in Western thought. It may be said that the aesthetical thought that Tagore develops is the outcome of the elements of truth that he perceives in India and the West.

As already explained, the traditional aesthetical theory of India is spiritualistic. Rabindranath too constructs his aesthetical thought in accordance with this theory. He holds that art is not a matter of feeling only but a *bodhi*, an illumination of the spirit. He thinks after Indian aestheticians that aesthetic experience is contemplative.

Tagore's conception of beauty is derived from the metaphysical principle of the Upaniṣads. According to such principle, the self is present in everything. As our self is in all we have a desire to make all nature our kin. Tagore says:

> The function of our soul is to fraternize with others.
> – *Panchabhuta* 32

Through this fraternizing activity, self-enlargement and thereby self-knowledge become possible. *Bṛhadāraṇyaka Upaniṣad* II.4.5 says:

> Verily, it is not that thou lovest everything because thou desirest everything, but thou lovest everything because thou desirest thine own self.

Thus, the delight which is due to the realization of one's own self by fraternizing itself with the whole world is a joy which is purer and more deeply satisfying than pleasure in the ordinary sense. Aesthetic experience, according to Tagore, means experience of this delight.

When man realizes himself through self-aggrandizement, he really contemplates his self. That the universal spirit realizes itself through self-expansion has been the doctrine of many Western philosophers like Hegel and Schopenhauer. Beauty,

Tagore says, is a product of man's contemplative nature. For aesthetic experience, he adds, self-culture and concentration are necessary. But immediately he warns us that self-culture requisite for having aesthetic experience is not a product of intellect, since intellect gives us knowledge of the object as distinguished from the subject. But aesthetic experience which is the same as intuitive experience does not look at the self as distinguished from the not-self; here the objects remain united with ourselves. Thus, aesthetic experience is not knowledge given by the intellect.

We have seen that beauty, according to Tagore, is born of man's desire to make his self united with the rest of the world. Beauty, then, is a tie between self and matter. And this tie can be firmly established if the objects of the universe are loved for their own sake. Aesthetic enjoyment should be emancipated from all interest and desire. Hence Rabindranath takes the principle of the disinterestedness as a fundamental differentia of aesthetic experience. Kant, A.C. Bradley and other Western philosophers also have made the principle of disinterestedness central in aesthetic experience. But according to Rabindranath, aesthetic experience is not totally "will-less", the very term in which Schopenhauer describes it. In the *Bṛhadāraṇyaka Upaniṣad* we find, "thou lovest everything because thou desirest thine own self". The self, in order to realize itself, fraternizes itself with the things of the world. So, the love of the worldly objects is not wholly disinterested, but interested in a deeper sense.

Again, Tagore holds that the aesthetic delight is not a kind of pleasure. The term "pleasure" hints at the satisfaction of some "sense". But the aesthetic enjoyment of which our poet speaks is the antithesis of pleasure, it is *ānanda* (spiritual bliss).

IV. Rabindranath and Santayana

a. Rabindranath's conception of beauty is, then, spiritual. It speaks of self-enlargement and self-realization. It includes the not-self within the self. But Santayana's conception of beauty is diametrically opposite to the view of Tagore. The former reduces beauty to a simple and primitive psychological experience. He says:

> [Beauty] exists in perception and cannot exist otherwise. A beauty not perceived is a pleasure not felt, and a contradiction. – 1896: 47

Santayana takes beauty as a pleasure, as a kind of sensuous experience. But Rabindranath treats beauty as a kind of spiritual experience.

Santayana says that beauty is "a pleasure" which can be experienced by us. But our point is that we cannot experience pleasures, but we have experiences which are pleasant. Again, to Santayana, aesthetic pleasure stands as substantial, since he speaks of the contemplation of it. But here what is mentionable is that pleasure, whether aesthetic or not, is not an element in experience, but a quality of experience. It is adjectival, not substantial. Further, Santayana sometimes gives to aesthetic pleasure the name of an emotion or a feeling. In one place of *The Sense of Beauty* he says:

> Beauty is a value ... it is an emotion, an affection of our volitional and appreciative nature. – Ibid.: 51

But our objection against Santayana is that pleasure cannot be the name of a distinct feeling or emotion with a quality of its own. We can never become conscious of a pleasure, but only of an experience or a mental state or condition which is more or less pleasant.

From the above discussion, we conclude that aesthetic pleasure cannot stand as a substitute for aesthetic delight. For Rabindranath aesthetic experience is *ānanda*, it is more than ordinary sensuous experience.

b. Rabindranath and Santayana differ from each other as to the basis of art. Santayana, as we have seen (pp. 177-78), refers to a natural basis of art. He says:

> All art has an instinctive source and a material embodiment. – 1905, IV: 9

An automatic instinctive activity is transformed into art when it is performed with purpose and guided by consciousness. An incipient action like gesture, when it is modified with purpose and expressed consciously, gives rise to an art which we may call the art of dance.

Tagore gives a spiritualistic account of the origin of art and literature. The basis of art, he says, lies in the principle of unity. He learns from the Upaniṣads that what lies at the root of all things in the universe is nothing but the self which is indivisible and one. The one spirit has been manifested in infinite ways. Tagore's aim is like that of the mystics. He wants to see the one in many, to fraternize his self with the world of not-self. When the outer world of not-self is appropriated to the inner world of self, one feels a more pervasive mode of being and gets delight in such a feeling. Art arises out of the deep feeling of union of one's self with the rest of the world. Tagore says:

> The union of the human heart with the universe beyond, soothes the sorrows of man and out of this union arises literature. – *Sahityer Pathe* 70

But, here the poet says that everybody has not got the same capacity to feel the oneness with the outer world, since everyone is not endowed with the faculty of imagination through which the feeling of union is made possible. We find the poet saying:

> Everybody has not the same capacity to feel and enjoy this union with the universe. For the power through which the union becomes not merely one of the senses, but one of the mind and soul, is the power of imagination. – Ibid.

c. Both Rabindranath and Santayana hold that art is not imitation, but creation. But this is an apparent agreement between them. According to Santayana, art is always a new construction, it gives an ideal form upon matter. The function of the artist is to appropriate matter to ideal uses. Of course, Santayana speaks of imitative art (p. 186). Here imitation includes similarity, but it is more than similarity. In an imitative art the forms of things are reproduced in a fresh substance to a new purpose.

To Rabindranath also, art is not imitation, but not in the Santayanian sense. Art, according to him, consists in giving an ideal form to what was in the mind, to the feeling of oneness with the outer world. Artistic creation is always new, since the artist is by a spiritual vision. To know that the one infinite spirit is manifested in everything in the universe, even in a blade of grass or an atom of dust is to have a vision which is perfectly spiritual in character. Art should always try to reveal this spiritual ideal which lies hidden in the actual or the natural. Of the spiritual or ideal vision which should be embodied in any true art, Radhakrishnan says in *The Philosophy of Rabindranath Tagore*:

> Without this philosophic vision no great poetry can exist. Poetry may charm us by its wit, surprise us by its skill, thrill us by its richness, amuse us by its variety, lull us into sleep by its rhythm and satisfy our craving for extraordinary incident; but let it lack the vision, it sinks to the level of verse and ceases to be poetry.
>
> –1918: 145-46

d. Both George Santayana and Rabindranath Tagore are humanists. Both hold that art is for the sake of human life. For Santayana, the artist should portray an ideal picture of life which cannot be found in the actual world we live in. Art is "a rehearsal of rational living" (1905, IV: 119). The world fancied by the artist gives us a glimpse of perfect life, life in unison with peace and equanimity. Such a life would be an ideal to human mortals who in their actual lives meet with unhappiness and rivalry.

But Rabindranath's humanistic art has a spiritual side which is absent in Santayana's. That art lies unrelated to human life is meaningless to Rabindranath. He says that art is the expression of the essential nature of man. By the essential nature of man is meant his spiritual nature, his contemplative self. Art, Tagore says, never expresses man in actuality, besmeared with sorrows and pains and sins. Art reveals the greater self, the self which is beyond all sorrows and evils, the self in which intellect, desires and experiences are mixed into a perfect unity. What is eternally true in life is not the actual self that we suffer, but the real or ideal self which is one, infinite and ubiquitous. Shelley also writes:

> A poem is the very image of life, expressed in its eternal Truth. – 1840: 109

e. If, according to Tagore, art be the expresssion of man's self-realization, if it be the revelation of the feeling of union of the self with the rest of the world, it, then, expresses a basic Upaniṣadic truth which is, viz. "That Thou art", the meaning of which is that what is at the root of all perceptible things of the universe is the self which is indivisible and one. This truth which is revealed by art is not achieved through intellect, but through a mystic process called intuition. This intuition is also called imagination. What intellect gives us is an actual truth. It gives a knowledge of the object as distinguished from the subject. But what intuition gives us is a truth which is higher than the actual truth. It gives a vision of the unity of self and not-self. The truth with which art deals does not lie in a faithful reproduction of facts but in realization. What Tagore accepts as real is this artistic truth. Naturalistic truth given by intellect is not called by him truth, but fact.

Now, let us see what Santayana says about the truth of art. Art, Santayana would not say, reveals the actual truth or what Rabindranath calls "fact", since art lies in the region of imagination. If art does not reveal fact or the natural truth, does it express the spiritual truth? But this problem cannot arise in respect of Santayana, since he does not treat art in a way in which Rabindranath treats it.

When art, according to Santayana, does not express truth, either naturalistic or spiritualistic, then what does it reveal? Santayana says, "What nature does with existence, art does with appearance" (1905, IV: 119). The artist by his imaginative power would draw an ideal picture out of the materials found in the natural world. Santayana says:

> In every poet, indeed, there is some fidelity to nature, mixed with that irrelevant false fancy with which poetry is sometimes identified. – Ibid.: 81

The artist's world, being fancy-born, is one of appearance which seems to be insignificant in comparison to reality. Santayana writes:

> A play of appearance is accordingly some little closed circle in experience, some dream in which we lose ourselves by ignoring most of our interests, and from which we awake into a world in which that lost episode plays no further part and leaves no heirs. – Ibid.: 143

Though art is concerned with appearance, though its idealization of reality seems to be insignificant, rational art, says Santayana, is possible and can serve as a significant ideal to human life. A rational poet, by dint of his extraordinary genius, gives all existence an ideal setting which, although it is a fiction, will not be falsified in any of its elements. Santayana says that the poetry of a rational poet

> would be an ultimate truth in its practical scope. It would present in graphic images the total efficacy of real things. – Ibid.: 80

Part Three
Ethics and Religion

10

Moral Philosophy and Theory of Value

I. Introduction

SANTAYANA'S moral philosophy is set forth in *The Life of Reason* (1905), one of his notable earlier works. His moral philosophy develops from the pre-rational through the rational to the post-rational stage. Humanism is not only the temper, but also the core and substance of *The Life of Reason*. The aroma of Santayana's ethics is best smelt in his theory of value which has cast a great influence upon the present-day writers. The present chapter is, therefore, mainly focused on Santayana's theory of value in general and his moral philosophy in particular.

A point needs to be mentioned before we enter directly into the discussion of the ethical problems which are met in *The Life of Reason*. The later writings of Santayana do not deal so much with the moral problems as with the epistemological and metaphysical ones. The dominant doctrines of the earlier and later periods of his writings are so noticeably different that we venture to conclude that Santayana's philosophy is devoid of a common line of thought. In this critical appreciation of Santayana's moral philosophy the writer likes to ask: does the moral tone of Santayana's earlier works vibrate in his later writings too? The answer, of course, comes from Santayana himself. And on our part, a probe into his writings seems to justify what he says. He says:

> After all, there has been no change in my deliberate doctrine; only some changes of mental habit. – 1905, I: 7

We may think that the attitude of Santayana in his later writings is a non-moral one in that he moves beyond the region of good and evil, and in that for him the true good lies in the disintoxication from all human loves and ideals. But as detachment is itself a moral ideal of high excellence and as an attempt to get hold of the ideal of detachment involves the most intense voluntary effort, Santayana's moral tone remains dominant in all his works. The terms of his morality seem to have changed in his earlier and later works, but it may be said that the same moral tone prevails throughout.

II. Development of Santayana's Moral Philosophy

The pre-rational, the rational and the post-rational are the three stages through which Santayana's moral philosophy develops. This is a triadic development. The pre-rational (i.e. non-rational) and the rational constitute the antithesis and the thesis respectively of this developmental process. Out of these two opposite moments, develops the third moment, the post-rational, the synthesis, which is neither pre-rational nor rational but which amounts to the reconciliation of these two.

A. PRE-RATIONAL MORALITY

Ethics which is to be rational cannot be so, if it does not spring from what is not rational, or if the pre-rational elements do not precede it or are totally denied. Rational ethics would be impossible "if pre-rational morality were annulled" (Schilpp 1940: 563). By pre-rational morality, Santayana means the life of impulse. Instead of extirpating or annulling the life of impulse he makes it the basis of true morality. In this connection Santayana's notion of morality can be compared to the ethical views of the post-Socratic Cynic School, the Stoic School of the Hellenistic age and the eighteenth-century philosopher Immanuel Kant.

The Cynics, the Stoics, Kant and Santayana

The Cynics, the Stoics and Kant advocate the rigoristic or ascetic view of morality. They are all in favour of developing a pure life of reason devoid of sensibility or the life of impulse. They argue that irrational and uncontrolled impulses or affects are opposed to reason; in contrast to the affects, virtue belongs to the rational constitution of the soul and true happiness lies in independence of or freedom from impulses or passions. Like them, Santayana also develops what is called rational ethics, but unlike them he does not overthrow the life of impulse. The Cynics, the Stoics and Kant treat sensibility as accidental to the essential nature of man, since it is a relic of animal nature in him. But in contrast to them, Santayana's speciality lies mainly in ascertaining the life of impulse as one essential part of human nature. Moreover, the antagonists of Santayana hold that reason is something opposed to impulse, while he takes the view that vital impulse is not alien to reason, it rather assists in "the birth of reason". He goes on to say that the true life of reason can be brought forth not by the extirpation, but by the inclusion, of impulses. "The Life of Reason is the happy marriage of two elements, impulse and ideation" (1905, I: 18). The life of reason can be led only when impulses are modified by reflection. And in such modification lies true happiness also. Santayana also opines that moral progress consists in leading the life of reason. The life of reason should not be taken as a means in human progress; it is rather "the total and embodied progress itself" (ibid.: 17). The life of reason does not consist in the mere "betterment in sentience" which is the Epicurean ideal. In order to effect the life of reason the pleasures of sense are to be "intelligently enjoyed and pursued" (ibid.). Santayana wants to establish his view by saying that reason is an abstraction without impulse; rational morality is rooted in pre-rational impulses. Rational morality grows like a plant, being nurtured by sap taken by its roots from the soil of irrational impulses.

Santayana's view of rational morality resembles that of the eudaemonist. The eudaemonist contends that to occupy the rational viewpoint is not to eliminate all our desires and embrace the Kantian viewpoint of mere formal self-consistency. He believes in rational morality as that in which all our desires and impulses are placed in their right relations to one another.

The fact that moral phenomena have a biological basis is not challenged. But what Santayana mainly ignores is the social ground of morality. We can argue with John Dewey and George Herbert Mead that apart from social environment neither intelligence nor the values expressed in the life of reason are conceivable. As a purely biological organism the human animal, apart from all social surroundings, cannot develop a moral sense. The individual man is known only as a member of some society. What we call his virtues are chiefly exhibited in his fellows. It may be said that Santayana's youthful connection with Herbert Spencer's philosophy serves as one of the conditions for the underestimation of the social ground of morality. This underestimation is also due to his stern individualistic attitude.

B. RATIONAL MORALITY

Morality, then, according to Santayana, passes from the pre-rational to the rational, from the life of impulse to the life of reason. In his "Apologia Pre Mente Sua" he states what he understands by rational ethics. By rational ethics he understands "rather reasonableness itself" (Schilpp 1940: 562-63). This reasonableness or rather reason, for its origin, requires the fusion of two things, viz. impulse and reflection. "Vital impulse, however, when it is modified by reflection ... is properly called reason" (1905, I: 16).

The life of impulse and the life of reflection are fused together to constitute the life of reason. Everybody should lead a rational life. For this, what is necessary is to act in accordance with nature, where by "nature" is meant the nature of the agent. Thus, Santayana's first and ultimate commandment of morality is the Socratic dictum: "Know thyself". A man should know his own vital impulses and needs; he should try to interpret them; and lastly he should, according to that interpretation, control and modify them by reflection or thought. In such ethical functions consists virtue or the true life of reason. Moral life, for Santayana, does not mean the life of non-activity or rest. With Aristotle he argues that "life is reason in operation" (ibid.). Indeed, there are no holidays from virtue.

Rational Morality and Art

Here we should not forget to mention that Santayana speaks of the pragmatic side of rational life:

> Man's rational life consists in those moments in which reflection not only occurs but proves efficacious. – Ibid.

His life of reasons should not be "visionary". He should not be content with the mere idea of his own nature. He should also act according to that idea. And such action rarely comes to be unsatisfying and fruitless. The following line rings with the pragmatic tone of his morals:

> The rational man ... is constituted by ideas which have ceased to be visionary and actions which have ceased to be vain. – Ibid.: 18

As the life of reason has efficacy, it can, therefore, be called art. Every art is the product which expresses an idea or purpose. Like art, moral life or the life of reason is also a "result". It consists in the rational constitution of the impulses.

Santayana seems to be right when he says that moral life consists in activity. But by making morality an art, he seems to confuse activity with capacity. Art lies in capacity or in the possession of a particular kind of skill. A good painter is one who can paint beautifully; a good man, on the other hand, is not one who can, but one who does, act rightly. Goodness is not a capacity but an activity.

There is another fundamental distinction between art and morals. In art the ultimate appeal is to the work achieved, whereas in morals the ultimate appeal is to the inner aim. Actually, the essence of virtue or moral life lies in the attitude of the will. In the case of virtuous action, as Kant says:

> A good will is good not because of what it performs or effects, not by its aptness for the attainment of some proposed end, but simply by virtue of the volition. – 1797, vol. I

From the above discussion, what follows as a rule is that morals should be distinguished from art. But Santayana opposes this rule when he treats rational morality as art.

The Ideal to Be Followed in Our Rational Life

From Santayana's rational ethics we come to know the ideal which is to be followed in our rational life. The ideal is the perfect and harmonious adjustment of all phases and interests of life. Harmony is the formal condition of the ideal and the only end. Santayana here appears to speak like a perfectionist. But he is not a perfectionist, for his morality is always fixed to this earth. The ideal is "a resultant or synthesis of impulses already afoot" (1905, I: 169). Thus, Santayana's ethics is naturalistic and not perfectionistic.

Now, is there only one ideal or many ideals? In Santayana, the ideal is declared to vary. He says:

> I wish, individuals and races, and nations to be themselves, and to multiply the forms of perfection and happiness, as nature prompts them. The only thing which I think might be propagated without injustice to the types thereby suppressed is harmony; enough harmony to prevent the interference of one type with another, and to allow the perfect development of each type. – 1922: 258

He has not recognized any abstract ideal in the sense of the supreme good. The ideal which has no concern with the actual demands of living beings carries no value. The pursuit of such ideal "would be not the acme but the atrophy of moral endeavour" (1905, I: 169). Santayana contrasts the abstract ideal with the chimera of an absolute reality.

> As an absolute reality would be indescribable and without a function in the elucidation of phenomena, so a supreme good which was good for nobody would be without conceivable value.
> – Ibid.

By discarding the supreme ideal in the abstract sense he accepts many ideals in the concrete sense. But the ideals

> are neither more numerous nor more variable than the living natures that generate them.
> – Ibid.: 19

An abstract ideal in the general sense cannot, while a concrete ideal in the particular sense can, be realized, since the former has not, while the latter has, deep roots in the world. The individual alone is judge of what shall be his ideal, since he alone feels the impulses which his ideal is to direct and harmonize. Santayana's rational ethics is both naturalistic and individualistic.

Santayana and Emerson

Individualism in Santayana's ethics suggests Emerson. The latter, like the former, bears an individualistic attitude. But between them there is a marked difference which we should not fail to notice. Santayana's ethics, as we have seen, is naturalistic, while Emerson's ethics has an idealistic basis. Emerson's ethics depends upon his notion of Being. Being by which is meant eternal truth is in its essence everywhere one and the same. Ralph Waldo Emerson conceives an identity of the human soul with the supreme soul. Hence, for each human being the flash of immediate insight into truth, universal and divine, is perfectly, possible. Ethics which Emerson speaks of is naturally one of self-dependence. Speak your latent conviction and it shall be the universal sense, since the human soul and the world soul are identical. What another announces I must find true in me or wholly reject. The right is what is after my constitution, the wrong is what is against it. Emerson's strong individualism inclines to lower the value of humanitarian activities to which modern times including Santayana assign much importance.

Santayana's individualism does not lead to moral licence and anarchy, since he has imposed upon it certain checks and balances. In the construction of an ideal, the vital impulses of one should not be merely harmonized, but it is to be seen whether that harmony will lead "to the maximum satisfaction possible in the whole community of spirits affected by our action (1905, I: 167). Santayana's morality may be self-centred, but its breadth renders this self-interest innocuous in practice.

MORAL JUDGEMENT

Let us now pass from Santayana's notion of the ideal to that of the criterion by which the truth or falsity of a moral judgement is to be determined. Satisfaction is, according to Santayana, the moral criterion and his moral philosophy is undoubtedly hedonistic. His relation to hedonism will be discussed shortly. From the criterion of satisfaction we come to know wherein lies the good of a man. The good of a man consists in the comprehensiveness (Santayana 1913: 146) of the satisfaction of his animating impulses. In this connection a probe into Santayana's distinction between "real" and "apparent" goods is necessary. The "real" good lies in the comprehensiveness, permanence and biological utility (1957: 248) of the interest of the subject in the object. In comparison to the real good the apparent good is less pervasive. To tell an occasional lie is an apparent good since its propriety lies in serving an occasional purpose, but it is no real good since it interferes with the acquisition of other goods more comprehensive or more permanent. But to love my neighbour is a good which does not interpose in the achievement of other goods more satisfying. Hence, such a good is not apparent, but real. The apparent good is, while the real one is not, relative to the interference with the more comprehensive goods.

A moral judgement, according to Santayana, is a judgement upon, not about, an action. It is a judgement upon an action with reference to a moral standard, viz. the standard of comprehensiveness of satisfaction. An action is judged to be true if it involves the long-range interests of a man. It is false if by it is expressed his short-range interests.

Though moral judgements are true or false in the above sense, Santayana is very careful to set them free from the realm of truth. In his theory of knowledge he takes essences as descriptive. The psyche feels a vital demand for its adaptation to the ambient world and an urgency for its part which is called intent converts an essence into description of a thing. As in epistemology, so in moral experience, essences intuited are expressions of the states of the psyche. But moral essences are not descriptive, but are merely expressive. Descriptive essences are causally connected with the objects external to the psyche, whereas moral essences stand in no such causal connection. Moral essences, being merely expressive, cannot render moral experience either a truth or a falsity. Any moral essence is selected or preferred as it expresses the state of the psyche. Preferences which are felt can be neither true nor false. Moral judgements which speak of preferences are neither true nor false.

> The nerve of moral judgement is preference: and preference is a feeling or an impulse to action which cannot be either false or true. – Santayana 1938: 67

A question may arise to the student of ethics whether there is any utility of moral judgement when it cannot be called either true or false. Santayana says:

> ... moral judgements of some sort are inevitable in man. He cannot help having some radical preference. However sublimated this perference may be, it will express his vital feeling ... . – Ibid. 73

Moral judgements, then, are expressive of vital feeling, and as such are essential. It may, however, again be said that preference which is the "nerve" of moral judgement indicates a truth in it. But Santayana asserts that the vital feeling which is expressed by preference is "morally groundless".

> ... there is no meaning in saying that the preference so uttered is a truth in itself.
> – Ibid.

Santayana's Naturalistic Ethics

As we have seen, Santayana's ethics tends to be naturalistic. A natural science observes the phenomena with which it deals, classifies them, and last of all, explains them. A phenomenon is explained when it is related to other phenomena within a particular system. Santayana's rational ethics becomes naturalistic in the above sense. Reason, instead of extirpating desires and impulses, makes them the contents of moral life. The life of reason arises from the observation and explanation of them. Rational morality is a system in which all impulses are placed in their right relations to one another.

Now, like all natural sciences, Santayana's naturalistic ethics becomes positive. It deals with "what is" instead of dealing with "what ought to be". Santayana explains moral phenomena by the actual facts, i.e. by the prior biological phenomena of animal life. But moral facts, as we know, are to be accounted for by the moral ideal which always transcends the actual facts. Santayana, of course, speaks of an ideal which should be followed in our rational life. But such ideal, according to him, does not transcend the actual facts. The ideal, he says, is "a resultant or synthesis of impulses already afoot" (1905, I: 169). Thus, the impulses account for the ideal instead of being explained by the latter. We can conclude by saying that Santayana speaks of an ideal in the particular sense instead of referring to the ideal of the Highest Good.

Santayana's Moral Philosophy and Hedonism

Santayana's philosophy is hedonistic. His frank hedonism is expressed in the following lines:

> To deny that pleasure is a good and pain an evil is a grotesque affectation. ... The more pleasure a universe can yield, other things being equal, the more beneficent and generous is its general nature; the more pains its constitution involves, the darker and more malign is its total temper. – Ibid.: 47

Though Santayana's position is hedonistic, he is neither a psychological hedonist nor an ethical hedonist. First, he cannot be a psychological hedonist, since he is an epiphenomenalist. He holds that matter does everything. The claim of causality is complete on body's side, so that mental processes are merely accompanying phenomena which have no causal agency, i.e. which make no difference to the outcome. Psychological hedonism holds that pleasure alone can be the final and efficient cause of action. Now, for Santayana, final-cause terminology in the sphere of matter which is coextensive with the field of action is mythological. It may be claimed that pleasure, when it is not the final cause of action, can be the efficient cause of it. But here also the epiphenomenalist holds that no conscious event is causally efficacious. Thus, pleasure, which is a mental phenomenon, is a concomitant action, but by no means a cause of it.

Nor is Santayana an ethical hedonist. Ethical hedonism takes pleasure as the only good which we ought to seek. No doubt, Santayana takes pleasure as a good, but not as the only good. He says that goods are numerous, individual and irreducible. Moreover, by subscribing to the view that good is an indefinable essence, he avoids hedonism at a single stroke.

So, Santayana is neither a psychological hedonist nor an ethical hedonist. His position with regard to hedonism is rather Aristotelian. Like Aristotle, Santayana asserts that pleasure, though it is undoubtedly a good, cannot be made itself the end of our actions. Pleasure or agreeable feeling is a concomitant of the good life, but it is not the whole of it. The good life is the happy life. Santayana makes a distinction between pleasure and happiness. Both pleasure and happiness are satisfactions of impulses. But in contrast with pleasure, happiness is a satisfaction of long-range impulses. Happiness is serene, disciplined and lasting, while pleasure is ecstatic, unrestrained and momentary. Happy is he who has achieved an ideal harmonious with his nature. Happiness includes pleasure, but not vice versa. Happiness which means a harmony among the impulses is the only ideal that we should strive for.

With regard to Santayana's hedonism an important question is whether it is egoistic or altruistic. Self-centredness is of the very essence of the psyche. It pursues only a selected set of private objectives. Thus, egoism, says Santayana, "is not the thin and refutable thing" (1913: 150). But does he not also speak of the happiness of the greatest number? Does he not say that the ideal is lost sight of "when a man cultivates his garden-plot of private pleasures?" (1905, V: 270). Do we not hear from him that

> any system that, for some sinister reason, should absolve itself from goodwill toward all creatures, and make it somehow a duty to secure their misery, would be clearly disloyal to reason, humanity and justice?
>
> – 1905, I: 156

Then, ultimately, Santayana is not an egoist. Now, the problem is: how does the psyche, an automatic self-seeking machine, act disinterestedly? To be disinterested means to be interested in the good of others. How is it not possible for the psyche to acquire this generosity? In his *Some Turns of Thought in Modern Philosophy* (1933) Santayana says that generosity is one of our primitive passions. Then for the animal psyche it is quite natural to respond to the passion of generosity. To seek the good of others is an impulse as real as others.

When the psyche gives rise to the spirit, it is possible then to pass from egoism to altruism, from uncompromising pursuit of private objectives to generosity or sympathy. The ultimate good of the spirit is sympathy. In the mind's essence-directed stage which is the spiritual life this sympathy is retained as tolerance and quiet understanding. Thus, the development from egoism to altruism coincides to an extent with the progression from the moral to the spiritual life. Here, we come to the last stage, the post-rational, of the development of Santayana's moral philosophy.

C. POST-RATIONAL MORALITY

The moral life is the life of action. No enduring satisfaction is possible here. The characteristic perfection, which lies in having "expressed and discharged all that was latent in us" (1933: 100), is not possible in the moral life. The spirit sees everything from the standpoint of universal sympathy.

> ... in its outlook ... it is initially universal and addressed to anything and everything that there may happen to be.
>
> – Schilpp 1940: 26

It does not adopt the standpoint of preference which is characteristically the psyche's own. Preference is the ground of value judgement and since the spirit is moved by universal sympathy and not by preference, it rescinds all distinction between good and evil, that is, transcends all value judgements. The spirit, by absolving itself from preferential attitude, absorbs itself in the intuition of essences for their own sake. This is spirit's "essence-directed stage". This stage can be compared to Spinoza's third kind of knowledge where everything is looked at under the form of eternity. The spirit contemplates essences in their eternal form. The contemplation is very like aesthetic enjoyment. The spiritual life involves "disintoxication clarifying those passions which the life of reason endeavours to harmonize" (ibid.).

The logical groundwork of Santayana's theory of the spiritual life is his epiphenomenalism according to which consciousness has no place in the direction of action. Feeling discontented with the world of experience – with moral action and social living, the mind or consciousness looks beyond and finds its highest good in the contemplation of the play of essences.

The Life of Reason and the Life of Spirit

From Santayana's notion of the spiritual life it is quite natural to conceive that spirit, according to him, is antagonistic to reason. But he pronounces:

> Between the spiritual life and the life of reason there is accordingly no contradiction: they are concomitant. – Ibid.: 27

Spirit and reason have a common root in organic life. They spring from the power of active adaptation possessed by animals. Though spirit and reason are not antagonistic to each other, "yet there is a difference of temper and level" (Schilpp 1940: 27) between them. What reason establishes, is not destroyed by spirit.

> Spirit is not a power: it comes to fulfil, not to destroy ... spirit merely heightens and universalizes the synthesis which reason makes partially, as occasion requires, in the service of natural interests. – Ibid.: 27-28

Reason engages itself in the task of harmonizing one's own natural impulses. Spirit also performs the same job, but it does so, not by taking one's impulses to the exclusion of others' interests, but by taking the interests of all. The function of synthesis here is made from a universal standpoint.

The spiritual life is not, thus, quite separated from the life of reason or the moral life. The spiritual life must have a "moral bias". Santayana refers to the *Gītā* in the *Mahābhārata* in order to show the relation between rational and post-rational morality. He says after the *Gītā* that it is quite possible for a person to "live the life appointed for him", but at the same time "with detachment" (ibid.: 571). *Karma-yoga* in the *Gītā* commends a life of activity and yet it gives no room for the play of selfish impulses. Santayana, by following the *Gītā* teaching, accepts both the ideals of life, the negative ideal of renunciation and the positive one of active life. To quote a pretty long portion from his writing.

> You cannot be detached without being previously attached; you cannot renounce or sacrifice anything significantly unless you love it. And if you withdraw from any action it must not be from timidity or laziness; that would be giving up one vain impulse for another still vainer and more physical. Your detachment will not be spiritual unless it is universal; it will then bring you liberation at once from the world and from yourself. This will neither destroy your natural gifts and duties nor add to them; but it will enable you to exercise them without illusion and in farseeing harmony with their real function and end. Detachment leaves you content to be where you are, and what you are. – Schilpp 1940: 571

Thus, Santayana shows a chain of relation among the different stages in the development of morality. Rational morality is based upon the pre-rational which supplies the former with the materials which are to be harmonized in order to effect the life of reason. And post-rational morality or the spiritual life becomes possible when it is based upon the life of reason. Santayana says:

> ... without any moral bias, it would seem to me a useless reproduction of the truth absolute. – Ibid.: 570

D. CRITICAL REVIEW

An important criticism is levelled against Santayana, namely, that he has not been able to make his epiphenomenalism consistent with his faith in reason. According to the epiphenomenalist theory of mind, mind or reason has no causal agency, it is important to change the flow of events in the natural world.

> Consciousness is not itself dynamic, for it has no body, no idiosyncrasy or particular locus, to be the point of origin for definite relationships. – 1905, I: 145

If there is no causal agency on the part of consciousness or reason, how, then, can it be able to harmonize the natural impulses? Santayana, however, would answer that consciousness is not dynamic, it is made so by matter which is by definition called flux. If that be so, it must be said that mind expresses only the blind movement of irrational matter. But it is not understood how the life of reason can be constituted by the blind movement of matter.

Sterling P. Lamprecht shows that Santayana seems to remain in his different but conflicting moods in giving emphasis at one time upon the engaged life of reason and at another upon the detached life of the spirit. To quote from Lamprecht's essay "Animal Faith and the Art of Intuition":

> 'Santayana seems in one mood when he writes: "I frankly cleave to the Greeks and not to the Indians, and I aspire to be a rational animal rather than a pure spirit" (*Realm of Essence*, p. 65). He seems in quite another mood when he writes: "I myself have no passionate attachment to existence, and value this world for the intuitions it can suggest, rather than for the wilderness of facts that compose it"' (Santayana 1923: *Scepticism and Animal Faith* p. 171).
>
> – Schilpp's Edition 1940: 119-20

These two contradictory statements, Lamprecht concludes, can in no way be reconciled. For coming to such a conclusion he cannot be made guilty, since it is true that Santayana himself has not always spoken out what he intends to mean. The present writer thinks that the statements, quoted by Lamprecht in order to show their mutual contradictions, are consistent. The thread of connection can be discovered if we can solve the riddle of "pure spirit" mentioned in the first statement. What does Santayana exactly mean by "a pure spirit" which he does not aspire to be? "Pure spirit", according to him, is non-existent. Instead of pure spirit, he conceives an actual spirit, a spirit which is tied with the life of action. To quote him:

> Pure spirit does not exist, spirit according to my theory being a function of the psyche; but if you conceive a spirit without any natural place, time, or point of view, and without any moral bias, it would seem to me a useless reproduction of the truth absolute, which actual spirit lives by seeing only in perspectives and on actual occasions. –Ibid.:569-70

Thus, by discarding pure spirituality, he accepts the spiritual life and "values this world for the intuitions it can suggest". He seems to maintain a single mood when he speaks at different times of the busy life of reason and the detached spiritual life.

Humanism in Santayana's Moral Philosophy

In the earlier works, especially in *The Life of Reason*, Santayana seeks to develop humanism in moral philosophy. He has never deserted his humanism throughout his whole career. Only we find a shift of interest in his earlier and later works.

> After all, there has been no change in my deliberate doctrine; only some changes of mental habit. I now dwell by preference on other perspectives, in which the same objects appear with their relative bulks reversed and inversely hiding one another; what lay before in the background – nature – has come forward and the life of reason, which then held the centre of the stage, has receded. – 1905, I: 7

In his earlier works, the humanistic principle which is the principle of the life of reason remains most vivid and occupies the centre of his attention. But in his later works, specially in *Scepticism and Animal Faith* (1923) and in *The Realms of Being*, (1942) his interest is shifted to the natural philosophy, and to the ontological and epistemological principles which, instead of going against humanism, support and justify it. But how can materialism justify the life of reason? Let us seek Santayana's answer here:

> Certainly materialism cannot justify moral ideals morally. ... But materialism justifies the life of reason martially, as a fighting organization and explains its possible strength and dominance. – Schilpp 1940: 24

What are called the instruments of reason from the moral point of view are, in a primary sense, the ground and cause of reason. Matter is controlled by reason, since "reason is matter organized" (ibid.). When our passions which remain and continue to work are synthesized by reason, we come to possess the life of reason.

Santayana's essentialism, as we know, holds a prominent place in his later works. He says that the ultimate good lies in the contemplation of essences. This contemplation makes us oblivious of the engaged life of reason. It may be thought that Santayana's essentialism leads us into a post-humanistic stage. But it has already been referred to in the introduction of the present chapter that the life of contemplation, which involves disintoxication from all human affairs, is still an ideal which is perfectly human and an endeavour to come to the stage of contemplation is a human undertaking. On the whole, Santayana's humanism remains unabated throughout his earlier and later writings.

There are some modern philosophers, among whom the name of Irwin Edman may be mentioned, who have stressed two opposite stages in Santayana's moral philosophy. These two stages are humanism and post-humanism which coincide with the life of reason and the life of spirit respectively. Critics point out that the spiritual life transcends everything human, all commitments, all allegiances and all preferences. In such a life occurs a detachment or disintoxication so complete that this stage can hardly be called humanistic. Irwin Edman says that essences, which are contemplated in the post-humanistic stage, carry no significance to the spirit, since they themselves have no significance in their own terms (Schilpp 1940: 310). But Santayana is misunderstood by Edman. Essences are quite meaningful to Santayana. First, in the contemplation of them the spirit gets enjoyment or happiness. And we cannot forget that Santayana identifies intuition of essences with aesthetic appreciation of them. Second, if essences have no significance in their own terms, they would have remained unnoticed to the spirit. Moreover, all essences are expressive of the state of the psyche. Anyway, it can be said against Edman that the spiritual life which consists in the contemplation of pure essences is not a post-humanistic stage, but a humanistic one; it is a life which falls within human aspiration.

There is another fault in Edman's exposition of Santayana with reference to the latter's usage of the term which signifies the post-rational stage. Edman's frequent use of the term "spirituality" instead of the term "spiritual life" has occurred in his essay "Humanism and Post-humanism" (Schilpp 1940). Santayana thinks that there is no harm in taking spirituality as the quality of spiritual life. But to him, such a term taken by itself seems to be abstract, bearing no relation to human life. Hence, he prefers to use the term "spiritual life" which is the culminating phase of human life. Spirituality is "an attribute in the air", while "spiritual lives are facts"; and Santayana says that "if there be any choice between the two expressions, I incline to prefer the second" (ibid.: 569).

Santayana's humanism is confined to man. He is a poet before he is a philosopher. His poetry interests us because of humanism which it expresses. In his poetry, we find his sympathy with all human interests that are honest: love, beauty, religion, art. Again, his poetry expresses his recognition of human suffering which implies his deep human sympathy. As in his "Mid-night":

Immortal is the soul that sings
The sorrow of her mortal birth.
Oh cruel beauty of the earth!
Oh love's unutterable strings!

Moreover, in his poetry his humanism is accompanied by an inevitable naturalism which comes to the foreground in his later writings. As in one of his sonnets:

The soul is not on earth an alien thing.

Poetry, to Santayana, has a universal and moral function. It should not remain an idle play of fancy. It must be relevant to the ideals and purposes of life. The actual charm of poetry lies in that relevance.

> As its elementary pleasantness comes from its response to the demands of the ear, so its deepest beauty comes from its response to the ultimate demands of the soul. – 1900: vi

Thus, poetry, if it is to be meaningful and if it is not to be arrested in its development, should be tuned with the string of humanism.

Santayana is not only a poet, but also a philosopher. He may be best described as a "philosopher poet". For each philosophical poet, the whole world is gathered together. The vision of philosophy is sublime. So an honest philosopher should sympathetically consider everything that concerns life. In his approach to philosophy, Santayana is a critical humanist. His criticism is related to his underlying attitude towards life. He judges and criticizes literature, philosophy, culture and civilization by the quantum of happiness they yield. As a critic he is always a moral philosopher.

> I was not studying history or psychology for their own sake: my retrospect was to be frankly selective and critical, guided by a desire to discriminate the better from the worse. – 1905, I: 10

His humanism is that of a sympathetic retrospect and of a moral judgement. The retrospect of past philosophies is made with a realistic outlook. Each human discourse, each philosophical view of the world, each religious myth, each form of government, everything is examined concerning what it does or does not contribute to the life of reason. What is to be mentioned here is that we are deprived of knowing from Santayana the way in which intelligence functions or the way in which values are discriminated.

With respect to the critical retrospect of past philosophies the neo-humanists make an ally with Santayana. Paul Elmer More, a new humanist, considers Santayana's *Interpretations of Poetry and Religion* (1900) as "the wisest and most fascinating work in constructive criticism that has appeared in English for several years.[1] Norman Foerster, in order to compile a bibliography of humanistic literature, has headed his list with *Interpretations of Poetry and Religion*. Both the new humanists and Santayana have found more than a little fault with modern romanticism and the cult of the indeterminate. They always adhere to the humanist point of view as the touchstone of their critical philosophy.

In some respects Santayana sympathizes with the old humanists against the new humanists. The old humanists do not cling to austerity, they

> believed in the sufficient natural goodness of mankind, a goodness humanized by frank sensuality and a wink at all amiable vices. – 1931: 4-5

But the modern humanists do not offer a natural explanation of human goodness. Their notion of "ethical imagination" is above all natural explanation. They want to offer a universal moral "criterion, apart from all places, persons, and times, by which everything should be judged" (ibid.: 29). Their supernaturalism leads to absolutism which Santayana cannot tolerate in his moral philosophy. The rigidity of rational morality will be determined by its natural humanism,

---

1 *Harvard Graduates Magazine*, IX (September 1900), p. 19.

> Call it humanism or not, only a morality frankly relative to man's nature is worthy of man, being at once vital and rational, martial and generous; whereas absolutism smells of fustiness as well as of faggots. – Ibid.: 73-74

Santayana, as a humanist, adopts the classical point of view and raises his criticism against that kind of romanticism which refuses to be harmonized with classicism. Barbarism is one kind of romanticism which is incompatible with classicism. The barbarian is the man who merely feels and acts, valuing in his life its force and feeling, but being careless of its purpose and form. Thus, barbarism refuses to be harmonized with the classical sense of purpose and form. Rational morality, according to Santayana, is possible through the transformation of romanticism into classicism, of matter into form:

> This transformation of sense and emotion into objects agreeable to the intellect, into clear ideas and beautiful things, is the natural work of reason; when it has been accomplished very imperfectly, or not at all, we have a barbarous mind, a mind full of chaotic sensations, objectless passions, and undigested ideas. – 1900: 198

Santayana says that Walt Whitman and Robert Browning are "poets of barbarism". They express sensations and emotions without fitting them into a rational system of any sort. Whitman

> has approached common life without bringing in his mind any higher standard by which to criticize it; he has seen it, not in contrast with an ideal, but as the expression of forces more indeterminate and elementary than itself. – Ibid.: 181

Santayana admits that Whitman bears in his poetry a stamp of humanism, but that is not humanism in the truest sense of the term:

> Whitman's insight into man did not go beyond a sensuous sympathy. – Ibid.: 184

Happiness, for which man longs, does not lie in the sensuous life, but in the rational constitution of life. Browning's strength too lies in his clear representation of the immediate flux of life:

> He remained in the phenomenal sphere: he was a lover of experience. – Ibid.: 198

But the ideal which consists in the harmonization of impulses did not exist for him.

Unlike Whitman and Browning, Goethe makes an attempt to fit romanticism into a framework of classicism. Goethe emphasizes on life, as all romanticism does. But he has a classical position. To be happy one must recognize the limits of one's nature and must make oneself by means of calculated choice. This is the classical point of view which Santayana adopts in *The Life of Reason* (1905).

IV. Santayana's Theory of Value

Santayana, a prolific writer as he is, has to his credit a theory of value which creates a landmark in his moral philosophy. Indeed, the whole of his moral philosophy, nay, the whole of his philosophy, is a discourse on value. Hence, it would be rather pedantic for anyone who, by selecting some pieces out of the whole body of his philosophy, points out that herein lies his theory of value. But there seems to remain no other way than being pedantic for one who undertakes the sympathetic consideration of the great author's doctrine concerning value.

The main questions as to Santayana's theory of value are:

1. What is the unit of value?
2. What is the origin of value?
3. What is the standard by reference to which we can make comparisons of value?

What we must hope from Santayana is whether his answers to these questions supply us with a satisfactory theory of value.

Like Moore, Santayana asserts that "good" is a non-natural quality which is not definable and analysable. Thus, "good" is an essence. When the individual psyche finds a positive interest in an object, the non-natural quality "good" will attach to that object. All things cannot be valuable for the psyche, since it acts according to the rule of preference. The fact that some things are preferable relative to the nature of the psyche is the ground of morality. To see all things as equally valuable does not express the life of the psyche but the life of the spirit. To take equal interest in all things which is possible only in the spiritual life is the same thing as to say that the spirit sees all things from the standpoint of disinterestedness or universal sympathy.

From the above, it is evident that the source of values "lies in the specific potentialities and demands of life in various individuals" (Schilpp 1940: 577). This natural demand may be called an interest. For Santayana, the theory of value means the interest theory. From his interest theory we may come to the "unit of value". The subject *S* stands in a relation of interest *R* to an object *O* so that *SRO* is the unit of value. Interests which are identified with natural demands and impulses cannot be themselves good. They are merely "commitments"; and "they may be painful and biologically erratic" (ibid.). But they may give rise to values. Due to having a natural demand or an interest of the psyche for an object, the non-natural quality "good" accrues to that object. Though interest in the above sense is not value, it can be so if it be taken in the sense of the goal of aspiration.

The unit of value which has been referred to does not remain the same in various contexts. That is to say, the unit of value which is applicable to one person may not be applicable to another person. Different persons are not "abstract egos"; they are endowed with different impulses and aspirations.

> In the real world, persons are not abstract egos, like *A* and *B*, so that to benefit one is clearly as good as to benefit another.
> – Santayana 1913: 150

Unlike Russell, Santayana makes his ethics entirely individualistic and is concerned with the concrete interests of the individual person. He cannot advocate an abstract interest theory:

> Actual egoism is not the thin and refutable thing that Mr. Russell makes of it. What it really holds is that a given man, oneself, and those akin to him, are qualitatively better than other beings; that the things they prize are intrinsically better than the things prized by others; and that therefore there is no injustice in treating these chosen interests as supreme. The injustice, it is felt, would lie rather in not treating things so unequal unequally. – Ibid.

Thus, Santayana prefers the concrete interest theory to the abstract interest theory. If he starts with the concrete interests of the individuals, then he shall have to face a difficulty. The concrete interests are many and different, and even in an individual person they vary so largely that they are not compatible with one another. The diverse and incompatible interests do not supply us with a single source of value. Of the different interests of a person we can name the following which are most important: pleasure, desire and preference. These three interests are so characteristically different that with respect to them we do not get any single source of value unless they are robbed of those characteristics in which they differ; and to do so is definitely to advocate an abstract interest theory which Santayana would not obviously permit in his moral philosophy.

Pleasure itself seems to be a value, when it is disembodied. But when it is embodied, the content of pleasure acquires value. Unlike pleasure, desire cannot be a value in its own right. Desire involves an activity towards the attainment of some object. If the supposed object can terminate the desire, that object acquires value in virtue of the desire for it. Lastly, preference is a different sort of interest. In the case of preference two objects are present to the individual. The accepted object acquires a positive and the rejected object a negative value. Thus, we see that pleasure, desire and preference play different roles in the sphere of value and themselves do not form a common interest from which value is said to arise. With respect to different interests we get different units of value.

In *The Sense of Beauty* (1896), however, we may try to ascertain a single source of value. Beauty Santayana defines as "pleasure objectified" and he refers to sensuous, formal and expressive contents in which such pleasure is found. In the field of art and beauty he seems to be consistent in ascertaining a single source of value. But he mentions other fields of interest also. In one chapter of *Reason in Art*, he writes:

> Thus the fine arts are seldom an original factor in human progress. If they express moral and political greatness, and serve to enhance it, they acquire a certain dignity; but so soon as this expressive function is abandoned they grow meretricious. – 1905, IV: 148

The expression of "moral and political greatness" is the satisfaction of interests other than "objectified pleasure" mentioned in *The Sense of Beauty*. Thus, with respect to Santayana, we come to our previous conclusion that instead of confining himself to one type of interest he speaks of the diversity of interests.

On the interest theory, then, we do not get any social standard of value, since the standard of value lies in individual preference. Social sanctions, on this theory again, become meaningless. The value of social life cannot be established in terms of value defined as the satisfaction of particular concrete interests.

If the concrete interest theory is advocated by Santayana, two facts, viz. the fact of moral anarchy and the fact of incommensurability of values, are presented as a challenge to him. Santayana, in order to avoid moral anarchy, asserts that human beings, in spite of all individual variety, have some interests in common, a sufficient constitutional similarity. In his *Platonism and the Spiritual Life* (1957) he says that though human nature varies indefinitely, human morality is the inevitable hygienic bias of a race of animals. Different individuals are regarded as members of the same species, since their characteristics overlap in a certain measure. Each individual selects his own good, since his psyche is prone to do that. But the core of the different individual goods coincides to make social organization and social morality possible. What is to be noted here is that social morality becomes possible here by abandoning the concrete interest theory.

Let us now see what is the attitude of Santayana as regards the other fact. In *The Winds of Doctrine*, he mentions that values are incommensurable (1913: 148, 150). Comparisons of value are made; but the standard of comparison has its locus in the individual will. Thus, we get different standards of value and values remain incommensurable. But Santayana maintains that successive values can be compared. To do so, they should be represented. The good of another is laid in the mind in the form of an ideal representation: a representation which is essentially imaginative. Accordingly, comparison is made and in persons, who have strong imitative sympathies, the represented alien good may be apprehended.

The concrete interest theory of Santayana, as we have seen before, does not provide us with a single source of value, though an attempt in that line has been made in *The Sense of Beauty*. If the interest theory is left aside and if we consider "the life of reason" only, we may expect to find out the key to Santayana's theory of value. The life of reason consists in the integration of impulses and value lies in that integration. Long-range impulses, desires that are life-enhancing, comprehensive and compatible are combined in a system by reason which is itself a "formal interest, the interest in harmony" (1905, I: 174). This harmonized mass of interests constitutes the ideal which is called the rational life. Such ideals

> remain the only possible moral standards for man, the only tests which he can apply for value ... . – Ibid.: 177

That impulse which is life-enhancing and conducive to the rational system is to be pronounced as "good"; otherwise, it will be an evil.

In this connection, we may make a comparative reading of Santayana with S. Alexander. Both assert that values are relative to human beings. Again, both of them opine that values are what satisfy us. To Alexander, ethical value lies in the satisfaction of a social impulse in man. He says:

> We may add that the value of the good act or character is thus the relation between the act in question and the impulse it satisfies and that value is experienced by us as the pleasure of having our social impulse gratified. – Drennen 1962: 525

While Alexander lays stress on the satisfaction of the social impulse, Santayana emphasizes the satisfaction of reason; "to give reason satisfaction is made the measure of good" (1905, I: 181). Reason can be satisfied in two ways, viz. (1) in its capacity to harmonize impulses, and (2) in the concurrence of an impulse with the harmonized mass of interests. What is noteworthy is that Santayana, like Alexander, does not narrow the scope of ethical value to a single impulse. For Santayana, one who leads the life of reason is happy; but for Alexander, one who finds his social impulse gratified is happy.

We learn from Santayana that human nature is "a variable". Reason, being a function of human nature, should also be instable. Consequently, the human ideal cannot remain unchanged. The variability of human nature gives rise to different ideals which may come into conflict with one another and we miss a common standard of value. This may be taken as a charge against Santayana.

Santayana admits not merely the instability or flux but also the constancy in human nature. An individual, since his nature is "a variable", is confronted with many ideals at different times. But these ideals are not conflicting, since each ideal is due to the function of reason. Each successive ideal in one's life expresses better harmonization of impulses. The latter ideal is possible not by annulling the former ideal, but by retaining it. Thus, constancy is maintained in human nature. Santayana says:

> A succession of generations or languages or religions constitutes no progress unless some ideal present at the beginning is transmitted to the end and reaches a better expression there; without this stability at the core no common standard exists and all comparison of value with value must be external and arbitrary. Retentiveness, we must repeat, is the condition of progress. – 1905, I: 185

Moral progress does not consist in an advance towards an external end. It lies, for Santayana, in an inner direction – in the perfection of human nature. And the perfection can be reached by a more and more concrete harmonization of impulses. Here lies the value for the life of reason. This value is intrinsic. It is said that the one ideal is retained by another ideal which gives a better expression of the life of reason than that of the same given by the former ideal. Thus, Santayana seems to have admitted degrees of harmonization or integration; and since value lies in integration, it has also degrees. The complete good lies in the fullest possible integration of impulses. In the ultimate analysis, value, for Santayana, is actuality.

V. Conclusion

The foregoing discussion leads us to conclude that Santayana's *The Life of Reason* is an important American contribution to moral philosophy. He retraces the flowering of man's rational life out of the chaos of primitive feeling. He is a humanist in the sense that his concern is only with man. *The Life of Reason* with its five volumes is the work based upon one-term theme, viz. man. Eloquent and subtle, he describes how man first comes to recognize his instincts, decipher his experience, control his conduct and realize his ideals. *The Life of Reason* is, indeed, the expression of an exceptionally sensitive intellectual perception.

But Santayana cannot claim *The Life of Reason* as entirely his own, since most of its contents are gathered from his native country Spain and the ancient Greeks. His eclecticism in the field of ethics as in other spheres cannot be denied.

The Life of Reason exhibits the human scene against the background of an encompassing Nature. In this book Santayana takes for his ultimate goal a steady and integrated vision of man and nature. His thought for such a goal carries a clear mark of Spanish heritage. The Spanish philosophers, being led by a sense of actuality, are serious about man and nature rather than about the infinite and the abstract. The genius of Spain, says Madariaga, is "homocentric" and "considers man as a whole" (1923: 24). And the genius of Spain, Santayana inherits as a born Spaniard, and this permeates *The Life of Reason* with its subject matter of man and nature.

For Santayana, morality is life itself. His ethics is not puritanic. The puritan distinguishes between good and bad impulses and wants to lead an austere life by suppressing the bad ones. But Santayana gives an equal primacy to all impulses. They are all irrational and are inherently neither good nor bad. Again, unlike the puritan, Santayana considers all vital impulses to construct, out of them, the true ethical ideal which is called by him the Life of Reason. Thus, by taking morality as life itself and by cherishing the tendency to keep all the passions and impulses on an equal footing, he introduces himself as a true Spaniard. Again, as a true Spaniard, he makes an art of life, so that in his hands morality has never lost an aesthetic persuasiveness.

Thus we see that in his ethics the Spanish inheritances are much prominent. He himself has acknowledged the influences that Spain lays upon him. In "Apologia Pro Mente Sua" he avows:

> As to my native Spain, it has never crossed my mind to renounce my formal allegiance to it. ... – Schilpp 1940: 602

In moral philosophy, Santayana also harks back to the ancient Greeks. The naturalistic basis of his morality is mainly Hellenic. Democritus and Heraclitus supply this basis. Nature is conceived as a mechanism and as a flux. Democritean atomism describes "the practical and efficacious structure of the world". "We owe to Democritus this ideal of practical intelligibility" (1905, I: 24). On the other hand, Heraclitus, "the honest prophet of immediacy", finds the immediate in constant change.

> ... with the flux observed and mechanism conceived to explain it, the theory of existence is complete. – Ibid.

If the materialistic foundation is supplied by Democritus and Heraclitus, the course of rational life which constitutes the theme of *The Life of Reason* is marked out by Plato and Aristotle. *The Life of Reason* shows two trends:

1. an idealism in its highest reaches tempered by the emotional and the aesthetic, and
2. a systematic treatment of rational activities.

The former is Platonic, while the latter is Aristotelian. Plato's attempt to reduce ethics to some rigid standards and Aristotle's notion of "final cause" are not accepted by Santayana. Santayana, in one fundamental respect, comes nearer to Aristotle than to Plato. As a work of imagination Plato's philosophy holds the first place, but he "outran at times the limits of the Hellenic and the rational" (ibid.: 26). In comparison to Plato, "Aristotle's has the decisive advantage of being the unalloyed expression of reason" (ibid.). "In Aristotle", Santayana thinks, "the conception of human nature is perfectly sound" (ibid.). He concludes that

The Life of Reason finds its classic explication in the philosophies of Plato and Aristotle.

Now, a reader may be prone to ask: Where does Santayana's originality lie if *The Life of Reason* is already made by the Greeks? His originality, first of all, lies in the attempt to reconstruct ethics in accordance with Greek principles. He is not merely zealous to accept the principles of the life of reason given by the Greeks. He wants "to restate old truths in new words" (ibid.: 27), to restate rational ethics in the light of modern history, since he is aware of the change of the facts of human life and human conscience. "We must dress in our own clothes" (ibid.). Santayana wants to ponder over recent history with a Greek mind. Here lies the uniqueness of his thought. Moreover, his instillation of individualism in *The Life of Reason* is modern Spanish rather than classical Greek.

11

Theory of Religion

I. Introduction: Nature and Supernature

GEORGE Santayana, in his *Reason in Religion* (1905, vol. III), has made a painstaking analysis of religion, based on the model of Christianity. This analysis represents a comprehensive attempt to discover the rational worth of religion in a natural world. Santayana obviously advocates the natural basis of religion as of philosophy in general. He, who professes to be a naturalist, considers the supernatural basis of religion as a myth, without any substantial reality. Santayana is a naturalist in religion, since according to him, religion concerns human life in its natural conditions and moral aims as against all supernatural determinations. Supernatural machinery, found in religion, should be symbolic of natural conditions and aims. Otherwise, such a machinery is of no value.

In his view of religion, Santayana seems to appear to us a "natural idealist". His "idealism" is a fundamental concern with the realm of imagination, with the ideal products of human vision. His "naturalism" is a sober recognition of the natural basis of those ideal fulfilments. Imaginative vision is neither inwardly speculative nor fanatically exclusive. It has, on the other hand, a central role to play in the Life of Reason.

Now, one may be disposed to ask whether Santayana banishes the notion of supernaturalism lock and barrel from the religious sphere. Let it be answered that instead of giving up the notion of supernaturalism, Santayana retains it as an extension of naturalism. There is, according to him, a connection between the realm of nature and that of supernature, so that the two together "compose the total reality with which human knowledge, morality and sentiment must reckon" (1931: 30). On this account supernaturalism is a completed naturalism. Thus, nature and supernature, according to Santayana, do not stand opposed to each other. There is no dualism between the two. On the other hand, there is a dynamic continuity of nature and supernature, taking account of facts and forces which lie "hidden from our near-sighted and imperfect science" (ibid.). The realm of supernature is not the conceptual realm of mathematics. The former realm is the extension of the natural into the unknown. The supernatural is the deeper or remoter part of nature.

> This almost tangible supernatural world is only the rest of nature, nature in her true depths and in her true infinity.
> – Ibid.: 32

So, Santayana's stand as a naturalist remains undaunted, since he accepts supernaturalism as a "completed naturalism". Fiction arises only when the supernatural is described in myths, and Santayana distrusts this fiction.

As a result, it is found that Santayana's standpoint in respect of religion is naturalistic. In our critical estimate of Santayana's religious doctrine in the following chapter we shall find what consequences follow from the religious standpoint adopted by him. Let us for the moment discuss Santayana's religious view.

II. Santayana's Religious Theory

A. RELIGION AS AN EMBODIMENT OF REASON

Santayana thinks that religion is the more direct and conscious pursuit of the Life of Reason than is art, science or society.

Religion, he declares, approaches rationality so far as its purpose is concerned. This leads him to consider religion as an embodiment of reason. Religion resembles reason in some respects:

1. Reason, as we know, has a moral function. It makes right eternally different from wrong. This rational function is adopted by religion also. Absolute moral decisions are made by it. The sanction and the transformation of ethics are largely due to it.
2. In another respect, religion is found to exercise the function of reason. A person may be inspired by the objects suggested by reason and by losing what is accidental in himself he may immortalize what is rational and human. By following the path of reason, one may be free from the tribulations of life. The possibility of freedom from the tribulations of life is also held out by religion. Religion seems to direct man towards something eternal. It seems to ensure peace and happiness by bringing an ultimate harmony within the soul and an ultimate harmony between the soul and every other thing the soul depends upon. Thus, both religion and reason coincide in the task of liberating man from his personal limitations.

Though religion is the embodiment of reason in the sense described above, some important points of difference between religion and reason should not escape our notice. First, we come to possess so many religions, but reason, the instrument of reflection, is not many but one. Second, religion has concreteness in the sense that it "consists of conscious ideas, hopes, enthusiasms, and objects of worship" (1905, III: 12). On the other hand, reason exists in us ideally as "a mere principle or potential order" (ibid.). The materials which we gather from experience are endowed with the perfect order which reason introduces into them. Reason imparts a form or an ideal constitution to experience.

We have seen after Santayana that religion is near to rationality in its purpose, but the former falls short of the latter in its accomplishments. Religion leaves room for certain myths or fictions which confuse intelligence so greatly that true happiness is never achieved. Santayana wants that religion should be rational. Rational religion, according to him, would preserve the fundamental religious attitudes and practices, such as prayer, mythology, piety, spirituality and charity; but it must detach them from the illusory objects around which they have spontaneously grown in clusters and link them to the real features of the world, disclosed by science and philosophical criticism.

B. IMAGINATIVE APPROACH OF RELIGION

That religion fails in its aim to attain the Life of Reason is due to the fact that its approach is imaginative. Religion imparts a poetic interpretation of life. Poetry arrogates to itself literal truth which it does not actually possess. A query may crop in our mind; why does religion adopt the course of imagination instead of that of understanding? The answer to this question is made clear from the distinction which Santayana has drawn between the faculties of understanding and imagination. Understanding is "a kind of wit with a practical use" (1900: 5). Ideas of understanding are those which prove serviceable in practice and can be verified by sense. On the other hand, verification in sense and serviceableness in practice do not apply to the sphere of fancy. The sphere of science, led by understanding, has a practical validity which is totally lacking in the sphere of imagination. Santayana treats both understanding and imagination as fictions, but while the former is an "applicable fiction", the latter is not so.

The religious minds feel the greatness of the problems of life and the necessity of a solution to all the questions that arise in connection with those problems. They seek deeper harmonies between the self and the world. What they aspire after cannot be provided by understanding which has "its basis in sense and its demand for verification" (1900: 6). Santayana declares that only the imagination will supply to religion and metaphysics

> those large ideas tinctured with passion, those supersensible forms shrouded in awe, in which alone a mind of great sweep and vitality can find its congenial objects. – Ibid.

The solution to all the problems of life, since it is furnished by fancy, remains ideal to us, admitting no verification in sense.

C. RELIGION AND POETRY

The imaginative approach of religion makes it akin to poetry where is also found a free play of imagination. But the value of imaginative exercise, says Santayana, is greater in religion than in poetry, since the former deals with sides of life which are in greater need of imaginative touch than those pleasant things which ordinary poetry deals with. Santayana writes:

> Poetry is called religion when it intervenes in life, and religion, when it merely supervenes upon life is seen to be nothing but poetry. – Ibid.: v

Both the poet and the religious man dwell on imagination. But the latter does, while the former does not, probe more deeply into sides of life. By taking an imaginative flight, religion communicates a symbolic representation of moral reality which has an important function in vitalizing the mind. But since this imaginative achievement is not literally true, it always remains a deception which can be harmful to the conscientious persons living in the world.

The imaginative exercise of religion, though deceptive, is not without value since it has necessity in a life which is smothered by so many tribulations. Religion may be conceived

> as having come to relieve situations which, but for its presence, would have been infinitely worse. In the thick of active life, or in the monotony of practical slavery, there is more need to stimulate fancy than to control it. – 1905, III: 15

Santayana's remarks about the relation of religion to poetry find their echo in Mill and Irwin Edman. To Mill

> religion and poetry address themselves ... to the same part of the human constitution: they both supply the same want, that of ideal conceptions grander and more beautiful than we see realized in the prose of human life. – 1874: 103

Irwin Edman, the editor of a recent collection of Santayana's writings, has been influenced much by Santayana's doctrines. Edman, like Santayana, believes that religion is poetry,

> a lyrical and dramatic symbolism by which the significance of life, the movement of nature, the aim and direction of human life are represented. –1929: 227-28

Religion, when it is called poetry, has an imaginative approach. Yet the two philosophers, Santayana and Edman, do not forget to mention its naturalistic basis.

> The nature that man thinks about he admits long before he has thought and in the intervals when he is not thinking. It is the nature in which acorns grow into oaks, boys into men, relations into communications. It is the nature in which the tongue utters speech and the body flowers into the entelechy of soul. It is the nature wherein bodily life comes to a glow of realization in consciousness, blossoms into dreams, ideals and purposes. – Kallen and Hook 1935: 147

The higher values are contingent upon nature, specially they are relative to human nature. This naturalistic faith dominates in the religious doctrines of both Santayana and Edman.

> Faith in the possibilities of experience intelligently to redirect itself, to find the materials for its ideals in nature consciously controlled, to make the objects of faith the objects of fulfilment and realization that creative and imaginative thinking may first discern out of the suggestions Nature itself generates – this is the temper of the only possible naturalistic faith. – Ibid.: 152

This naturalistic temper, Santayana would call, a religion of disillusion.

D. VALIDITY OF RELIGION

Santayana possesses a mind which is naturally antagonistic to accepting anything uncritically. This attitude of Santayana is, no doubt, commendable. He, with his searching mind, makes an honest attempt to determine the rational worth of religion, especially of its various elements. Of the elements or ingredients of religion, Santayana refers to superstition, mythology, prayer and sacrifice. We shall now come to see how our philosopher discovers the rational worth of these elements.

i. Superstition

Of the ingredients of religion, first comes superstition which Santayana takes to be "belief in the miraculous". In every superstition some notions or ideas stand united in a loose causal connection. It has a miraculous power to arouse fear in people's minds or to lead them to perform experimental actions.

Rational Element in Superstition: What Santayana specially maintains is that superstition contains a rational element within itself and thus makes its place in religion more abiding and certain. Immediate intelligibility underlies the meaning of rationality. A superstition is called rational since its ground is immediately intelligible. Santayana has cited an example which can be quoted here:

> Thus, if the water of Lourdes, bottled and sold by chemists, cured all diseases, there would be no miracle, but only a new scientific discovery. In such a case, we should no more know why we were cured than we now know why we were created. But if each believer in taking the water thinks the effect morally conditioned, if he interprets the result, should it be favourable, as an answer to his faith and prayers, then the cure becomes miraculous because it becomes intelligible and manifests the obedience of nature to the exigencies of spirit. – 1905, III: 22

Thus a superstition the ground of which is immediately intelligible is rational to that extent.

Superstition Does Not Mean "Disbelief in Law": There are persons who are of the opinion that superstition or belief in the miraculous means disbelief in mechanical law. But Santayana repudiates such a view. To him a mechanical law "is only a record of the customary but reasonless order of things" (ibid.: 21). In holding such a view he adopts the Humean standpoint. Like Hume, he says that the relation between two things is not causal but customary, so that "the appearance in part of any usual phenomenon makes us look for the rest of it" (ibid.: 18). Santayana continues that if there be any causal relation between two objects, we must find or understand the ground of such relation. But to our utter disappointment we "are absolutely without insight into the machinery of causation" (ibid.: 17). This leads us to infer that the customary order of things is "reasonless".

We have seen after Santayana what superstition means. It has a just ground for it, i.e. its ground is immediately intelligible. Now, it will be quite illogical to say that a superstition or a belief in the miraculous is disbelief in law. Superstition has a rational element in it, since we can find out a reason or ground which it is based upon, whereas a mechanical law is reasonless since it is a record of the customary order of things.

Error of Superstitious Minds: It is an error of a superstitious mind to think that everything in the natural world is morally conditioned or determined. Santayana takes it as a "rash confidence in the moral intelligibility of things" (1905, III: 22). He says that a thing is morally conditioned when a person considers it from the standpoint of his particular interests. But this does not mean that every natural object has its determination in the moral sphere. In the words of Santayana:

> For moral significance is relative to particular interests and to natures having a constitutional and definite bias and having

> consequently special preferences which it is chimerical to expect the rest of the world to be determined by. – Ibid.

Superstitious minds are "deep" and "penetrating" when they speak of a moral category. But such minds are "ignorant" and "narrow" when they bring the natural order under the moral.

> Superstitious minds are penetrating and narrow, deep and ignorant. They apply the higher categories before the lower … . – Ibid.

Explanation of the lower in terms of the higher reverses the scale of mechanical causation, which alone is scientific or it is inverted mechanism, as Bergson calls it. Such an inversion, says Santayana, is valueless, since the function of a higher category can work only being based upon the lower.

> Poetry anticipates science, on which it ought to follow, and imagination rushes in to intercept memory, on which it ought to feed. – 1905, III: 23

Superstitions in religion deceive us, because here we are governed by the said rule of inversion.

ii. Mythology

Mythology is a conspicuous aspect of religion. In mythology, Santayana carefully observes, an expression of a primitive habit of thought has been illustrated. The nature of primitive thought is poetical in form and prosaic in function. It is eager to know objects as they are and distinguishes the objects from the experience which reveals them. Though the primitive man has a tendency to observe nature, he has "no adequate power to analyse, remmèmber and abstract" (ibid.: 39). His observation of nature becomes coloured by his imagination, so that he cannot distinguish between what is efficacious and what is not so.

Santayana says that myths are not believed in, but they are conceived and understood. When we demand belief for an idea, we mean that the idea has scientific truth, i.e. it has a practical efficacy. But the myths lack scientific truth. They are the imaginative constructions out of the materials experienced by the senses. Or, in other words, they are the things observed through the coloured glass of fancy: they are the fancied visions of nature. We are, then, forced to conclude that illusions are incident to mythology. But the myths with their illusory character do not lead us to a dangerous end since illusions involved in them are not complete and can be corrected by further experience.

Santayana has distinguished mythical thinking from science. Both of them have their roots in reality: they are based upon experience of the objects. The main point of distinction between the two is that mythical thought cannot, while science can, serve the purposes of transitive thought or action. The former is "no vehicle for experience" (1905, III: 92), although it is rooted in experience. By standing firm upon experience it constructs imageries, it

> flowers want only into the air, transmuting into unexpected and richer forms the substances it sucks from the soil. – Ibid.

But a scientific hypothesis, unlike mythical thinking, involves a transit of experience from one end to another. It, being based upon perceptions, points to further perceptions of the same kind.

> Science is a bridge touching experience at both ends, over which practical thought may travel from act to act, from perception to perception. – Ibid.

Moral Suggestion of Mythology: One salient feature in mythology, we have noted, is the poetic or imaginative conception of things. A myth being an imaginative expression of things does not set them

> before us in the very terms they will wear when they are gradually revealed to experience. – Ibid.: 42

But Santayana observes that a myth is not building castles in the air; its sterling quality lies in displaying some important function in human life. It moralizes men by presenting an ideal standard for action. Its religious value lies precisely in such function.

We have seen after Santayana that experience of objects is at the root of the construction of a myth. The mythology of Vedic India is poetic naturalism, or the imaginative observation of things of nature. If we be inspired by the fact how a myth comes to be constructed, we are sure to be scientific, i.e. our hypotheses about phenomena will tend to be expressed more and more in terms of the phenomena themselves. Santayana here makes an aim that we should be inspired by the inner suggestions (which are moral) expressed by the myths. On its inner side, a myth makes us acquainted with "an ideal standard for action and a perfect object for contemplation" (1905, III: 49).

iii. Sacrifice

Sacrifice and prayer are the religious acts by which men seek harmonious relations with the gods, culminating in fellowship, self-denial and service. Santayana says that the beginnings of these two acts go back to primitive religion. In dealing with them he alludes to the historical development of religion.

Early religion springs from fear. Whenever the primitive man finds the tendency of life checked or disturbed by some external power, he attributes divinity to it and, out of fear, pays tribute to it in order to propitiate it. Thus, Santayana shows that worship or cult, not fable or myth, lies nearer to the roots of religion.

> The work of expression, the creation of a fabulous environment to derive experience from, is not, however, the first or most pressing operation employing the religious mind. Its first business is rather the work of propitiation; before we stop to contemplate the deity we hasten to appease it, to welcome it, or to get out of its way. – Ibid.: 27

So, Santayana regards propitiation as the most earliest form of sacrifice. D. Miall Edwards also says:

> In view of the prominence of fear in primitive religion, we ought perhaps to regard propitiation as the most primitive form of sacrifice … .
> – 1929: 119

It is true that all philosophers do not accept propitiation as the primitive form of sacrifice. As for example, Robertson Smith believes that the primitive form of religion consists in the craving for participation or communion with a deity. In this he has been followed by Otto Pfleiderer. But the theory is not backed by much evidence.

Santayana also speaks of an attitude expressed in the sacrificial rite, viz. the attitude of gratitude or thanksgiving to the gods for favours received. The deity to whom sacrifice is offered proves a kind and responsive being. In offering to him

> a few sheaves of corn, some barley-cakes, or a libation from the vintage, the public is grateful rather than calculating.
> – 1905, III: 30

Santayana lays stress on the fact that the higher development of the sacrificial idea is not to be found in the attitude of thanksgiving. Sacrifiice which is demanded by a god from us means renunciation of "the foolish and inordinate part of our wills" (ibid.). And the god which demands such a kind of sacrifice is our own ideal,

> the goal that determines for us how we should proceed in order to realize as far as possible our inmost aspirations.
> – Ibid.: 31

By giving up the inordinate part of our nature, we come to see ourselves morally improved. But sacrifice as a rite does not contain ideas exclusively moral. The purification which results from the sacrifice is, so to speak, "an emotional catharsis rather than a moral improvement" (ibid.). Like Santayana, the cry of the Hebrew prophets is also for the purification of the mind and will, for "a clean heart and a right spirit within".

iv. Prayer

Along with sacrifice naturally goes prayer to God. Prayer in some form or other is as universal as religion. Santayana says that "prayer expresses need" (ibid.). Prayer is the instinctive cry of the human soul to a power that can help it in its time of need. In primitive religion prayer is not distinguished from the magical spell. There prayer, like magic, is expected to do work. Thus, primitive religion assigns material efficacy to prayer.

But Santayana observes very truly that the essence of prayer is misunderstood if it be given material efficacy. He speaks of the rational side of prayer. Though prayer springs from a pressing need, it is directed towards "ideality, poetry, in the sense in which poetry includes all imaginative moral life" (1905, III: 34). Here, prayer involves a transit from the pre-rational to the rational, from a particular need to the general need of the spirit and of mankind.

Now, the question is: How is this transition possible? Santayana answers this. Since prayer expresses need, it will naturally dwell on what would satisfy that need. Now, the object most wanted is often particular. But any particular good is not detached from the field of relations, and so when we dwell on a particular good, we naturally come upon others which are related to it.

> An earnest consideration, therefore, of anything desired is apt to enlarge and generalize aspiration till it embraces an ideal life; ... Prayer, inspired by a pressing need, already relieves its importunity by merging it in the general need of the spirit and of mankind.
>
> – Ibid.

We may long for a particular good and that good may be realized also. But the comprehensive ideal which is prayed for is hardly realized. The rain wished for may fall but the kingdom of heaven does not come. Hence, Santayana says that what is regarded as possible in prayer is a denial. But though prayer accomplishes nothing material, it constitutes something spiritual. Prayer may not bring the kingdom of heaven but "it may cultivate hope and resignation and may prepare the heart for any issue ... " (ibid.: 36).

E. THE MAJOR RELIGIONS

In estimating the validity of religion, Santayana considers also the major traditions of religion. First comes within his purview the Hebrew religion.

i. The Hebrew Religion

Santayana points out that the Hebrew religion is to be credited for its wholesome emphasis upon morals. The great prophets are Israel's abiding glory. They themselves loved virtue and hence declared that the favour of heaven could be won by following the path of virtue. They believed virtue to be the only path to happiness. Moreover, they realized that social or public events depend on men's character and conduct, not on omens or sacrifices. Thus, we see that they had a sense for both moral and political philosophy and they gave a moral value to religion.

Though the Hebrew religion gets high marks for its great emphasis upon morals, according to Santayana, it suffers from a grave defect. It is censured for its dogmatic and intolerant spirit. The Jews did not tolerate the equal prerogative of other nations' laws and deities. Such intolerance is not due to their critical insight. Out of "pure bigotry, conceit, and stupidity" (1905, III: 58) they thought their God Jehovah as their only God and did not want other nations also to have a god. It may be pointed out in this connection that the Jews did not believe in a metaphysical absolute, but only in a personal god eternally acting and continuously interested in his creatures, specially bound up with their own history.

ii. The Christian Religion

a. Catholicism or Pagan Christianity: Hebraism takes the name of Christianity when it is blended with Greek thought and pagan habits. By the infusion of Greek thought Christianity becomes at once speculative, universal and ideal. The Greek thought finds its expression in the Christian doctrine of incarnation. While for the Greek thinkers God is the "Idea of the Good", the Nous or Logos, the divine Intelligence, incarnate as they always believe in the whole world and yet truly the essence of divinity, for the Jews and the Christians, God is a supreme person who reveals His Will to His lawgivers and prophets. Christians believe in addition that God took the form of man and led a human life on earth. Santayana says here that the incarnation of God in man and the divinization of man in God are pagan conceptions. If these expressions of pagan religious philosophy were excluded from Christianity, the latter would have lost its spiritual aspiration.

It is an improvement in Christianity as a religion that it is mixed with pagan philosophy and ritual. The Christianity of the gospels is itself post-rational. It, with its historical outlook, admits a non-natural future for the individual. Paganism has a genius, i.e. the faculty of expressing spiritual experience in myth and external symbol. Now, when Christianity comes to be united with paganism, the expression of spiritualism is reinforced. This Pagan Christianity is called Catholicism. Catholicism gives genial interpretations of life, aims to pass beyond visible nature and comes to believe in a realm of spirit.

b. Barbarised Christianity: The influence of Christianity is found to spread over the barbarians of the North who threatened the Roman empire. The Northmen accept Christianity, not because their religious needs are represented by it, but because it forms part of a culture and a social organization the influence of which they cannot resist. Though they have been converted, their conversion was only skin-deep.

> A non-Christian ethics of valour and honour, a non-Christian fund of superstition, legend and sentiment, subsisted always among mediaeval peoples. – Santayana 1905, III: 79

As a result, Catholicism fails to eradicate from the barbarian souls anything opposed to it which subsists there.

Opposition to the church comes from those northern barbarians whose religious natures are not satisfied by the Catholic doctrine. From their religious restlessness come forth Gothic art, chivalrous sentiment and even scholastic philosophy which Christianity regards, out of its own folly, as its own emanations. The barbarians are only indoctrinated, they are only introduced into an alien spiritual medium, but they are not inwardly tamed. Their "inward rebellion against something greater and overshadowing, yet repulsive and alien" (Santayana 1905, III: 82) becomes expressed in the form of Protestantism, when they come into direct contact with Christianity.

c. Protestantism or the Teutonic Religion: Apparently, Protestantism is a form of Christianity, since it also retains the Bible. But inwardly, the Protestant religion is independent of Roman Catholicism. It is simply the natural religion of the Teutons. The Teutonic religion is anterior to Christianity and can survive it. The former opposes to the Gospel upon which Christianity is based. The Gospel speaks of a supernatural realm, regards earthly ties as a burden and takes contemplation and solitude as the only resort of spiritual freedom and peace. But the Teutonic religion is the exact opposite of what the Gospel says. To such a religion, contemplation is nothing but idleness and solitude and selfishness. What are to be credited to religion, according to it, are success and prosperity, married and industrious life, profitable enterprise and practical ambition.

Thus, Protestantism is materialistic and aims at raising men to a conventional well-being. We find two characteristics expressed in the Protestant religion, viz. (i) "confidence in one's own impulse and destiny, a confidence which the world in the end sure to reward", and (ii) "abomination of all contrary religious tenets and practices" (ibid.: 87), of asceticism, of idolatry and myth, and finally of traditions and institutional authority. Protestantism speaks of the inner cooperation of man with the world and speaks of success which results from laborious activity.

> The point is to accomplish something, no matter particularly what; so that Protestants show on this ground some respect even for an artist when he has once achieved success.
> – Santayana 1905, III: 88

Thus, Protestantism

> misses the inner appeal of Christian charity which … begins by renunciation and looks to spiritual freedom and peace.
> – Ibid.: 84

In this sense, it is "the religion of inexperience" (ibid.: 88). It errs when it considers the will omnipotent, since the will will never face failure and disappointment. Such a religion again does not distinguish the field of inevitable failure from that of possible success.

F. PHASES OF RELIGION

In Section IIA of this chapter we have said that, according to Santayana, religion should be rational. He says that religion will be rational, when it will attach itself, through different attitudes and practices, to the real features of the world, disclosed by science and philosophical criticism. True religion should always be human. Rational religion has two phases: (i) piety or loyalty to necessary conditions, and (ii) spirituality, or devotion to ideal ends. Mysticism is yet another phase of religion which Santayana dislikes, but cannot ignore.

i. Piety

Piety, says Santayana, means reverent attachment to the sources of man's being. It is a sentiment of gratitude directed towards those conditions on which life and its interests really depend. Such conditions are parents, family, ancestors, country, humanity at large and the whole natural cosmos. The sentiment of dutifulness towards these forces would be moral if it be accompanied by the clear knowledge of their nature and relation to ourselves.

Piety is an "irrational suasion", because it involves a natural obligation to be loyal to those necessary conditions on which our life is based. Due to such natural obligation, an emotional peace is attained. Though piety is an irrational persuasion, our attachment or allegiance has a rational justification. Santayana observes:

> ... considering the animal basis of human life, an attachment resting on that circumstance is a necessary and rational attachment. –1905, III: 129

Piety thus involves a physical bond. But it should not disturb the intellect in its proper function. We should not, under guise of tenderness, attribute to our father or child greater stature or cleverness or goodness than he actually possesses. It is a defect instead of being a part of true loyalty.

We have already explained that Santayana supports or rather accepts the natural basis of religion. If that be so, what should be, according to him, the object of piety? It is obvious that the gods cannot be the object of piety, for they are supernatural and Santayana discards the supernatural basis of religion. Some are of opinion that mankind is the object of piety. But Santayana does not accept the religion of humanity. He says:

> But this religion of humanity is rather a desideratum than a fact: humanity does not actually appear to anybody in a religious light. – Ibid.: 131

Santayana's adverse view of the religion of humanity reminds us of Auguste Comte for whom religion consists in piety to humanity.

a. Santayana and Comte: The attitude of both Santayana and Comte is more or less the same, i.e. both agree in denying the supernatural basis of religion. In this sense, the theory of positivism is characteristic of the philosophies of both. In Comte's opinion, in the scientific age of ours, we cannot believe in the existence of anything which is supersensible. Hence, God of traditional religion, being essentially a supersensuous reality, cannot be believed to be real in this age. But the necessity of religion cannot be denied, since religion embraces the whole of existence. And when religion exists, there must be something which is to be worshipped. As it has been seen before, God cannot be the object of worship. Neither can a single human being be worshipped. Can humanity at large which is a synthesis of all human beings be the object of worship? But actual humanity cannot be adored. By abstracting the defects which lie in it, we can reach the conception of Ideal Humanity and worship it. This is, in short, Comte's view of religion.

But Santayana, starting from the same point as Comte does, does not, like the latter, reach the same conclusion. Santayana, with his penetrating outlook, finds that humanity which, according to Comte, is the representation of specific human virtues, cannot be the object of worship. Virtues, like patience and courage, says Santayana, are necessary to existence. Moreover, Santayana says that if we worship humanity, we shall be deprived of that which makes us akin to the divine – our aspiration: "Man is not adorable, but adores" (1905, III: 132). Santayana continues that this object of adoration is to be found within ourselves. He says:

> In this sense the religion of humanity is the only religion, all others being sparks and abstracts of the same. – Ibid.

b. Cosmic Piety: But while Santayana speaks of an indwelling ideal, does he not come closer to the Indian view of religion? He, most convincingly, says that spirituality constitutes the aspiring side of religion. We shall come to it shortly. Meanwhile, let us hold the thread of our previous discussion. Santayana wants to see religion standing on a natural ground. And in this respect the sort of piety he advocates is the cosmic piety which he also calls the philosophic piety. The object of such piety is the universe. He says:

> Why should we not look on the universe with piety? Is it not our substance? Are we made of other clay? All our possibilities lie from eternity hidden in its bosom. –1905, III: 133

We should grow within ourselves the sentiment of gratitude towards the universe, the maker of us. In it there is room for every hope and aspiration. And when it is "the source of all our energies, the home of all our happiness" (ibid.), why should we not attach ourselves to it and commend it? Santayana further asks,

> [as] we should abstain from judging a father's errors or a mother's foibles, why should we pronounce sentence on the ignorant crimes of the universe, which have passed into our own blood? – Ibid.

Thus, he looks upon the universe with true veneration.

c. Santayana and William Wordsworth: Santayana's "cosmic piety" bears resemblance to the "natural piety" of Wordsworth. Piety is a term frequently found in Wordsworth's writings and it expresses his own religious attitude. Both Santayana and Wordsworth have recognized that man is intimately bound up with nature. Both have insisted upon the feeling of gratitude, the touchstone of all true religion. This feeling of gratitude is a living sense of benefits received and is so far a feeling of dependence.

The similarity that is shown to be existing between Santayana and Wordsworth is apparent. Actually we find that they differ among themselves in respect of their doctrines of piety. To Santayana cosmic piety means the feeling of gratitude towards Nature, because it is the maker of us and because upon it depends all our fate. Thus, cosmic piety, according to Santayana, is nothing but the sentiment of gratitude shown to Nature. But Wordsworth's natural piety is a complex term which involves three phases or aspects and at the last phase comes the sense of gratitude. In order to comprehend Wordsworth's natural piety we shall have to understand the three phases involved by it. The first phase is the passive stage in which we are advised to be receptive, to reap "the harvest of a quiet eye that broods and sleeps in his own heart". Thus, in the first stage our attitude to Nature is one of receptiveness, of humility and passivity. The second phase is complementary to the first stage. The mind of man is akin to the spirit of nature. The poet Wordsworth:

> Considers Man and Nature as essentially adapted to each other and the mind of Man as naturally the mirror of the fairest and most interesting properties of Nature."[1]

This union of the human mind with nature is the source of purest joy, which is also religion.

But there is the last stage of spiritual love, where the mind by its creative imagination penetrates in love and holy passion to the outstanding thought of God the Eternal. In the last phase we find a remarkable change in the poet's mind. In him the change is from the poet advocating the simple joy and freedom of Nature to the sage defending abstract and conventional truths. His attitude is demonstrated in the following lines from the conclusion of *The Prelude*:

> *... but, the dawn beginning now*
> *To re-appear, 'twas proved that not in vain*
> *I had been taught to reverence a Power*
> *That is the visible quality and shape*
> *And image of right reason; that matures*
> *Her processes by steadfast laws; gives birth*
> *To no impatient or fallacious hopes,*
> *No heat of passion or excessive zeal,*
> *No vain conceits; provokes to no quick turns*
> *Of self-applauding intellect; but trains*
> *To meekness, and exalts by humble faith.*

---

[1] Preface to the second edition of the *Lyrical Ballads*.

Thus, in the last phase of natural piety, we see how the poet enters from the religion of Nature to that of Scriptures. But we should not be led to think that the poet severs the religion of Nature from the religion of Scriptures, since he takes the one as an endorsement of the other. Each of them finds its expression in joy, peace and love, which overflow in the feeling of gratitude, in the living sense of benefits received.

The above discussion of Wordsworth's natural piety facilitates its comparison with Santayana's conception of piety. We see after Wordsworth that gratitude is shown not to Nature, but to a Power, the "image of right reason" or God, whereas Santayana holds the opposite view. The latter says that gratitude is to be shown to irrational Nature, the maker of us. Moreover, Wordsworth speaks of the union or the adaptation between man and nature, which results in the purest, divine joy. But from Santayana we do not get a promise of such union between man and nature. Thus, we see how Wordsworth's natural piety differs from Santayana's cosmic piety.

ii. Spirituality

As piety is retrospective, spirituality is prospective. The former looks back to the sources of life, while the latter looks forward to the end towards which we move. Spirituality, which constitutes the aspiring side of religion, cannot be possible without the previous existence of piety. While we discuss the spiritual phase of religion, the following questions need to be answered:

1. What is meant by spirituality?
2. Why should we aspire after the Ideals when we show our loyalty to the universe?

We shall begin our discussion with an attempt to answer the second question.

a. Normal Madness: At one extreme of rational religion lies piety, at its other extreme spirituality. Now, how is the transit from the reverent attachment to the universe to the contemplation of Ideals possible? Or, to put it in another form, how is the transition from natural basis to ideal contemplation possible? The answer is to be found in the concept of "normal madness" which Santayana has used in his *Dialogues in Limbo* (1925) and in also other books. The concept of normal madness is not properly interpreted by many of the readers of Santayana. It is a natural thought to us that madness is folly and that normal madness is the folly which occurs at any time in the world. It is also conceived by us that the opposite of madness is sanity. But this conception is erroneous since sanity is also a form of madness which is shared by all persons living in the world. Now, what, according to Santayana is madness? And what is the antithesis to madness? Santayana calls all life madness and the antithesis to madness, says he, is death. But in what sense is all life called madness? Santayana calls all life madness, because, judged in comparison with substance or matter, it is impotent and ineffectual. Matter or substance has omnisicient power. Our ineffectiveness is proved by the fact that we cannot create matter. Nature has its vast range of which only a portion is known by us. Science, which has made a great advancement in the present age, is only exploring nature instead of creating it.

As we know, Santayana gives supreme importance to matter which breeds everything. Substance is what produces human sensations, emotions and ideas. It is what supports life or consciousness. Though all life or consciousness, sensations, emotions and ideas come from unknown matter or substance, they make no difference to the course of nature. If they at all disappear from the world, substance would move on its inevitable course without direction from our conscious aims. Thus, Santayana speaks of the efficacy and potency of matter. And what it effects are only decorations of it. These are shadowy experiences for a time. These are called normal madness, since, judged in comparison with matter, they are ineffective and impotent.

Normal madness, Santayana holds, assumes different forms of which three are mentioned in his *Dialogues in Limbo:*

> images in sense, love in youth and religion among the nations. – 1925: 46

Images, love and religion are decorations upon the structural forces of nature. Since these are experiences, ineffective, shadowy and, therefore, illusory, all knowledge about them comes to futility and emptiness.

If, in the face of the efficacious substance, all knowledge is pathos, then what ought we to do? One answer which we can give to it is that we ought to do just as we do, since we can do nothing else. But there is another answer, the answer given by Santayana. He says that we may transfer our hopes and our ideals, at least in imagination, from the realm of matter to the realm of spirit. By this transfer we may at least make them into essences which it is a joy to contemplate. Though they are inevitably futile in guiding affairs and prove their inefficacy and momentariness when they are compared to substance, they remain, however, uncorrupted, real and beautiful in contemplation.

We have so far answered our first question: How do we pass from natural basis to ideal development? Our next question is: What is spirituality which constitutes the aspiring side of religion? What is it that we contemplate ideally?

By spirituality Santayana means life in the ideal. In his *Reason in Religion* he says:

> A man is spiritual when he lives in the presence of the ideal and whether he eat or drink does so for the sake of a true and ultimate good. He is spiritual when he envisages his goal so frankly that his whole material life becomes a transparent and transitive vehicle, an instrument which scarcely arrests attention but allows the spirit to use it economically and with perfect detachment and freedom. –1905, III: 135

In his "Apologia", written in 1940, Santayana writes:

> There would be no spirituality, though there would have to be spirit, in enjoying the food and drink on the table. Spirituality would appear if we began to enjoy these things disinterestedly and impersonally, in view of the ultimate good that might flow from their substance and their appearance; in other words, if we enjoyed them convivially, pictorially, intellectually.
>
> – Schilpp 1940: 566-67

From these two quotations, one taken from his writings in early life and the other taken from those in his later life, it is clear that by spirituality Santayana means unworldliness, but this unworldliness follows from the true knowledge of the world. In the latter quotation we notice another thing. He contrasts piety, or reverence for the sources of life, with spirituality, or sense for what he calls Ideals. When he speaks of grace at table, he regards the available goods piously; but when these goods are enjoyed "convivially, pictorially, intellectually", these are regarded spiritually or as ideals.

b. Ideals: Now, what does Santayana understand specifically by ideals?

In *Interpretations of Poetry and Religion* (1900) Santayana has freely referred to "ideals", and has insisted that Platonic Ideas and dogmas of religion are ideal only. Ideals belong to poetry and religion, not to material facts. They are called ideal both positively and negatively. They are ideal negatively in being negative and in that sense unreal. And they are ideal positively in being better than the reality and expressing demands made by human nature but not fulfilled by nature at large. Since ideals perfectly correspond to the demands of human nature, they are more interesting than other facts.

The Ideals, says Santayana, are not means but ends. But they are not ends in the sense of forming the final state of an object, as for example, a finished poem. They are ends in the sense of being the good of that finished work. This means, when a finished poem is best understood at some supreme moment, the vision and emotion that awaken in the mind are called ideals. Thus, this moral ideality is relative to appreciation.

Santayana says that all ideals are essences, but all essences do not exist as ideals from the first. What is at first given is only an essence. It may be presented repeatedly and we may see it with indifference. But when we become interested in it more and more, then that essence appears to us in a new setting, i.e. in a form of beauty. Only then that essence will be called ideal. To quote from Santayana:

> The essence given was at first graphic only: later it was re-exemplified in a form of beauty, containing the original essence but suffusing it with a new magic: it had become an ideal.
> – Schilpp 1940: 568

The corollary that follows from the above discussion is that spirituality, according to Santayana, is life in the ideal, a contemplative state in which essences appear to the spirit in a form of beauty. This state of contemplation is the suspension of busy life and can be compared to "the equilibrium of a divine repose". In this aspect Santayana and the Indians perfectly agree. But the point in which they disagree is that while the Indians, not being merely content in asserting the contemplative state or final peace as an ideal, long also to be merged in primal substance and identify the ideal with this longing, Santayana, on the other hand, does not accept this Indian viewpoint. He says that the spirit cannot long to be merged in primaeval substance which is an unlimited potentiality. The spirit cannot long to be so, since it, being a psychic faculty, has a specific range and as such cannot dare to embrace an unlimited potentiality. Moreover, potentiality is a "blind commitment" and it cannot be identified with the ideal which is an essence appreciated and enjoyed.

We see, then, after Santayana, that spirituality is the quality of spiritual life and forms the summit of such a life. Since to him life is always acceptable, he prefers spiritual life. Here, it may be asked whether Santayana would call the spiritual life the life of reason. The answer is in the negative. According to him, rationality and spirituality are the two concomitant dimensions of life, one lateral and the other vertical. The life of reason is the life of action. It consists in the rational constitution, i.e. in the proper harmonization of all phases and interests of life. The thoughts of the rational man are absorbed in instrumentalities, in business or politics or war. Such experience of his is not spiritual. But the same actions may be food for a spiritual life if they are enjoyed disinterestedly and impersonally. The spiritual life means the life of "disintoxication clarifying those passions which the life of reason endeavours to harmonize" (Schilpp 1940: 26). To quote the words from a letter of Santayana written to Justus Buchler of Columbia University on 1 July 1936:

> The vertical or spiritual dimension is what inward religion has always added to life in the world, or in the cloister, which is a part of the world: that element may be more or less emphatic or genuine, according to a man's temperament or experience, but it is always an element, optional, private, like the love of music or like love at large.[2]

iii. Mysticism

Santayana takes mysticism as the most primitive of feelings. The mystical feeling arises in consciousness, though it remains unexpressed and mute, "when instinct guides without kindling any prophetic idea to which action may be inwardly referred" (1905, III: 189). The mind rises to a mystical state when its intelligence is exceeded by its will and emotions. According to Santayana, the mystical state of consciousness is non-intellectual in character. On this point, he differs from William James. James, in his famous book *The Varieties of Religious Experience*, has stated different marks of the mystical states of consciousness. He also

2 *The Journal of Philosophy*, 21 January 1954, p. 56.

says that by these marks the mystical states of consciousness can be distinguished from non-mystical states of consciousness. Like Santayana, James also maintains that mystical states of consciousness are what defy expression. But unlike the former, the latter holds that they are

> illuminations, revelations, full of significance and importance, all inarticulate though they remain .... –James 1902: 380-81

Although they are unplumbed by the discursive intellect, they are not, for that reason, non-intellectual, because they are also states of knowledge.

Mysticism, says Santayana, appears incidentally in religion, science and art. But it should not be regarded as the basis of anything. It is not in the least superhuman. It is "an exaggeration of a rational interest in the highest abstractions" (1900: 18). The mystic's interest lies in such abstractions as the divine, the universal, the absolute, even the one. Such abstractions are

> terms of human thought having as such a meaning in language and a place in speculation. – Ibid.

The mystic feels ecstasy in these abstractions. And his state of consciousness follows the disappearance of intellect and remains ineffable.

Santayana is so discontent with the term "mysticism" that he regards it as a "possible overtone of religion" (1905, III: 188). But that he himself is a mystic will be shown in our critical review of his religious theory.

12

A Critique of Santayana's Religious Theory

IT IS only logical that Santayana's religious view is naturalistic, for naturalism forms the basis of his whole philosophy. The source of human life with all its faculties is the universe, and religion as an important feature of human life must, therefore, be naturalistic. For example, naturalism forms the basis of his discussion of cosmic piety in his *Reason in Religion* (1905).

I. God or the External World

According to Santayana, all religions are a work of human imagination. Behind such a view his naturalistic temper works. He believes that matter or substance alone is potent or efficacious and that all other experiences, as compared to matter, are ineffective. But here ineffectiveness is not his last word. We may have recourse to imagination in which we transfer our hopes and ideals from the realm of matter to that of spirit and by such transfer we make them into essences which it is a joy to contemplate. We find here a good reason as to why, according to Santayana, the works of imagination alone are good.

Is there any place for God in Santayana's naturalistic religion? In his mind the ideas of God and the external world are interchangeable. If these ideas are laid bare of pictorial and emotional associations in human experience, we are left with the core of both ideas, viz. the conviction of a primordial power or "efficacious reality". The ideas of God and the external world are interchangeable insofar as they both refer to the same "efficacious reality".

Santayana contends that we cannot have any insight into the nature of causal operations. But what we cannot at all ignore is the conviction that there is a primordial power or efficacious reality which interrupts as well as sustains the order of experience. It may be said that the order of experience is influenced by the idea, or rational construction, of the external world. But we must concede that our notion of a material thing is a logical construction and that this construction is in no sense a "duplicate" of a "thing" in the external world. The primordial power by which our lives are sustained connot be taken as the idea, or rational construction, of the external world. What Santayana finally says is that matter is the only reality with an efficacious character, and such efficacious reality intrudes upon and controls the field of experience.

That matter is efficacious or potent is not disputed. What, however, is disputed is a clear understanding of how the field of experience is controlled by the blind movement of matter. To influence the order of experience what is essential is the presence of consciousness. But, Santayana denies consciousness as the origin or ground of the order of experience, since consciousness itself, says he, springs from potent matter. Now, if consciousness or mind originates from and is guided by matter, its function consists only in expressing the movement of irrational matter and it is by no means possible for it to influence the order of experience.

II. Place of Revelation in Santayana

As we see, what occupies Santayana's thought most is his conception of matter as the efficacious reality. Naturally, the fact of revelation is not viewed by him from a lofty standpoint. As we have already pointed out in course of expounding his religious theory, religion, according to him, should be rational. And it can be rational when it, by denuding itself of all illusory objects, attempts to know the real features of the external world, disclosed by science and philosophical criticism. Here, rational religion is reduced to the scientific level and in that case the distinction between the two remains indistinct and blurred.

In religious doctrines we sometimes find the use of the word "revelation" made in the widest sense. In the widest sense of the word, the order of nature is a revelation, because it unfolds a meaning which has its ultimate source in God. Now, this sense of the word revelation can be applicable to Santayana's theory if the word God be taken as potent matter, and we can think of God as matter, since, on Santayana's theory, the ideas of God and matter are interchangeable insofar as they refer to the same efficacious reality. But still a difficulty lurks here. The "meaning" that is unfolded by the order of nature cannot be accounted for by the blind movement of irrational matter.

The possibility of revelation is generally admitted by those who accept the theistic conception of the universe. But Santayana is an atheist. If by "revelation" is meant disclosure of something by supernatural means, in Santayana's theory we find an instance of "revealed" knowledge. We have noticed after Santayana (p. 260) how the spirit, being based on imagination, apprehends ideals intuitively. We have already referred to (pp. 261-62) what he means by "ideals". When essences appear to the spirit in a form of beauty, then they are called "ideals". Essences are disclosed to the spirit through supernatural means, i.e. through intuition. Such disclosure may be called, then, revelation.

In one place of his *Reason in Religion* Santayana says:

> The very disappearance of intellect may be taken for a revelation.
> –1905, III: 189

Here he wants to mean that revelation does not come through intellect, which is an instrument for having empirical knowledge of the world. From his statement it also follows that revealed knowledge is possible only through a means other than intellect. Then in the case of revealed knowledge he gives a latent reference to supernatural means which he calls intuition. And what are revealed through intuition are "ideals", devoid of existence and of anything found in the natural world. Thus, Santayana accepts the possibility of knowledge of the supernatural. And the admission of such knowledge means the denial of his previous assertion of the existence of the natural only.

What appears to us as revealed knowledge from Santayana's theory may not do so after a close scrutiny. Intuition, as Santayana, says is not supernatural but natural. Its organ is the psyche which is material (vide Chapter 3, pp. 60-61). Now, if such is the character of intuition, it is not understood how it is possible for it to know essences which constitute a separate realm other than the realm of matter (vide Chapter 3, p. 65). Intuition, being itself material in its origin, cannot serve as the faculty of knowing the realm of essence.

III. Is Matter the Only Existent Reality?

The potent matter, says Santayana, is the only existential reality, and consciousness is the by-product of matter. The Indian materialists also, commonly known as the Cārvākas, hold a similar view. But should we really call matter as the only existent and potent reality? And should we say that consciousness is an epiphenomenon? Here we should seek answers from a study of four kinds of experience which cover the whole reality. If these experiences reveal matter as the only existential reality, then what Santayana believes can be taken as true.

The first kind of experience is the waking experience in which the knower and the known, the subject and the material object, stand in an intimate relation. In such experience both consciousness and matter are present independently. The second kind of experience is the dreaming state in which the external objects are not physically related to the mind or consciousness. As dream-objects are dependent upon a person's experience acquired in his waking life, they do not, therefore, maintain an independent status like the objects in the external world. In the dreaming state what seems to be independently real is the knowing mind or consciousness. But at the same time we should not say that dream-objects are unreal. What are called unreal cannot have appearances, as for example, the son of a barren woman or a winged horse. But dream-objects appear in consciousness and hence unreality cannot be attributed to them.

In the third kind of experience which is a state of dreamless sleep what shines only is consciousness or knowledge. In such state the object of knowledge is not so manifest. After dreaming a dreamless sleep a man says, "Last night I enjoyed a good sleep, devoid of dreams". Such experience is a state of contentless knowledge which is also a state of pure joy. In such experience what alone remains as a shining star is consciousness only. This state of experience proves that consciousness can remain without objects. Such consciousness is also of the nature of bliss (*ānanda*). The nature of consciousness which is apprehended in dreamless sleep is fully manifested in meditation which is a fourth and last kind of experience.

Thus, in all kinds of experience, what invariably exists is not matter, but consciousness. Practically speaking, without consciousness no knowledge or experience is possible. And it is also noticed from our brief study that experience is possible when no objects exist. Consciousness which is existent, or existence-consciousness is the only truth which is to be found in any religion worth the name. Existence-consciousness is the primal being which cannot be the by-product of anything. It is called the Supreme Reality or, as the Advaitins in India say, *Brahman*.

IV. Santayana's View of Immortality

For Santayana, mind is dependent upon body and psychical process is always associated with neural process. If that be so, then on the advent of death as a physiological fact all signs of psychical activity cease and the hope of a survival after death is excluded. Thus, Santayana has abandoned the idea of "existential immortality". But a little before it has been observed by us that consciousness or self is the only existential reality which is different from matter and cannot be the by-product of the latter. Death is a fact in the material world, and consciousness, being itself not material, cannot cease on the advent of death. So, existential immortality of consciousness or self is justified by our theory.

As a naturalist, Santayana denies existential immortality of the self or spirit, but as an idealist he speaks of ideal immortality of the spirit. By upholding the theory of ideal immortality he distinguishes himself from those who adopt a naturalistic standpoint in religion. Santayana says that man's destiny is single in relation to matter, but still man can achieve ideal immortality or can escape death ideally. But how is it possible? When man is embedded in the natural, how can he transcend it? We have seen after Santayana that the spirit has a function of its own other than the material function which it has to perform to meet the need of the psyche. And the characteristic function of the spirit lies in taking a flight, on the wings of Plato, to a transcendental realm where it envisages eternal essences. Though this experience of the spirit is transitory, though its detachment from the world of flux and from its personal destiny is for a short period, yet it gains an ideal immortality in the sense that it envisages the eternal.

We have seen after Santayana that ideal immortality lies in the contemplation of eternal essences. He also observes that ideal immortality of the spirit lies in the knowledge of its own destiny:

> The animals are mortal without knowing it, and doubtless presume, in their folly, that they will live for ever. Man alone knows that he must die; but that very knowledge raises him, in a sense, above mortality, by making him a sharer in the vision of eternal truth.
>
> – 1938: x

Indeed, conscious determinism is freedom. And what Santayana says here has also been observed by Blaise Pascal and Baruch Spinoza. Pascal says that man is superior to the mountain which crushes him, in that he is aware of the fact. And Spinoza argues that by knowing the law of his fate man rises superior to it. We cannot forget that Santayana's conception of ideal immortality is the very pinnacle of his idealism.

V. Santayana's Theory of Spirituality vs Our Theory of the Same

Santayana's religious theory has an aspiring side which is called spirituality. His contention is that spirituality is not the whole of the spiritual life. On the other hand, it is one of the two aspects of the latter, the other aspect being piety. Spirit springs from the material psyche, when the latter intends to adapt itself to alien things (vide Chap. 4, pp. 79-80). Naturally, the spirit has a piety to the psyche, i.e. it meets the demands of the latter. Through the spirit the psyche adapts itself to the world of objects, and thus empirical knowledge becomes possible. Though spirit is grounded in animal life, it does not restrict itself to the pragmatic function only. It has a reflective capacity by which it overleaps this function and associates itself with the moral and aesthetic function. In this latter function consists the spirituality of the spiritual life.

As already shown (p. 260), Santayana means by spirituality "life in the ideal". It is a contemplative state in which essences appear to the spirit in a form of beauty. This state of contemplation can be compared to the Stoic indifference; it consists in freedom from disturbance of mind or passion. But the spirit cannot remain in the contemplative state for a long time; its piety to the psyche pulls it amidst the busy life in the world. The contemplative state is purely imaginary and as such cannot have the truth which is claimed by the active life lived in the material world. Though the contemplative state is imaginary, Santayana asserts its necessity. It is a state which makes us oblivious of the tribulations of life, a state which can be compared to "the equilibrium of a divine repose".

From the above, it is manifest that Santayana, in his religious theory, has laid stress upon detachment of spirit, but at the same time does not speak of the renunciation of the world. Detachment of spirit and not renunciation of the world is what is demanded from us. Santayana has truly pointed to the core of the spiritual life. But the way in which he presents his view of spiritual life cannot be accepted from the viewpoint which we have taken of the spirit or consciousness. Our previous study of the varieties of experience shows how consciousness is the only existential reality. But, to Santayana, consciousness is the epiphenomenon, while the efficacious matter is the only existential reality. Renunciation of the world is not possible for the spirit, since it is embedded in the material psyche which is its organ. When the spirit belongs to "the essence-directed stage", it looks at the things of the world with detachment or disinterestedness.

In contrast to Santayana's view, our theory holds that the non-conscious cannot be the cause of the conscious.

> Our judgements of value, our convictions of truth, our appreciations of beauty are the proof that we are not products of merely physical forces. – Radhakrishnan 1929: 56-57

The fundamental consciousness which is the basis of all reality is not the finite consciousness but the ultimate one. It is of the nature of non-objective consciousness.

> The *Ātman* is throughout nothing but intelligence; intelligence is its exclusive nature, as the salt taste is of the lump of salt.
>
> – Śaṅkara's Bhāṣya iii.2.16

As spirit is eternal, it should be devoid of activity which is by its nature non-eternal. An activity is motivated by desire, and cannot function without modifying the individual who is its agent. The *ātman* by itself cannot be the locus of activity; there can be no agency without the limitation of the *ātman* by a body. Here, it can be observed how Santayana differs from our theory. He does not deny activity to spirit. Spirit is the function of matter, says he. Of course, he adds that spirit loses all activity in its ideal or contemplative mood.

The eternal nature of consciousness tends to prove that it has no limit. From our consciousness of limits we apprehend that consciousness is more than the limit. Moreover, consciousness and limit are opposed in nature. Limit is the nature of a thing and consciousness is no thing. Here, again, Santayana differs from us. For Santayana, the spirit is both limited and free. It is limited, because it originates from the material psyche. The limitation of the spirit is shown by its piety to the psyche. Spirit is free in the sense that it is not itself matter, although the latter breeds the former. Spirit is intelligence, while matter is blind. The former has a reflective capacity by which it can have a vision of the eternal forms. Thus, spirit canstitutes a separate realm of its own and in that sense it is free.

When Santayana observes that spirituality, which is an aspect of the spiritual life, constitutes the aspiring side of religion, he wants to mean that in sprituality the character of religious experience has been fully expressed. We should, then, go deep in our explanation of his view of sprituality or the contemplative state of the spirit. In the contemplative state, the spirit dwells on "ideals". This spiritual condition can be called "the essence-directed stage" to which the spirit belongs for the time being. The phrase "for the time being" is used, since the spirit's inability to remain long in a contemplative mood is due to the fact that it has to serve the material psyche in the latter's adaptation to alien things. In the contemplative state of the spirit essences appear to it in a form of beauty. Here, the spirit gets an experience which can be characterized as aesthetic. Then, on Santayana's view, religious experience and aesthetic experience seem to be the same thing. Shall we subscribe to this view? For having aesthetic experience, says Santayana, what is necessary as the only condition is emotional consciousness. But do we not seek the religious object by the totality of our faculties and energies?

The religious object which we seek to realize in our whole being is called "God". But here God to whom we offer the nosegay of love is completely independent, is the spirit in him objectified. Then self-realization is the theme of the spiritual life. While Santayana refers to the spirit's "essence-directed stage", our theory speaks of the spirit's "self-directed stage". This point of distinction is the vital one which is to be borne in mind.

Spiritual experience can be had only through the perfection of body and mind. The proper development of the natural impulses of an individual helps to express the spirit in him. Santayana is on the right track when he finds a line of continuity between the life of reason and the life of spirit. The life of reason is not the end in itself. It is the condition and instrument of the life of spirit in man. Unless reason harmonizes the affects or impulses of human life, the spiritual life cannot be enjoyed. As the expression of the spiritual, the perfection of body and mind is an integral part of man's complete living. In *Taittirīya Āraṇyaka* (x.66) we read:

> *pṛthivyāpas tejo vāyur ākāśā, me śuddhyantām śabda sparśa rūpa gandhā, me śuddhyantām ... mano akkayavkarmaṇi me śuddhyantām ... ātmā me śuddhyantām, jyotir aham viraja vipāpmā bhūyasām* ।

> May the earth, water fire and ether that compose my body become purified; may sound, touch, vision, taste and smell become purified ... may my thought, speech, actions become purified ... may my soul become purified so that I may become the effulgent spirit, free from sullying passion and sin.

In spiritual experience the tension of normal life disappears, giving rise to inward peace, power and joy. Santayana also says that in the contemplative state the spirit forgets its origin in the material psyche and thereby all the pains and tribulations of the engaged life of action and enjoys life which is full of peace and joy. Some have expressed this state of inward peace and joy negatively and some in the positive fashion. The word "ataraxy" used by the Greeks is a negative expression of such a state of spiritual experience, while the Hindu term *śānti* (peace) is a positive expression of the same.

The actuality of spiritual experience cannot be questioned, although profounder intuitions do not normally occur. To quote the words of Radhakrishnan:

> When we experience the illumination of new knowledge, the ecstasy of poetry or the subordination of self to something greater, family or nation, the self-abandonment of falling in love, we have faint glimpses of mystic moods. – 1929: 93

Spiritual experience is called intuitive consciousness or *anubhava*. *Anubhava* is the ineffable experience beyond thought and speech. It is the state of consciousness which is accompanied by what Russell calls "the true spirit of delight, the exaltation, the sense of being more than man" (1910: 73).

Anubhava which consists in the personal experience of universal consciousness (*ātman)* is called mysticism. Religion in the mystic sense is what our entire self is, feels and does. Santayana takes the mystic consciousness as obscure and confuses it with the instinctive. To quote him:

> ... when instinct guides without kindling any prophetic idea to which action may be inwardly referred; when life and hope and joy flow through the soul from an unknown region to an unknown end, then consciousness is mystical. – 1905, III: 189

The words "unknown end" suggest obscurity and ignorance in the case of mystical consciousness. But the mystical consciousness (*anubhava*) is not devoid of an unknown end. On the other hand, it consists in the direct contact with a real object, with the spirit (*ātman*). Mysticism assumes the indivisible oneness of human life, whose apprehension cannot be contrary to reason.

Our contention is that mystical experience is not different from spiritual experience. The inward essence of religion is spirituality and this side of religion is emphasized by mysticism. We then differ from Santayana when he says that mysticism constitutes a phase other than the phase of spirituality.

Santayana observes that all religion is a work of imagination. It is true that imagination has a place in religion, but it cannot be taken as a solid rock upon which religion is based. Religion, we should not forget, is rooted in spiritual experience. Spiritual experience has a character of ineffability. It transcends expression. There is no experience by which we can limit it, no conception by which we can define it. While the tools of sense and understanding fail to describe *anubhava*, creative imagination with its symbols and suggestion may be of assistance. If the myths and symbols are interpreted literally, we shall fail to penetrate into the real meaning suggested by them. In interpreting the myths we shall go behind the works to the moods they symbolize. The illusory character of the myths is not denied, since they are the products of creative imagination. But they have their utility in this that through them is communicated to us the religious feeling experienced by the seers. Moreover, it is through the medium of myths that the ineffable realization of seers and saints percolates down to the common mass of people. Hence, Santayana is not justified when he says that rational religion should consist in the abolition of all myths and symbols.

VI. Santayana's Religious Standpoint

The discussion made hitherto reveals to us the fact that Santayana is an atheist. His denial of God is a necessary corollary from his general philosophical standpoint which is known as materialistic. Of course, he suggests that matter may be called God so far as they both refer to the same "efficacious reality". Though in his view matter and God are interchangeable terms, he cannot still be regarded as the one, eternal Being or Consciousness. He always sticks to his position that matter is the Ultimate Reality and consciousness springs from matter.

On going through Santayana's lecture, "Ultimate Religion", delivered at the Hague during the tercentenary celebration of Spinoza's birth, one may conceive the theistic position of Santayana. But theism goes against the whole philosophical outlook adopted by Santayana. It is necessary to find out what Santayana says in his "Ultimate Religion". Man's "ultimate religion", says he, must be truthful in a Spinozistic sense, humble, disillusioned and cosmic. To love God is "to love things spiritually" (1936: 292). It is, in Santayana's chosen terms, a turning from existence to essence, from matter to spirit, from time to eternity. It is an actualization of spirit, which is aspiration become aware of itself. It is, hence, the ultimate religion for man.

Now, why this turning from matter to spirit? Because matter, the omniscient power, is beyond our spiritual control, and because, in relation to it our destiny is "tragically single". Hence, to get an "intellectual delight", to set the self free from the entanglement of matter (this freedom is, of course, not actual but ideal), we should adopt a disinterested outlook on all things in the world. To treat all things disinterestedly is to love them spiritually, to form all things of love into a single ineffable good or, what may be called, universal good. This "universal good" can be taken as what stands for "God". Thus has been conceived theistic position of Santayana. But it will be erroneous to think in that manner, since here "God", the preferred word for "universal good" is not the theistic God. "God" of the theist is not only immanent in the world but also transcendent to it. The "God" of Santayana, on the other hand, is fully immanent in the world, without being transcendent to it. For him, to love God is to love all things disinterestedly and to love all things disinterestedly is to love God; that is, Santayana adopts the Spinozistic conclusion which is: God is Nature and Nature God. This pantheistic absorption is surely not the theistic standpoint. Thus, we conclude that Santayana is not a theist.

Santayana's religious standpoint can be called materialistic pantheism as against idealistic pantheism of Gustav Fechner. Fechner holds that nature is only external appearance whose indwelling soul is universal consciousness. Universal consciousness as the inner reality determines nature as its phenomenon. But materialistic pantheism of Santayana holds the opposite view. According to it, matter or nature is the fundamental reality which determines consciousness. It should be mentioned in this connection that Santayana's materialistic pantheism is not the same as the traditional pantheism of Spinoza. In Spinoza, the substance is a psychophysical whole in which the physical and the psychical, nature and mind, are regarded as having equal status. But in Santayana we see, as mind comes from matter, so they cannot possess equal status in the system of the universe.

In the naturalistic religion of Santayana, what we find, then, is materialistic pantheism. Here we are acquainted with the notion of power which is manifested as blind, omnipotent matter, with its trampling march. This recognition of cosmic power is also found in the naturalistic thinkers of the nineteenth century, e.g. in Herbert Spencer and T.H. Huxley.

Santayana's naturalistic religion leads to two serious consequences. First, it leads to Agnosticism. In the face of the greatness of nature we are not encouraged to ask the questions, Why? Whence? Whither? Our only virtue will be "childlike piety" which is the submission to the perpetual laws of nature. The second consequence to which Santayana's naturalistic religion leads is that of fatalism. Our fate or destiny is determined by nature. For the moment we may escape from the omniscient matter and indulge ourselves in images, love and religion, but these experiences are not long-lived in comparison to matter, the only existential reality. That we indulge in those experiences is sheer madness or folly for us, since ultimately we are to follow the guidance of nature. Of course, we should not be led to think that Santayana is in favour of absolute determinism. When it is in our power to escape the almighty matter (for the time being) by our imaginative faculty, it should be admitted that we are partly free. This freedom of the spirit, though transient, ineffective or impotent in comparison to matter or substance, is a fact which cannot be denied.

In conclusion, we can say that Santayana's religious standpoint is not wholly naturalistic or wholly idealistic. His attitude to religion is a result of the combination of naturalism and idealism; that is, he is a "natural idealist" in his view of religion. His naturalism is expressed in his cosmic piety and his idealism in the contemplation of "ideals". A question remains to be answered: Is Santayana a mystic? The mystic, says Santayana, indulges himself in the speculation of abstractions. If that be so, we can ascribe to Santayana the title of the mystic. Santayana too loves to contemplate the "ideals" which are also "abstractions", since they are denuded of existence and of everything that the physical world contains. In fine, the spirituality of the spiritual life, which Santayana takes as the aspiring side of religion, is a kind of experience which is mostly mystical.

Appendix

On Santayana's Americanism

GEORGE Santayana (born on 16 December 1863, Madrid, Spain – died on 26 September 1952, Rome, Italy) was a Spanish-born American philosopher. He was not only a speculative philosopher but a poet also. The matter does not end here. His versatile genius made room for him as a dramatist, as an educator, as an essayist and as a novelist. Besides, his contributions to aesthetics and literary criticism made him prominent as a major figure in the history of modern American philosophy and literature.

George Santayana led almost a solitary life. And in his solitude he developed his philosophy and, practically speaking, made it the whole of his life. He never took "philosophy" as a vocation, as a skill or expertise in a job at which others who are called "philosophers" earn their livings, not a life they live. To cultivate philosophy in the sense of living a life, Santayana became aware of "three traps that strangle philosophy", in his own words,

> the Church, the marriage-bed and the professor's chair. I escaped from the first in my youth; the second I never entered, and as soon as possible I got out of the third.[1]

This statement is enough to establish the fact that Santayana lived his life for the sake of his philosophy, for the sake of

[1] *The Journal of Philosophy*, LXI(1), 2 January 1964, p. 68.

writing volume after volume on various matters, such as, on the realms of Being, on the nature and conditions of knowledge, on the sense of Beauty or on aesthetics, on political philosophy, on moral and religious philosophy and so on. What is to be primarily noted is that whatever he discussed or wrote had a naturalistic basis; for him what is called supernatural is not really transcendental to Nature, that is, what we designate as the Supernature is nothing but the infinite extension of what is termed as Nature. In "A General Confession" , in *The Philosophy of George Santayana,* Santayana adds:

> My naturalism or materialism is no academic opinion: it is not a survival of the alleged materialism of the nineteenth century, when all the professors of philosophy were idealists: it is an everyday conviction which came to me … from experience and observation of the world at large and especially of my own feelings and passions. – Schilpp 1940: 12

He continues:

> It seems to me that those who are not materialists cannot be good observers of themselves: they may hear themselves thinking, but they cannot have watched themselves acting and feeling; for feeling and action are evidently accidents of matter. – Ibid.

The Santayana collection in the Columbia University Library is large and ranges over the full length of Santayana's writing career. While talking or writing, Santayana used the same beautiful style and cadenced sentences. What was most outstanding about Santayana was one of perfect composition and perfect timing. He never ended a lecture in the middle – the way both James and Royce were in the habit of doing. In Santayana's lecture there was a beginning, a middle and an end. In short, in his way of talking, of delivering a lecture in a class, even in his way of writing he always delivered "a disciplined version of himself" (ibid.: 64).

When, in the year 1872, Santayana's father took him to Boston and left him in his mother's care, he was only a nine-year old boy. At that age he did not know a single word in English. During his first winter in Boston he was sent to a Kindergarten where he picked up English by ear before knowing how it was written. Then in his life the Brimmer School, the Boston Latin School and Harvard College followed in order. He joined the Harvard philosophical faculty as a professor although he "always hated to be a professor" (Schilpp 1940: 6). At the Harvard University he worked with William James, Josiah Royce and George Herbert Palmer as their colleague. He left the University in 1912. Santayana lived in America for long forty years from 1872 to 1912. It would be quite natural for us to think that a person who lived in a country like America for four decades at a stretch would surely be influenced by some "ism" or "isms" of that country. Professor Baker Brownell who was once a student of Santayana found "American present" in him. To this Santayana replied:

> It is a true honour to be claimed when one might so easily be disowned ...
> – Ibid.: 600

No doubt, his reply to Brownell in this regard would be interesting for us. The quality of Americanism, in Santayana's own words:

> he finds present and important in my philosophy, in something he calls naturalism, but which he does not describe clearly.
> – Ibid.

Naturalism which Santayana professed was cosmological naturalism or materialism. For his professed naturalism he was indebted to Democritus, Lucretius and Spinoza. This kind of naturalism as professed by him was not American; what Brownell wanted to mean by Santayana's naturalism was something social or psychological; in such naturalism the crucial factor is mind. In this connection Santayana referred to what was called "the animality of the mind". "I believe", in his own words:

> profoundly in the animality of the mind; this is my critical, as distinguished from my cosmological or dogmatic naturalism; and if this be what Brownell refers to, I agree that it characterizes my philosophy and my instinctive way of thinking in a marked degree. – Schilpp 1940: 601

But Santayana claims that this critical, satirical naturalism of his is not American at all. To use his words, "I have seen no sign of it in American philosophy" (ibid.).

We can delineate, following Santayana, his Americanism, by dividing it into two parts – the involuntary and the voluntary. His "long residence, education and twenty years of teaching in the United States" all these belong to the involuntary part of his Americanism. All these happened in his life due to circumstances; and though "they were not done by choice", there was "no hardship in any of these things; they had good sides"; and he "sometimes enjoyed them frankly and unfeignedly" (ibid.).

As to the voluntary side to his Americanism, Santayana sums up this in a single word – Friendships. He had "American friends more numerous, more loyal, more sympathetic, and with two or three exceptions more beloved than" his "friends of other nationalities"; and, as a result of that he developed "American manners and tastes more natural to" him "than any others" (ibid.: 601-02). Also he felt most at ease with American people, with a few exceptions, of course. In this connection Santayana also uttered that he never had any contact "with the deeper layers and broad currents of American life" (ibid.: 602). He himself said that by his America he meant "Harvard College, a part of Boston, and an occasional glimpse of New York" (ibid.). He, however, did not hesitate to accept the fact that that his "intellectual relations and labours" joined him closely to America; he emphatically pointed out that he must be counted as an American writer, if he were counted at all (ibid.: 603).

Bibliography

A. Writings of Santayana

1894: *Sonnets and Other Verses*, Cambridge and Chicago: G.S. Stone and Kimball.

1896: *The Sense of Beauty: Being the Outline of Aesthetic Theory*, New York: Charles Scribner's Sons; also published by The Modern Library, New York.

1899: *Lucifer: A Theological Tragedy*, Chicago: Stone & Co.

1897: F.H. Bradley, *Appearance and Reality*, 2nd edn, p. 1, London: Oxford University Press.

1900: *Interpretations of Poetry and Religion*, New York: Charles Scribner's Sons; also published by Harper and Brothers, New York.

1904: "What Is Aesthetics?", *The Philosophical Review*, 13: 320-27.

1905: *The Life of Reason*; or, *The Phases of Human Progress*, New York: Charles Scribner's Sons (5 vols); volumes are separately published by Collier Books, New York.

vol. I – The Life of Reason: Reason in Common Sense.

vol. II – The Life of Reason: Reason in Society.

vol. III – The Life of Reason: Reason in Religion.

vol. IV – The Life of Reason: Reason in Art.

1906: vol. V – The Life of Reason: Reason in Science.

1910: *Three Philosophical Poets*, Cambridge, MA: Harvard University Press.

1911: "Hypostatic Ethics", *The Journal of Philosophy, Psychology and Scientific Methods*, 18(16): 421-33.

1913: *Winds of Doctrine*, London: J.M. Dent and Sons.

1915: *Egotism in German Philosophy*, New York: Charles Scribner's Sons; also published in London by J.M. Dent and Sons.

1918: "Literal and Symbolic Knowledge", *The Journal of Philosophy, Psychology, and Scientific Methods*, 15(16): 421-44.

1920a: *Character and Opinion in the United States*, London: Constable and Co.

———b: "Three Proofs of Realism", in *Essays in Critical Realism*, London: Macmillan.

1921: "On My Friendly Critics", *The Journal of Philosophy*, 18: 701-13.

1922: *Soliloquies in England and Later Soliloquies*, London: Constable & Co.

1923a: *Scepticism and Animal Faith; Introduction to a System of Philosophy*, London: Constable & Co.

———b: *Poems*, New York: Charles Scribner's Sons.

1924: "Some Meanings of the Word Is", *The Journal of Philosophy*, 21(14): 365-77.

1925a: "The Mutability of Aesthetic Categories", *The Philosophical Review*, 24: 281-91.

———b: *Dialogues in Limbo*, London: Constable & Co. (also published by Charles Scribner's Sons, New York, 1926).

1927: *The Realm of Essence: Book First of Realms of Being*, New York: Charles Scribner's Sons, also published by Constable & Co., London.

1930a: *The Realm of Matter: Book Second of Realms of Being*, New York: Charles Scribner's Sons (also published by Constable & Co., London).

———b: "A Brief History of My Opinions", in *Contemporary American Philosophy*, ed. Adams and Montague, New York: Macmillan.

1931: *The Genteel Tradition at Bay*, New York: Charles Scribner's Sons.

1933: *Some Turns of Thought in Modern Philosophy*, New York: Charles Scribner's Sons, also published by the University Press, Cambridge, the UK.

1935: *The Last Puritan*, London: Constable & Co.

1936: *Obiter Scripta*, London: Constable & Co.

1938: *The Realm of Truth: Book Third of Realms of Being*, New York: Charles Scribner's Sons, also published by Constable & Co., London.

1940a: "A General-Confession", in *The Philosophy of George Santayana*, ed. P.A. Schilpp (The Library of Living Philosophers), Chicago: North Western University.

———b: "Apologia Pro Mente Sua: A Rejoinder", in *The Philosophy of George Santayana*, ed. P.A. Schilpp, Chicago: North Western University.

———c: *The Realm of Spirit: Book Fourth of Realms of Being*, New York, Charles Scribner's Sons, also published by Constable & Co., London.

1942: *Realms of Being*, one volume edition, New York: Charles Scribner's Sons.

1944: *Persons and Places: The Background of My Life*, London: Constable & Co.

1945: *The Middle Span*, New York: Charles Scribner's Sons.

1946: *The Idea of Christ in the Gospels*, New York: Charles Scribner's Sons.

1951: *Dominations and Powers*, New York: Charles Scribner's Sons.

1953: *My Host the World*, New York: Charles Scribner's Sons.

1957: *Platonism and the Spiritual Life*, New York: Harper Torchbooks.

B. Writings about Santayana and Other Writings

Alexander, S., 1914, The Basis of Realism, *Proceedings of the British Academy*, 6: 279-314.

———, 1920, *Space, Time and Deity*, vol. II, London: Macmillan.

Ames, Van Meter, 1952, "The Zenith as Ideal", *The Journal of Philosophy*, 49(7): 201-08.

Bergson, Henri, 1913, *An Introduction to Metaphysics*, tr. T.E. Hulme, London: Macmillan.

———, 1914, *Creative Evolution: A Metaphysical Essay*, London: Arthur Mitchell.

Bode, B.H., 1922, "Critical Realism", *The Journal of Philosophy*, 19: 68-78.

Bradley, F.H., 1897, *Appearance and Reality: A Metaphysical Essay*, 2nd edn, London: Macmillan.

Buchler, Justus, 1954, "One Santayana or Two?", *The Journal of Philosophy*, 51(2): 52-57.

Calkins, Mary, 1926, "On Certain Difficulties in the Modern Doctrine of Essence", *The Journal of Philosophy*, 23(26): 701-10.

Collingwood, R.G., 1938, *The Principles of Art*, Oxford: Clarendon Press.

Croce, B., 1949, *Saggi Filosofi*, vol. I, Gius, Laterza & Figli Publication.

Cory, D.M., 1954, "God or the External World", *The Journal of Philosophy*, vol. 51(2): 57-61.

———, 1963, *Santayana: The Later Years*, New York: George Braziller.

———, 1964, "On the False Steps of Philosophy: George Santayana, with Prefatory Note", *The Journal of Philosophy*, 61(1): 6-19.

Descartes, René, 1959, *Regulae ad Directionem Ingenii*, III, Paris: Vrin.

Drake, Durant et al., 1920, *Essays in Critical Realism: A Cooperative Study of the Problem of Knowledge*, London: Macmillan.

Drennen, D.A., 1962, *A Modern Introduction to Metaphysics: Readings from Classical and Contemporary Sources*, New York: The Free Press of Glencoe.

Ducasse, C.J., 1929, *The Philosophy of Art*, New York: L. MacVeagh.

Edman, Irwin, 1929, "Religion and the Philosophical Imagination", *Adam, the Baby and the Man from Mars*, Cambridge, MA/Houton Mifflin.

———, 1954, "Philosopher as Poet", *The Journal of Philosophy*, 51(2): 62-69.

——— (ed.), 1942, *The Philosophy of Santayana*, New York: Modern Library.

Edwards, D. Miall, 1929, *The Philosophy of Religion*, Calcutta: Progressive Publishers.

Gilbert, Katharine, 1926, "Santayana's Doctrine of Aesthetic Expression", *The Philosophical Review*, 35(3): 221-35.

Gilson, E., 1952, *Being and Some Philosophers*, Toronto: The Pontifical Institute of Mediaeval Studies.

Holt, Edwin B., 1914, *The Concept of Consciousness*, London: George Allen & Unwin.

Howgate, George W., 1938, *George Santayana*, Philadelphia: University of Pennsylvania Press.

Hume, David, 1739, *Treatise on Human Nature*, London: Longmans Green & Co.

James, William, 1902, *The Varieties of Religious Experience*, Longmans, Green & Co.

Kallen, H.M. and S. Hook (eds), 1935, *American Philosophy Today and Tomorrow*, New York: Lee Furman.

Kant, Immanuel, 1797, *Metaphysic of Morals*.

Keats, John, 1818, *Endymion: A Poetic Romance*, London: Taylor and Hessey.

Knox, Israel, 1958, *The Aesthetic Theories of Kant, Hegel and Schopenhauer*, London: Thames and Hudson.

Lachs, John, 1964, "Santayana's Moral Philosophy", *The Journal of Philosophy*, 61(1): 44-61.

Lamprecht, Sterling P., 1933, "Naturalism and Agnosticism in Santayana", *The Journal of Philosophy*, 30(21): 561-74.

Lamprecht, Sterling P., 1952, "Normal Madness and the Political Life", *The Journal of Philosophy*, 49(7): 208-14.

Lipps, Theodor, 1903, *Grundlegung der Asthetik*, Hamburg: Verlag von Leopold Voss.

Madariaga, Salvador de, 1923, *The Genius of Spain*, Oxford: Clarendon Press.

Mill, J.S., 1874, *Three Essays on Religion*, London: Longmans, Green, Reades and Dyer.

Moore, G.E., 1922, *Principia Ethica*, Cambridge: Cambridge University Press.

Nagel, Ernest, 1954, "Some Gleanings from the Life of Reason", *The Journal of Philosophy*, 51(2): 46-49.

O'Neill, G., 1921, "Poetry, Religion and Professor Santayana", *Studies*, 10(39): 451-63.

Olafson, Frederick A., 1954, "Skepticism and Animal Faith", *The Journal of Philosophy*, 51(2): 42-46.

Pepper, Stephen C., 1945, *The Basis of Criticism in the Arts*, Cambridge, MA: Harvard University Press.

Perry, Ralph Barton ,1935, *The Thought and Character of William James*, Boston: Little Brow & Co.

———, 1912, *Recent Philosophical Tendencies*, New York: Longman, Green & Co.

Perry, Ralph Barton et al., 1922, *The New Realism: Cooperative Studies in Philosophy*, New York: Macmillan.

Randall, John Hermann, 1931, "The Latent Idealism of a Materialist". *The Journal of Philosophy*, 28(24): 645-60.

———, 1954, "George Santayana: Naturalizing the Imagination", *The Journal of Philosophy*, 51(2): 50-52.

Ratner, J., 1923, "George Santayana's Theory of Religion", *The Journal of Religion*, III: 458-75.

Radhakrishnan, S., 1918, *The Philosophy of Rabindrananth Tagore*, London: Macmillan.

———, 1929, *An Idealist View of Life*, London: George Allen & Unwin.

Read, Herbert, 1951, *The Meaning of Art*, New York: Faber & Faber.

Runes D.D (ed.), 1943, *Twentieth Century Philosophy: Living Schools of Thought*, New York: The Philosophical Library.

Russell, Bertrand, 1910, *Philosophical Essays*, London/New York: Longmans.

———, 1912, *Problems of Philosophy*, New York: Oxford University Press.

———, 1921, *The Analysis of Mind*, London: George Allen & Unwin.

———, 1927, *An Outline of Philosophy*, London: George Allen & Unwin.

———, 1928, *Essays in Skepticism*, New York: Wisdom Library.

———, 1959, *My Philosophical Development*, London: George Allen & Unwin.

Schilpp, Paul Arthur (ed.), 1940, *The Philosophy of George Santayana,* New York: Tudor Publishing Company.

Schopenhaur, A., 1818, *The World as Will and* Representation, tr. Haldane.

Seal, Brajendranath, 1915, *The Positive Sciences of the Ancient Hindus,* London: Longmans, Green & Co.

Selby-Bigge, L.A. (ed.), 1949, *A Treatise of Human Nature,* Bk. I, Part-IV. Sect. VI, Oxford: Clarendon Press.

Sellars, R.W., 1929, "Current Realism", in *An Anthology of Recent Philosophy,* ed. D.S. Robinson, New York: Thomas Y. Crowell Co.

Shelley, P.B., 1840, *A Defence of Poetry,* in English Critical Essays (Nineteenth Century), London: Edward Moxon.

Singer, Irving, 1957, *Santayana's Aesthetics: A Critical Introduction,* Cambridge, MA, Harvard University Press.

Souriau, E., 1929, *L'Avenir de l'Esthétique,* Paris: Librairie Felix Alean.

Spinoza, Baruch, *Ethics* (a posthumous work)

Sullivan, Celestine J., 1952, "Essence and Existence in George Santayana", *The Journal of Philosophy,* 49(7): 220-26.

Ten Hoor, Marten, 1923, "George Santayana's Theory of Knowledge", *The Journal of Philosophy,* 20(8): 197-211.

Tolstoy, Leo, 1896/1904, *What Is Art*? tr. Aylmer Maude, New York: Funk & Wagnalls Co.

Whitehead, A.N., 1926, *Science and the Modern World,* Cambridge: Cambridge University Press.

———, 1929, *Process and Reality: An Essay in Cosmology,* Cambridge: Cambridge University Press.

Williams, Donald C., 1954, "Of Essence and Existence and Santayana", *The Journal of Philosophy,* 51(2): 31-42.

Wisdom, John, 1931, *Interpretation and Analysis in Relation to Bentham's Theory of Definition,* London: Kegan Paul, Trench, Trübner & Co.

Wordsworth, William, 1888, *The Prelude, or Growth of a Poet's Mind,* Boston: D.C. Heath & Co.

Author Index

Subject Index